G T O

PONTIAC'S GREAT ONE

Darwin Holmstrom Photography by David Newhardt

motorbooks

First published in 2009 by Motorbooks, an imprint of MBI Publishing Company, 400 First Avenue North, Suite 300, Minneapolis, MN 55401 USA

Motorbooks titles are also available at discounts in bulk quantity for industrial or sales-promotional use. For details write to Special Sales Manager at MBI Publishing Company, 400 First Avenue North, Suite 300, Minneapolis, MN 55401 USA.

To find out more about our books, visit us online at www.motorbooks.com.

ISBN-13: 978-0-7603-3985-5

Editor: Chris Endres
Designers: Simon Larkin and Chris Fayers
Jacket Designer: Simon Larkin

Printed in China

About the author

Darwin Holmstrom, senior acquisitions editor for MBI Publishing, has written or co-written over a dozen books on cars and motorcycles, including *BMW Motorcycles*, *GTO: Pontiac's Great One*, *The Harley-Davidson Motor Co. Archive Collection*, *Camaro: Forty Years*, *Muscle: America's Legendary Performance Cars*, and *The Complete Idiot's Guide to Motorcycles*.

About the Photographer

Photographer and writer David Newhardt was born in Chicago, Illinois, and attended Southern Illinois University, majoring in Professional Photography. He served eight years in the U.S. Navy aboard nuclear submarines before settling in Southern California. Newhardt worked at *Motor Trend* magazine for three years and has been on the masthead of other top automotive magazines. He has shot fashion photography, but finds that automobiles make better subjects. The author of seven books, Newhardt has supplied scores of other books with images. A longtime member of the Motor Press Guild, he lives in Pasadena, California, with his wife and two sons.

On the cover: No grille treatment from the muscle car era is as iconic as that of the GTO.

On the frontispiece: In creating GTO, Pontiac started not just a new model, but a new genre of American automobile.

On the title pages: Few cars before or after possess the presence of the 1967 GTO.

On contents page: hough not very accurate, the hood-mounted tach was a signature item that no owner wanted to be without.

On the back cover: As the originator of the breed, GTO was the car all automakers wished to surpass, though few did.

PONTIAC'S GREAT ONE

CONTENTS

ACKNOWLEDGMENTS

THE PHOTOGRAPHER

Photographing muscle cars in general, and GTOs in particular, is a wonderful way to make a living. The owners are passionate, the vehicles possess rugged good looks, and the soundtrack is second to none. To say that I had a ball photographing the automobiles in this book would be an understatement. But none of it would have been possible without the help of many individuals.

In no particular order, they are: Mike Guarise, Colin Comer, Cana Tinkle, Ken Lingenfelter, Eric White, Rich Dabrowski, Taft L. Taylor, Merrill Taylor, John Gust, Mike Tiffany, Joe Sparks, Bill Nawrot, John and Jenette Holmes, Bob Cupery, Bill Baker, Barry Troup, Carter Chee, Les Iden, Jack Blum, Joseph Church, Bernie DeMarkey, Doug Watt, Roger Becker, Bill and Rita Schultz, Tenney Fairchild, Dave Anderson, Jim Gannes, Keith Seymore, Jim Kennedy, Stefano Bimbi, Jan Laxton, Jack Blum, Otto Tharp Sr., John at Groucho's Performance, Bob Alling, Charles Bailey, Glenn Hammack, Irvin Hammack, Doug Emch, Scott Tiemann, Rodney Salmon, Irv Hammack, Jim Golata, Jerald Papesh, Chuck Cocoma, Mike Radke, General Motors Public Relations, Pam Ertman, Dean Jefferies, Benjamin J. Geer, Steven Dorris, Matt Stone, Arnie Beswick, the staff of Chicagoland Raceway, Les Quam, Dana Mecum, David Christenholz, Richard & Elaine Bonnefoi, Dan Paush, Bob & Judy Foxx, Michael Smyth, Len & Pat Cradit, Greg & Lara Williams, Randy Leffingwell, Brett Torino, and Faxon Auto Literature.

A huge thank-you to Eric Schiffer and Jim Wangers. I tip my hat to my editor, Chris Endres, for his sage advice and patient mien. The author of this tome, Darwin Holmstrom, and I have collaborated on a number of auto-motive books, and it's always a pleasure working with him.

Finally, thank you to my wife, Susan Foxx-Newhardt, for holding down the fort while I travel across the country "working."

THE AUTHOR

In addition to all the folks David Newhardt mentions, I'd like to thank David himself for providing the stunning photography in this book. The best part about working with David is that the man never loses his enthusiasm for photographing muscle cars. Every time he calls me to talk about the car he just shot, his excitement is infectious and I wish I'd been there with him.

I'd also like to thank our editor, Chris Endres, and our publisher, Zack Miller. But they are just the leading edge of an entire staff that works incredibly hard to make a book like this a reality, people like Melinda Keefe, Carmen Nickisch, Jenny Miller, Krystyna Borgen, our publicists Nichole Schiele and Blake Johnson, and many, many other dedicated people.

I have to thank my entire family: my grandma, aunts, uncles, cousins, brother, children, grandchildren, niece and nephews, and all of my in-laws, people who are always there to provide support. I'd especially like to thank my parents, Dean and JoAnne Holmstrom, and my wife, Patricia Johnson, who practically has a full-time job keeping my dumb ass alive. I don't make it easy for her. It's to these last three that this book is dedicated.

CHAPTER 1

WE'RE GOING RACING!

Historians rightly peg the birth of the Pontiac GTO to one spring day in 1963. That day Pontiac's Chief Engineer John DeLorean and his two favorite staff engineers, Bill Collins and Russ Gee, came up with the inspired idea of mounting a high-performance 389-cubic-inch V-8 engine in the Tempest, which was Pontiac division's version of General Motors' then new corporate A-body intermediate platform. But if that moment marked the birth of the GTO and hence the birth of the entire muscle car era, the GTO's (and the genre's) conception occurred much earlier.

Trouble of the GTO variety had been brewing at Pontiac since at least 1956, when a fellow named Semon E. "Bunkie" Knudsen assumed control of the division. Knudsen's appointment had almost been preordained. His father, William Signius "Big Bill" Knudsen, a Danish immigrant, had managed Pontiac division before he succeeded Alfred P. Sloan as the president of General Motors in 1937. Nineteen years later the younger Knudsen's assignment was simple: revive the division or it would be eliminated. At that time Pontiac was a brand without an image.

Fortunately for Pontiac, Knudsen, a man who genuinely loved cars, possessed two things that the empty corporate suits currently trying to save various automakers from extinction lack: an understanding of the product and an understanding of the market. He had the good sense to surround himself with the best possible people. Knudsen hired Elliot M. "Pete" Estes to be Pontiac's chief engineer. Born on January 7, 1916, at Mendon, Michigan, Estes attended General Motors Institute in Flint, Michigan, for four years and studied two years at the University of Cincinnati, graduating with a degree in mechanical engineering in 1940. He joined the General Motors Research Laboratories while attending General Motors Institute and became a research engineer in 1939 while still studying at the University of Cincinnati. Estes became a senior engineer in 1945. By the time Knudsen asked Estes to join him at Pontiac, Estes had been promoted to assistant chief engineer in charge of the body design, chassis design, and standards engineering departments. Before that, Estes had been at GM's Oldsmobile division, where he had worked on the company's original overhead-valve (OHV) V-8 engine program.

Edward Glenn "Fireball" Roberts drove Pontiacs to great success, including an impressive win at the 1962 Daytona 500. Fireball could handle road courses equally well, finishing an amazing second in the 24 Hours of Le Mans race. *David Newhardt collection*

Trouble of the GTO variety had been brewing at Pontiac since at least 1956.

The bright lights of a car show glamorized the inevitable joy the customer would feel with a new 1956 Pontiac in the garage. Little has changed in the ensuing decades, as auto shows continue to present vehicles as objects of desire. *David Newhardt collection*

Knudsen and Estes hired John Zachary DeLorean from the ash heap of the failed Studebaker-Packard Corporation. DeLorean, who would become one of the most successful and controversial figures the automotive industry ever produced, had his finger on the pulse of the U.S. auto market. Born into a working-class Detroit family on January 6, 1925, and son of a foundry worker for Ford Motor Company, DeLorean learned the auto industry from the bottom up. He earned advanced

degrees in both engineering and business. His education, background, and charm made him perfectly suited for success in the U.S. auto industry of the 1950s and 1960s, a time in which dynamic personalities like DeLorean's drove automobile manufacturing in America. His rise to the top was meteoric, and he made a lot of friends (and a lot of enemies) on his way up.

General Motors management gave Knudsen five years to turn Pontiac around or the division would be

That wealthy look at a healthy saving!

THE 870 CATALINA

Pontiac's mighty, new Strato-Streak V-8 and all-new shockproof chassis deliver a completely new kind of performance, control and roadability.

From instrument panel to rear window, Pontiac provides the roominess and luxury of costly cars.

When you buy a Pontiac, fine things happen immediately. Your pride gets a lift. You own one of America's most desired possessions—the objective, and the envy, of everyone with eyes for clean, modern beauty, rakish smartness and the splendor of luxury fabrics artfully keyed to the two-toned colors of the spacious bodies.

Motoring becomes exciting again. You drive the ablest performer you have ever headed down a highway—alive with new alertness . . . sweeping uphill or down with the same effortless ease . . . responding with crisp, compelling power to every call for action.

And you have the pleasant knowledge that you have also pampered your purse. Pontiac prices are practical for every new-car buyer! Take a ride and look at the price tag for '55's finest value!

PONTIAC MOTOR DIVISION OF GENERAL MOTORS CORPORATION

'55 **Pontiac**
STRATO-STREAK V-8

SEE THE RED BUTTONS SHOW, FRIDAYS—NBC-TV

Above: A car guy to the marrow, Semon "Bunkie" Knudsen earned an engineering degree from MIT in 1936, and when he took over Pontiac in 1956, he was tasked to improve sales–or else. He had the foresight to bring aboard like-minded individuals, such as Pete Estes and John DeLorean. The result was a forward-thinking division that soon claimed the industry's No. 3 sales spot.
Mike Mueller archive

Right: A talented engineer and a quick study, John Zachary DeLorean briskly rose through the General Motors ranks to become, at age 40, the head of the Pontiac division in 1965. He is widely regarded as the father of the GTO.
Mike Mueller archive

eliminated. Saving Pontiac would be something of a Hail Mary effort, but with the combination of automotive enthusiasm, engineering brilliance, and marketing savvy represented by Knudsen, Estes, and DeLorean, Pontiac had the managerial horsepower not just to survive but thrive.

It didn't take an automotive Nostradamus to understand that the demographics of the U.S. auto market were changing fast and hard. Between the years 1946 and 1964, Americans spawned approximately 76 million children. This baby-boom generation contained such a huge number of people that it required society to bend around it rather than demanding that baby boomers conform to the mores of society. The baby boomers would reshape the face of corporate America. Even the most literal-minded CPA

Above: The Star Chief was the upper-range offering from Pontiac in 1956. The "Silver Streaks" on the hood were last used this year, as new Pontiac division head Bunkie Knudsen pulled them off of the 1957 models. *David Newhardt collection*

Right: Elliot Marantette "Pete" Estes, right, was a gifted engineer, having attended the General Motors Institute, then working at Oldsmobile. He caught the eye of Bunkie Knudsen, left, who made Estes Pontiac's chief engineer in 1956. His long career at General Motors was capped as president from 1974 until his retirement in 1981. *Mike Mueller archive*

possessed enough imagination to understand that these shifting demographic numbers would have a profound impact on every facet of commerce in the coming years. Surprisingly few observers could fathom what shape this change would take.

Knudsen, Estes, and DeLorean were among the august group who understood the implications the baby boomers would have on the U.S. auto industry. Today the

Like many automobiles from the mid-1950s, the 1955 Pontiac sported a two-tone paint scheme and lavish chrome to titillate the eye. Pontiac was proud of its new "panoramic" styling, a fresh design approach meant to attract younger owners.

position of division general manager at General Motors is practically middle management, just one more layer in the infinite onion of GM's bureaucracy, but Knudsen became Pontiac division's general manager at a time when division managers wielded almost godlike authority over their respective divisions. When GM President Harlow Curtice appointed Knudsen to head Pontiac division, he granted Knudsen the authority to save the division by any means necessary.

Knudsen had no marketing or sales background, but he loved cars, and he knew what excited people who loved cars. Unlike most men who reach a certain age, Knudsen seemed to remember what had excited him in his formative years: speed and competition. In an article about Pontiac's then new general manager, *Automotive News* quoted Mr. Knudsen as issuing the following challenge to everyone associated with Pontiac: "We're going racing, and we're going to build some really exciting cars here at Pontiac, so you better get some new people on your staff who know and like cars." To be specific, Knudsen expressed interest in stock car racing and drag racing because drivers competed in stock-

bodied cars in both forms of racing. Without question a Pontiac winning on a National Association for Stock Car Auto Racing (NASCAR) oval track or a National Hot Rod Association (NHRA) drag strip inspired some buyers to purchase a similar car from a Pontiac dealership.

To fully grasp the revolutionary nature of Knudsen's stated intent to go racing, one needs to understand Pontiac's place in General Motors hierarchy in the mid-1950s. Every GM division occupied a different rung on the corporate ladder. With its inexpensive sedans, Chevrolet occupied the bottom rung, and with its luxury sedans and coupes, Cadillac occupied the top rung. Things got a bit confused at the next rung down, which was more or less shared by the near-luxury divisions Buick and Oldsmobile, but the situation got even more confusing when it came to Pontiac, which occupied the nebulous territory between Chevrolet and Buick and Oldsmobile. It wasn't a semi-luxurious brand like Buick or Olds, and it wasn't an economy brand like Chevrolet. And it wasn't much of anything else. The division had developed a reputation for reliability, much like Grandma develops a reputation as a reliable baby-sitter. With the

Owner-installed chrome valve covers sit atop the Strato-Streak 287-cubic-inch V-8 nestled in the engine compartment of the 1955 Pontiac. This model year saw the introduction of a 12-volt electrical system.

The public called them "chrome suspenders," while Pontiac referred to them as Silver Streaks. Whatever the name, the twin chromed trim pieces running the length of the hood were a stylistic touch confined to Pontiac.

With its huge 124-inch wheelbase and rocket-inspired styling, the Pontiac Bonneville was the ultimate aspirational Pontiac in 1957. Available only as a convertible, Pontiac built just 630 examples of the $5,782 flagship.

stodgy, conservative image Pontiac cars projected, Grandma was the most likely member of the family to drive a Pontiac. The cars might have been as dependable as Grandma, but they weren't any sexier.

When Knudsen took over GM's grandma division and said he planned to build exciting cars and go racing, it was like he'd announced he was planning to replace Grandma with Brigitte Bardot.

STRATO-STREAK V-8

Knudsen's plans to inject some excitement into Pontiac would have seemed more achievable had he inherited better raw material with which to work. Pontiac was one of the last manufacturers to abandon the antiquated side-valve engine architecture, only replacing its inline flathead sixes and eights with an overhead-valve V-8 in 1955. Dubbed the Strato-Streak V-8, this engine bore remarkable similarities to the Chevrolet V-8 introduced the same year, with one notable difference: rather than run the oil up to the rockers through hollow pushrod tubes, as on the Chevy V-8, the Pontiac used an oil passage that ran the entire length of the cylinder head to lubricate each ball pivot. This less-than-optimal system would not be corrected until the 1961 model year, when Pontiac would begin using hollow pushrod tubes to lubricate the top ends of its V-8 engines.

Never let it be said that Pontiac's stylists were reticent to slather chrome on the top-shelf 1957 Bonneville. Yet they didn't overdo the brightwork, creating a sleek, upscale look that rivaled Cadillac in dramatic presence.

Ignoring the flawed top-end oiling system, the Pontiac V-8 was as sturdy an engine as any on the market in the mid-1950s, with the exception of Chrysler's Hemi, which was such a complex design that each engine was practically hand assembled. The wedge-shaped combustion chambers in the Pontiac engine were fully machined, which helped equalize the compression ratio in each cylinder as well as reduce the hot spots that caused engine knocking. With a 3.25-inch bore and 3.25-inch stroke, the Strato-Streak featured a perfectly square bore-and-stroke ratio, resulting in a displacement of 287 cubic inches. Pontiac offered the engine in three states of tune, a 170-horsepower version, a 180-horsepower version, and a 200-horsepower version. This compared favorably with Chevrolet's Turbo-Fire V-8, which displaced 262 cubic inches and produced only 162 horsepower.

But it didn't compare as favorably with Chrysler's FireDome Hemi engines, the top-performing version of which produced 300 horsepower in the C-300, Chrysler's sporty high-performance coupe that was also introduced for the 1955 model year.

By the time Knudsen took the reins at Pontiac in 1956, the situation had improved somewhat. The Strato-Streak engine had grown to 316 cubic inches through a slight overbore. A tuned version with 10.0:1 compression and a pair of four-barrel carburetors cranked out 285 horsepower. In 1957 displacement grew to 347 cubic

inches thanks to an increase in both bore and stroke. The version of this engine with 10.0:1 compression and a mechanical camshaft generated 317 horsepower.

The most notable feature of the 317-horsepower version of the 347 was the Tri-Power induction system. Consisting of three two-barrel carburetors, the Tri-Power system replaced the dual four-barrel setup on the 1956 cars. Pontiac also released a fuel-injection system for the engine, but even though Pontiac's version of the Rochester fuel-injection system was more sophisticated than the version used by Chevrolet and infinitely superior to the Bendix Electrojection system used by Chrysler in 1958, Pontiac's fuel injection was an expensive option and few cars used it. The engine grew again in 1958, to 370 cubic inches, generating up to 310 horsepower when equipped with a dealer-installed cam, and again in 1959, to 389 cubic inches. The high output version of the 389 cranked out 348 horsepower when equipped with optional Tri-Power carburetion. A thorough redesign in 1958 incorporated freer-flowing exhaust manifolds and enlarged exhaust ports, making the 370-389 engines some of the best-breathing V-8s on the market. As a result, Pontiacs began to win lots and lots of races, both in the NASCAR Grand National series and at NHRA drag strips.

Knudsen, who had decided to build his new Pontiac image around youth and performance–and

In the mid-1950s, American automobile stylists were enamored with jet aircraft and rockets. The 1957 Bonneville borrowed heavily from the design language of the aerospace industry, including sizable tail fins.

You'll be surprised to learn this luxurious Pontiac
is powered by a V-8 that prefers regular grade gasoline

Pontiac has merged magnificent automobile design with an efficient new V-8 engine.

It's the Tempest 420E, especially built by Pontiac to give exceptionally good mileage on regular grade gasoline. At the same time, you get V-8 muscle and pep. You save up to five cents per gallon which considerably reduces car operating costs. Yet you still have all the power you'll ever need in normal city or highway driving. There's never been such an alliance between efficiency and beauty.

If you desire still greater power, Pontiac also offers the Tempest 420. It's a deep-chested engine wringing high-powered performance from premium gasoline. Either engine can be specified on any model at no extra cost. Only Pontiac gives you this unusual choice.

You'll be proud of this daring and different automobile and proud of yourself for making such a sensible investment.

See the Pontiac dealer nearest you for a demonstration.

THE ONLY CAR WITH WIDE-TRACK WHEELS!

Wheels are 5 inches farther apart. This widens the stance, not the car. Gives you a steadier, balanced, road-hugging ride. One of the many reasons Motor Trend Magazine voted Pontiac Car of the Year.

PONTIAC MOTOR DIVISION · GENERAL MOTORS CORPORATION

PONTIAC!

America's Number ① Road Car!

3 Totally New Series • Catalina • Star Chief • Bonneville

Period General Motors photographs used well-appointed models to emphasize the posh lifestyle that surely came with ownership of a new 1957 Bonneville. Auto manufacturers were selling more than automobiles; they were hawking a lifestyle. Love the hat. *David Newhardt collection*

that included an absolute must involvement with racing–was heard to say, "If those guys want to be fools and withdraw from racing, let them. But I've got a car to save, and I haven't got time to be a gentleman. We're going racing."

STRIPPING OFF THE SUSPENDERS

Once Knudsen had an improving and increasingly competitive engine, he needed a sexy car to put it in. Unlike the engine development program, which was already underway when he arrived, Knudsen would have to start from scratch when it came to building a car that didn't look like an octogenarian's transportation tool. Pontiacs of the mid-1950s looked as old and unstylish as the division's elderly customer base. Knudsen knew he would have to build some visually exciting cars if he was to succeed in turning the brand around.

The pair of chrome strips that ran over the hood and down the rear deck provided the most distinct aspect of Pontiac style. Pontiac referred to these chrome affectations as "the silver streaks," but most people called

them the "Pontiac suspenders" because they looked a lot like the suspenders many aged Pontiac drivers wore. The suspenders had defined "Pontiac" since they had first appeared in the 1930s. In fact, Knudsen's father, Big Bill, had been the person who approved the suspenders when he was Pontiac's general manager in 1932.

One of the first things Knudsen did after arriving was to strip this tired styling affectation from his division's cars. It really wasn't enough to make the Pontiac look stylish, but it at least let the public know that *something* was happening at General Motors' moribund Pontiac division.

The most exciting car under development when Knudsen took over Pontiac's helm was the Bonneville, a convertible scheduled for the 1957 model year. The Bonneville was named after the salt flats in Utah where top-speed runs were held each year. General Motors' legendary design chief Harley Earl was inspired to build the Pontiac Bonneville Special, a show car displayed at the 1954 Autorama show, after a visit to the Bonneville Salt Flats, though the 1957 Bonneville shared only a name with that futuristic design exercise.

Only two options were offered on the 1957 Bonneville: air conditioning and a continental tire kit. Surprisingly, just eight Bonnevilles were equipped with air conditioning. The long wheelbase and plush ride made it ideal for long trips on America's new Interstate Highway system. Considering the stylistic excesses that Detroit was rolling out, the Bonneville was a beautifully proportioned and restrained automobile.

Knudsen decided to make the limited-production 1957 Bonneville a showcase for Pontiac's version of the upcoming Rochester fuel-injection system. Pontiac introduced the Bonneville on January 11, 1957, in time to qualify for that year's race at Daytona Beach, Florida. Pontiac's new flagship was fast, taking just 8.1 seconds to get to 60 miles per hour and able to attain a top speed of 101.6 miles per hour, according to a *Motor Trend* magazine test. Considering that the car weighed a massive 4,285 pounds, these were impressive numbers. The Bonneville was heavy, and at $5,782, it was expensive. This was a whopping $2,677 premium over a base Star Chief convertible.

The new Bonneville was a much better looking car than its predecessors. In addition to being shorn of their antiquated chrome suspenders, all 1957 Pontiacs received a mild facelift under the direction of Irvin W. "Irv" Rybicki. But even when cloaked in more stylish bodywork, the high-tech, expensive Bonneville didn't set any sales records. In fact, it was one of the lowest-volume cars that Pontiac division has ever built; Pontiac sold just 630 copies of its high-tech fuel-injected convertible in 1957. In part the price contributed to low sales, but the fact that the Bonneville's fuel-injected 347-cubic-inch

engine generated just 300 horsepower–7 horsepower less than the much less expensive Tri-Power-equipped high-compression solid-lifter version of the engine–helped keep sales low.

The fuel-injected engine may have put out less peak power than the Tri-Power version, but that didn't keep the Bonneville from succeeding in stock car racing. On February 17, Cotton Owens drove a Bonneville owned by Ray Nichels to victory at the Daytona Beach NASCAR race, giving Pontiac its first ever NASCAR victory. This was helped in part by the departure of the Carl Kiekhaefer team from NASCAR's Grand National series. The Kiekhaefer team had dominated the series with its omnipotent Hemi-powered Chrysler 300s for the previous two seasons.

The 1957 Bonneville might not have sold enough copies to generate the sort of income that constitutes success on a bean counter's ledger, but it succeeded in its intended purpose, generating excitement about Pontiac. Between the Bonneville's high-profile Daytona victory and the glowing reviews that appeared in the automotive press, the car inspired many potential customers to visit a Pontiac showroom to see the division's new fuel-injected hot-rod for themselves.

Pontiac fitted the new Rochester mechanical fuel injection on every 1957 Bonneville, giving the division bragging rights. Performance was starting to raise its potent head at Pontiac, and by incorporating such an advanced induction system, word started getting out that Pontiac was building "Hot Ones."

With the Bonneville's 310 horsepower and 400 lb-ft of torque, its narrow bias-ply tires struggled to maintain a grip with the pavement under heavy throttle. Access to the trunk was compromised with the continental tire installation, but owners wanted to make a statement, not worry about luggage.

SUPER DUTY GROUP

Being a true racing fan, Knudsen had many friends in the racing world, influential people like Smokey Yunick and Mickey Thompson, and he knew how to reach out to the racing community. Pontiac already had a rudimentary NASCAR racing program in place when Knudsen took the division's helm. When he assumed control, he personally oversaw the stock-car and drag-racing programs. This hands-on approach, combined with Knudsen's racing contacts, meant that Pontiac became more intimately involved with the racing community than any other U.S. automaker. This personal connection did as much to cement Pontiac's image as *the* manufacturer of performance cars as did the cars themselves.

When Knudsen assumed power, Pontiac already offered a line of aftermarket racing parts such as a dual-four-barrel intake-and-carb setup as well as solid-lifter camshafts. Stock car racing had become so popular by that point that every American manufacturer wanted to be involved, even Pontiac. Apparently even the division's octogenarian customers were campaigning their suspendered cars at the local fairgrounds. Knudsen wanted these parts to be developed in-house, so he formed the Super Duty group in 1957. This group included Malcolm R. "Mac" McKellar, Russ Gee, and Bill Collins. Engineer Bill Klinger headed the group and Frank Barnard was in charge of distributing Super Duty parts. Knudsen gave the group two years to develop parts that would help Pontiac cars win in both stock car and drag racing.

At least that's what Knudsen told Klinger on the sly; the stated goal of the group, which was officially part of the engineering department, was to design parts that would stand up to heavy-duty service. That

It was inconceivable that a 1957 Bonneville owner would break a sweat. From power everything to factory air conditioning, this Bonneville was a delight to drive or ride in. This wasn't your grandma's Pontiac, which was the precise reason Knudsen brought the car to production.

was because Knudsen, in his official capacity as a senior manager for General Motors, couldn't come out and say the goal was to win races, thanks to the Automobile Manufacturer's Association's (AMA) ban on factory involvement in racing, instituted on June 6, 1957. This comprehensive ban prohibited manufacturers from fielding factory race teams, supplying pace cars, publicizing results, advertising speed-related features of their passenger cars, and helping anyone involved in auto racing.

The AMA, which was composed of the major U.S. automakers, initiated this ban as a gentlemen's agreement among its members in response to several high-profile racing tragedies, apparently without consulting Knudsen. In his book *Glory Days*, Jim Wangers describes Knudsen's reaction to the ban:

Knudsen, who had decided to build his new Pontiac image around youth and performance—and that included an absolute must involvement with racing—was heard to say, "If those guys want to be fools and withdraw from racing, let them. But I've got a car to save, and I haven't got time to be a gentleman. We're going racing."

Knudsen's Super Duty group steamed ahead with his race-development program, gentlemen's agreement be damned, and came up with some of the hottest performance parts a racer could buy at that time. They developed free-flowing intake and exhaust manifolds, heads with bigger valve ports and bigger valves to put in those ports, high-compression pistons, forged rods and crankshafts, and gear sets for the rear end in a wide variety of ratios, ranging from tall gearing for NASCAR superspeedways to low, stump-pulling gearing for quarter-mile drag strips. The most challenging Super Duty part to develop was a solid-lifter camshaft with extreme grinds that would stand up in normal use. This task proved especially challenging because Pontiac's V-8 engine retained that marginal oiling system up until the 1961 model year. The complete Super Duty package was made available for the 1960 model-year cars.

FOOTBALL PLAYERS IN BALLET SLIPPERS

The years between the introduction of the fuel-injected Bonneville in 1957 and the availability of the complete Super Duty package were challenging ones, not just for Pontiac but for the entire U.S. auto industry. The country found itself in a deep economic recession and auto sales suffered. Midpriced automakers such as Pontiac and

The 1957 Bonneville's fuel injection system used a cast manifold header and combined manifold heater and piping to present a neat engine compartment. The beefy engine propelled the 4,285-pound car at a healthy clip, helping Pontiac's glamour car to cover the quarter-mile in 18 seconds.

From the massive hood to the "rocket-fin" backup lights, the 1959 Bonneville was the rolling personification of a confident America. This was not a desirable car for an introvert. Only 11,426 Bonneville convertibles were built in model year 1959, ensuring that it was unlikely you would pull up next to one at a stoplight. Overall vehicle length was a whopping 220.7 inches, making a deep, deep garage a necessity.

DeSoto were especially hard hit; that year Pontiac sold just 217,000 cars. At the two-year mark it might have appeared that Knudsen's five-year resurrection plan for Pontiac wasn't going especially well, had it not been for the fact that every other brand was equally hard hit by the failing economy.

By the time the 1959 models came on line, the economy had improved dramatically, and the appearance of Pontiac's cars had improved even more. That year marked the first year that cars designed under Knudsen's stewardship hit the market.

Pontiac had developed competitive engines in the latter part of the 1950s. With the advent of the "Wide-Track" Pontiac styling, which debuted on the 1959 model-year cars, the cars themselves would have the attitude and street presence needed to reach the millions of baby boomers entering the U.S. auto market. Wide-Track styling was a corporate move toward the increasingly popular wider bodies being produced by other manufacturers. According to an unverified corporate legend, when Knudsen saw the new wider 1959 bodies on the existing 1958 chassis and saw how far out over the wheels the bodies hung, he is said to have exclaimed: "They look like football players in ballet slippers."

Whether or not this legend is true, Knudsen did in fact order engineers to redesign the chassis and move the wheels out toward the sides of the cars. Milt Coulson, a creative director at MacManus, John and Adams, Pontiac's advertising firm, coined the term "Wide-Track Ride" to describe the new look. With the advent of Wide-Track styling, Pontiac cars had muscular, aggressive stances that made them seem much better suited for Knudsen's stated racing ambitions than they did to

ferrying Grandma about. That the redesign led to a more stable, better-handling platform was a bonus, as was the fact that Wide-Track gave MacManus, John and Adams a terrific new marketing hook.

ENTER JIM WANGERS

The Super Duty group built parts for racers only and never intended its products for use on public highways. Pontiac didn't provide warranties for cars using solid-lifter camshafts–that is, cars equipped with the Super Duty package. This was because in normal street use, the lobes on the solid-lifter cams were so steep that the lifters beat the hell out of them at idle, scuffing the surface of the lobes and causing them to lose their coatings.

Initially the main focus of the Super Duty group had been to develop a package for stock car racers; they needed to develop some drag-racing-specific parts to meet

You want wide? Look no further than a 1959 Bonneville. Here is the birth of Wide-Track. On the road, it felt as if passengers were in another time zone. Let's just say that parallel parking could present some challenges.

the needs of the drag strip. For example, NASCAR only allowed one four-barrel carburetor, while the NHRA, the top drag-racing sanctioning body in the United States, allowed multiple carbs. That meant that the Super Duty drag-racing package would need to include Pontiac's Tri-Power system, at the very least, and likely would have to include a dual four-barrel system. Mac McKellar developed a camshaft specifically designed for use in the quarter mile, and the group provided a number of other parts also intended to live a brutal life one quarter mile at a time, like heavy-duty clutches and low-geared rear ends.

Not all Super Duty parts were meant for use in the engine bay. Less weight contributed as much to success

on the drag strip as did more horsepower, so the group developed lightweight body parts to help the powerful engines win races. These would eventually include aluminum bumpers, fenders, hoods, and braces, all of which would be available to any would-be racer through Pontiac's parts department.

Pontiac sold Super Duty parts through all of its dealerships, but few Pontiac dealers understood performance or even cared about it. Generations of Pontiac salespeople had honed the skills needed to sell homely cars to blue-haired retirees, and these skills didn't prove helpful when it came to selling drag-racing equipment to hormonally crazed young hot rodders. Most Pontiac parts men would have preferred to continue selling parts to the same post menopausal clientele rather than take the time to develop new skills. Customers learned about Pontiac performance and the Super Duty parts available at Pontiac dealers by watching Pontiac cars win drag races, through word of mouth, or in the enthusiast magazines, but when they went to the Pontiac dealership to purchase the parts, the parts men often didn't know what the customer was talking about.

Dealers didn't understand how profitable the sale of Super Duty parts could be, but a young ad man named Jim Wangers from MacManus, John and Adams would make it his personal quest to change that situation.

For 1960, the full-sized Bonneville used a full-width grille, which only emphasized the Wide-Track stance. Pontiac advertised how the Wide-Track feature delivered swayless stability and solid contact with the road.

The aggressive, forward-leaning grille looked like it was ready for high speed, and with up to 318 horsepower behind the brightwork, the top-shelf Bonneville melded performance and panache.

Wangers cut his teeth working on ad campaigns for Chevrolet and Chrysler. He was also a hardcore auto enthusiast and an amateur racer; when he wasn't working, he was drag racing. Wangers joined MacManus, John and Adams in 1958, just in time to work on the advertising campaign for the new Wide-Track Pontiacs.

Wangers developed a plan to train dealers in the art of successfully selling performance cars and performance parts. In early 1959 he met with Knudsen, Estes, and Frank Bridge, Pontiac's sales manager. Bridge hated Wangers' idea because he thought dealers had their hands full selling regular cars. Knudsen thought the idea was brilliant, but he couldn't second-guess Bridge because in addition to managing Pontiac's sales, Bridge's duties included spying on the young upstart Knudsen for GM's corporate management.

ROYAL PONTIAC

After Wangers' initial pitch for training Pontiac dealers in the art of selling performance, Knudsen met privately with him and directed him to find a dealership willing to be a test bed for his vision of a performance-oriented dealership.

The standard engine in the 1959 Bonneville used a 10.0:1 compression ratio and a Tri-Power induction system to generate 315 horsepower. An optional heavy-duty block featured 10.5:1 compression and could be fitted with either a single four-barrel carburetor or a Tri-Power setup, increasing horsepower to 330 and 345, respectively.

Looking like a brace of rocket nozzles, the taillights of the 1960 Bonneville captured the American automakers' fascination with everything aircraft. Actual aerodynamics didn't really affect the output of the stylists in the late 1950s; instead, lines and contours that tickled the eye determined the final result.

From the spectacular dashboard to the metallic-flecked carpet, the 1959 Bonneville was anything but subtle. Tri-tone leather upholstery was standard on Bonneville convertibles, and the flashy interior more than matched the exterior for visual impact.

Asa "Ace" Wilson Jr., a hard-living young man who liked women, liquor, and fast cars in equal measure, owned Ace Wilson's Royal Pontiac in Royal Oak, Michigan. Wilson jumped at the chance to become Wangers' prototype for a performance Pontiac dealership. He liked the idea of making his dealership the epicenter of Pontiac performance and understood how this would drive customers in what was becoming the most important demographic group to his showroom.

According to Wangers' plan, Royal would make certain it had all the best performance parts in stock, and salesmen would help customers select performance options such as manual transmissions, free-breathing exhaust systems, Tri-Power carburetors, H.O. engines with performance cams, and insulation deletion, which shed 90 pounds. When equipped with the Tri-Power setup, the top-rated 389 H.O. engine generated 348 horsepower and produced even more than that after receiving the full Royal performance treatment.

While that treatment included performance cams, those cams still used hydraulic lifters. Though much work had gone into the design of the solid-lifter camshafts for the Super Duty package, mechanical camshaft-equipped cars still destroyed their camshaft lobe surfaces in normal street use. Solid-lifter camshafts wouldn't prove reliable for street use until Pontiac began using hollow pushrod tubes to lubricate their rocker arms in the 1961 model-year cars, and the Royal Pontiacs were meant to function as reliable street cars as well as potent weekend drag racers.

Stocking the parts was easy; teaching the sales staff that money could be made in selling performance proved much more difficult. Like most Pontiac salesmen, Royal's staff was composed of salesmen who were much more comfortable selling conservative transportation to buyers in their golden years. They feared and loathed the young men who flocked to Royal to buy hot-rod cars, and they were too shortsighted to see the profit potential inherent in this new clientele.

Dick Jesse, one of Ace Wilson's top salesmen, was the exception to the rule. Jesse understood performance cars as well as the audience such cars attracted. Wangers took Jesse under his wing and schooled him in all things related to Pontiac performance. Soon young customers were lined up outside Jesse's door.

With Jim Wangers behind the wheel, the 1960 Royal Pontiac drag car lunges down the quarter-mile en route to the NHRA Top Stock Eliminator championship. Wangers' ability to walk the walk at the track added no small amount of credibility when he spoke about Pontiacs and performance. *Jim Wangers collection*

Though the rest of the sales staff didn't share Jesse's interest in high performance, they were jealous of all the attention (and sales commissions) he was getting from the new breed of young customers. Some of them tried to horn in on the performance market, but they weren't perceived as being authentically interested in fast cars, as was Jesse. The young customers still lined up outside Jesse's office, helping him keep his unofficial title of "Performance Sales Manager."

Royal always kept demo cars on the lot equipped with the very best Pontiac performance parts. Jesse used these cars as his most effective sales tools. If a customer wasn't sure about buying a high-performance Pontiac, Jesse would give him (back in those days virtually all customers for fast cars were male) a ride in a fast demo, often heading north of the dealership to a straight stretch of road through a cemetery. Since there was nowhere for the police to hide, it was a relatively safe place to get down on the car and demonstrate the nature of Pontiac performance in a most visceral manner. By the time they returned to the Royal sales lot, more often than not Jesse had a sale.

NATIONAL CHAMPIONS

As a drag-racing enthusiast and amateur drag racer, Wangers knew the importance of having Pontiacs successfully compete on the nation's drag strips. He'd convinced MacManus, John and Adams to advertise in the enthusiast magazines that catered to drag-racing fans, and now that his Royal Pontiac experiment was up and running, he decided to take his Pontiac performance gospel directly to the people, so Royal went drag racing.

The first Royal drag car, a red 1959 Catalina hard-top coupe, featured a stock 389 H.O. engine, which generated 341 horsepower and 425 lb-ft of torque. Frank Rediker, a brilliant mechanic who early on recognized the performance potential of turbochargers and superchargers, blueprinted and hand assembled many of the Royal race engines. Rediker worked at a local Oldsmobile dealership and worked on the Royal race engines in the evenings and on the weekends. He was assisted by his old friend Win Brown, another talented local hot rodder. Rediker and Brown developed many parts that would later become part of the Royal Bobcat package.

Wangers used his connections to get the team special retreads that had been created by a local Goodyear retread maker. These tires were undercooked. That is, they were not completely hardened, meaning that they were softer and stickier than any other available tires.

Drag racing in 1961 was a bit more relaxed than today. Notice the lavish pit area and the total lack of even a rudimentary roll cage in any of the cars.

Jim Wangers collection

Royal Pontiac used a pair of full-tilt Catalinas as tow vehicles, hauling the race cars from track to track. The team garnered plenty of ink, thanks to Wangers. *Jim Wangers collection*

Since many of the Super Duty package parts were still under development, the Royal team was forced to use aftermarket equipment such as an Isky E-2 cam on its 1959 drag car. They built a powerful engine, but the Achilles' heel of that first Royal drag car was its transmission and shifter. At the time Pontiac didn't offer a four-speed manual transmission; the cars came with three-speed manual transmissions shifted by horrible column-mounted shifters, and the only optional transmission was an automatic. The slow-shifting three-on-the-tree shifter, which was especially clumsy on second to third gear shifts, kept Royal's 1959 car from achieving much success. Eventually the team mounted 4.88:1 gears in the rear end, which allowed them to start in second

and make just one shift during the quarter-mile run. Using this method, the Royal Catalina managed a best quarter-mile time of 13.93 seconds.

For 1960 Royal campaigned a Coronado Red Catalina equipped with a 389-cubic-inch, 348-horsepower, Tri-Power-equipped H.O. engine. The engine received the full Rediker-Brown tune-up, significantly bumping its power output.

The Royal Pontiac had a definite advantage when it came to tires. Most drag racers at that time ran on Atlas Bucron tires. These were made of butyl rubber, which was softer and stickier than the rubber used on regular street tires and allowed the car to hook up better off the line. Wangers used his connections to get the team special retreads that had been created by a local Goodyear retread maker. These tires were undercooked. That is, they were not completely hardened, meaning that they were softer and stickier than any other available tires, even the Atlas Bucrons.

By 1960 Pontiac offered a complete line of Super Duty race parts through its catalog, and the Royal team took full advantage of Wangers' Pontiac connections to build the best drag racer possible. That meant building the lightest drag racer possible, and the Super Duty catalog featured numerous parts designed to shave weight off of race cars. The stock Catalina was a heavy car. Wangers and his crew mounted one of the first aluminum front bumpers that Pontiac had begun offering in its parts catalog, bringing the weight of the car down to right around 4,200 pounds, which was still heavy. Over the next few years the list of aluminum parts available in the Super Duty catalog grew to include fenders, hoods, braces, and wheels, bringing the weight of the big Pontiacs more in line with the competition.

With Jim Wangers behind the wheel, the Royal Pontiac 1962 Catalina sits among its competitors waiting for its turn on the track. Notice that virtually all of the lettering on the car is dealer related. This was in the era when you could actually see paint on the body. *Jim Wangers collection*

For 1962, Royal Pontiac used the Catalina as the basis for a potent drag racer. With a big engine in a midsized platform, it pointed the way for later muscle cars, such as the GTO.

For 1960 Pontiac finally offered the Borg Warner T-10 four-speed, floor-shifted transmission from Chevrolet's Corvette, though a poor-quality Inland linkage, which was standard equipment on all GM vehicles, connected the shifter to the transmission. Wangers and the Royal crew called the linkage "spaghetti" because it was so flexible and followed such a byzantine pathway between the shifter and gearbox. Still, it was better than the antiquated three-on-the-tree shifter setup.

Wangers, who had had quite a bit of success as an amateur drag racer in the past, drove the car himself that year, attaining the best results yet for Pontiac. When equipped with Bucron tires, cars usually found the best compromise between acceleration and traction by launching at 2,000 rpm; with the undercooked Goodyear retreads Wangers could launch at 2,500 rpm, giving him a significant advantage off the line. By the time the NHRA Nationals rolled around on Labor Day weekend that September, Wangers had won quite a few races and felt confident going into the Nationals, which were to be held in Detroit that year.

At the Nationals Wangers won the elimination round of the Super Stock class with a best run of 13.89 seconds at 102.67 miles per hour. On Monday, September 5, 1960, Wangers competed in the Top Stock Eliminator run off, which featured the 50 fastest cars from all classes. The temperature was considerably higher than it had been on Saturday night when Wangers won the Super Stock class, so Rediker decided to switch from 4.56:1 to 4.88:1 gearing to take advantage of the stickier asphalt. It proved a good move. Even though everyone's times were slower in the heat of the afternoon sun, Wangers won the Top Stock Eliminator class with a best run of 14.15 seconds at 100 miles per hour. Wangers and his Royal Pontiac team were the national drag racing champions.

SUPER DUTY 421

For 1961 Wangers' Royal Pontiac team had a powerful new tool, courtesy of the Super Duty Group: a 421-cubic-inch Super Duty race engine. With a bore of 4.094 inches and a stroke of 4 inches, this over-square engine shared few parts with any previous Pontiac engine. It had an 11:1 compression ratio, a pair of four-barrel 500-cfm Carter carburetors with manual choke and straight mechanical linkage, a McKellar Number 10 mechanical cam, and tuned aluminum exhaust manifolds, and it was conservatively rated at 405 horsepower, though most estimates are that true output was closer to 450 horsepower. In a 1962 road test, *Motor Trend* magazine calculated that the engine was producing 465 horsepower at the crankshaft and 505 lb-ft of torque.

Designed expressly for stock car and drag racing, Pontiac didn't install a single example of the Super Duty 421 in any cars on factory production lines for 1961. The race-only engine was installed in Pontiac's engineering garage, or else it was shipped to select dealers and installed by those dealers. Built in extremely limited quantities, the engine was available only to top drag-racing and NASCAR teams. Buyers had to sign agreements promising to use the engine for racing purposes only, waiving any factory warrantees and absolving Pontiac of all responsibilities for any mishaps resulting from the use of the engines.

Because the Royal Pontiac drag cars competed in the Super Stock class, it was necessary to retain the heavy bumpers and all of the exterior trim pieces. Royal's race car ran in the 12-second range.

Pontiac was stepping away from the styling excesses by 1961, introducing a svelte Catalina. The split grille had become a Pontiac feature, and it helped emphasize the Wide-Track look.

In addition to its larger bore and stroke and the improved top-end oiling system that was a feature on all Pontiac V-8s for the 1961 model year, the Super Duty 421 featured a redesigned block with larger main-bearing journals and four-bolt main bearing caps on the number 2, 3, and 4 journals, giving it the strength to stand up to the rigors of competitive use.

NASCAR DOMINATION

Prior to the AMA racing ban, NASCAR racing had played an important role in the development of American cars. Detroit began producing increasingly powerful engines to propel their cars to NASCAR winner's circles. In many ways, NASCAR racing drove V-8 engine development.

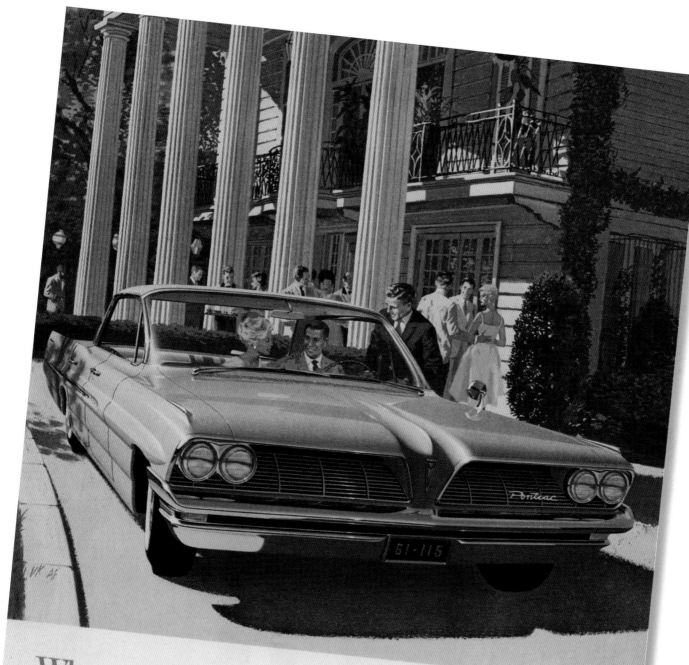

THE PONTIAC CATALINA VISTA FOR 1961

What comes in a Catalina? Wide-Track balance and
roadability! Trophy V-8 performance! Greatly improved gas mileage!
Yours only in a Pontiac. Yours easiest in a Pontiac Catalina. Yours
is ready now at your fine Pontiac dealer's.

PONTIAC—THE ONLY WIDE-TRACK CAR
Pontiac has the widest track of any car. Body width
trimmed to reduce side overhang. More weight balanced
between the wheels for sure-footed driving stability.

PONTIAC MOTOR DIVISION • GENERAL MOTORS CORPORATION

Tail fins were stepping off the styling stage in 1961, yet Pontiac's designers incorporated them in a tasteful fashion on the Catalina. Slender roof pillars ensured that visibility was superb, as well as creating a graceful greenhouse.

Though it was a pain to remove dead bugs, the thin slats were an elegant solution to filling the wide grille.

The Bonneville's performance at Daytona marked the beginning of Pontiac success in NASCAR. By the early 1960s, Pontiacs performed extremely well in NASCAR racing, thanks in large part to the availability of high-performance Super Duty racing parts. When the Super Duty 421 engine became available for the 1961 season, the select few racers who obtained the rare engine could build a competitive stock car using the parts available in the Super Duty catalog.

Super Duty Pontiacs won 30 Grand National races and the manufacturer's championship in 1961, though Ned Jarrett won the driver's championship in a Chevrolet Impala. The following year Pontiac was forced to either abandon the Super Duty 421 engine or offer it as a production option. To keep one brand from dominating the sport, NASCAR instituted a rule that would have a significant impact on the classic muscle car era; it required manufacturers to sell passenger cars with the same engines it raced.

This meant that the over-the-counter Super Duty parts Pontiac sold would no longer be eligible for NASCAR competition unless Pontiac installed it as a regular production option, so in 1962 Pontiac made its

421-cubic-inch Super Duty engine available as an option in some Pontiac models. These were still competition-only cars built in limited quantity. As had been the case with all previous Super Duty–equipped cars, they came with no factory warranty, and each car sold came with an elaborate list of instructions and warnings.

The list went on for five pages and includes a warning about burning holes in the cast-aluminum exhaust manifolds during sustained use. Pontiac wanted to make certain that no buyer accidentally bought a Super Duty car for commuting to work and picking up groceries.

These were thoroughbred race cars and highly successful ones at that. When properly set up, the Super Duty cars regularly turned in quarter-mile times of 12.5 seconds at speeds of 115 miles per hour or better. The engine proved itself in stock car racing, too. In 1962, Pontiac won its second NASCAR manufacturer's championship, and Bud Moore won the driver's championship in a Pontiac. Moore went on to win another championship in his number-eight Catalina the following year.

continued on page 50

The full-width bench seat allowed for three-across seating, but the center passenger might have had a difficult time twisting out of the way when the floor-mounted manual four-speed shifter was rowed.

With 389 cubic inches beneath the hood, the 1961 Catalina generated more than enough power to reduce the bias-ply tires to scrap. Emission controls were virtually nonexistent, leaving a mechanic plenty of room to work on the big V-8.

Twin 500-cfm carburetors sitting on top of a huge 421-cubic-inch V-8 helped the 1962 Super Duty Catalina to generate tremendous power. Rated at 405 horsepower, it actually generated in excess of 450.

1962 Model Super Duty Pontiac Special Notice

Super Duty Pontiacs are not intended for highway or general passenger car use and they are not supplied by Pontiac Motor Division for such purposes.

The Owner should recognize the following characteristics of the Super Duty Engines which make them unsuitable for general passenger car use.

The engine should be kept at a minimum idle speed of 1,000 rpm or above. This is necessary to ensure adequate lubrication of bearings and valve mechanism.

The ignition system is designed for high-speed operation. Consequently sustained low-speed operation will cause burning of the breaker points in the distributor.

As part of the maximum performance tuning of these engines, the exhaust heat is blocked out of the intake manifold. This results in extremely unpleasant operation during the extra-long warmup period. In fact, full warmup is never obtained during cold-weather operation.

The large capacity oil pan reduces ground clearance and would be subject to severe damage if driven over obstructions in the road.

Engine noise will be objectionable due to the large clearances required for expansion under maximum engine speed. Valvetrain and piston noise, in particular, will be most noticeable in normal driving conditions.

Winter starting and warmup operations will be particularly bothersome due to the thickness of the recommended heavy weight oil.

Finally, general operating expenses will be higher than normal due to the required use of "super premium" fuel and an engine oil supplement. Not only are these items more costly to purchase, but in many cases they may even be unavailable.

Caution

A competition package, #544990, shipped in the luggage compartment, contains the following items that must be installed before high-speed operation.

a. *Six quarts of SAE 30 oil and one 16 oz. can of Engine Oil Supplement should replace the factory engine oil. The original oil is suitable for low speed "car in transit" running only.*

b. *Resistor block #1931385 (.3 ohm) should replace factory-installed 2.2 ohm resistor #1941604 which prevents burning the distributor points during low speed operation.*

c. *High load valve springs #540362 and #540363 should be installed before exceeding an engine speed of 5,500 RPM.*

d. *High pressure fuel pump #5594901 is required to insure (sic) sufficient fuel for maximum operation.*

Above: Long, low, and wide, the 1962 Catalina Super Duty 421 was an ideal platform for a high-performance engine. A very limited number of Super Duty Catalinas wore aluminum front-end bodywork, earning them the name Factory Lightweight.

Right: With room for six adults, a tachometer strapped to the steering column, and a huge shifter jutting out of the tunnel, the 1962 Catalina Super Duty was ready for stoplight battles right off of the showroom floor. Yet with all the interior room, this was considered a midsized car.

All the painted bodywork seen here is aluminum. This factory option was designed to shave up to 150 pounds from the Catalina. Inset: As the 1960s wore on, American automobiles started wearing fewer chrome embellishments. But in 1962, the Catalina still sprouted "rocket spears" from the top of the front fenders. Maybe they helped cut the wind.

ROYAL BOBCAT

Bunkie Knudsen took Pontiac racing and succeeded beyond anyone's wildest dreams; within five years of his assuming control of the division Pontiac had earned national championships in both the NHRA and NASCAR. But the real measure of his success would be translating that racing success to sales at the dealership level.

Fortunately for Pontiac, Jim Wangers had a plan for achieving that goal. He'd already set up Royal Pontiac as a prototype for a performance-oriented Pontiac dealership. The next step was to create a performance car that would appeal to the growing youth market by taking the Royal Pontiac race image to the street. The resulting car would be one of the very first dealer specials–that is, series of performance cars modified at dealerships. Royal called the car the Royal Bobcat. In *Glory Days*, Wangers describes the reason he chose that name:

> *At the time Pontiac was using block letters to spell out Catalina, Star Chief, or Bonneville on their cars. They were placed strategically at the rear of each car. The block letters were all the same size and all standing alone. I played around with the letters Catalina and Bonneville to see I could find a new, catchy name. It didn't take long to come up with the word "Bobcat." It fit nicely in the same place on the car, and it looked like it came right out of the factory. Honestly, that's how we chose the name.*

Royal's performance special began life as a 1961 Catalina coupe equipped with the high-output Tri-Power version of the 389 engine, which generated 348 horsepower (though Royal switched to the 421-cubic-inch V-8 when a street version of that engine became available as a regular production option for the 1963 model year).

If a buyer wanted more power, Royal offered the Royal Bobcat tune-up package. This consisted of using thinner head gaskets to bump the compression ratio, progressive linkage for the Tri-Power carburetors, bigger jets in the carbs, a recurved ignition advance, and blocked intake heat-riser gaskets.

Most Royal Bobcats left the dealership with four-speed transmissions, though an automatic was optional, as were heavy-duty suspension components, tachometers, lower-geared rear ends, and Pontiac's innovative eight-lug aluminum wheels painted to match the colors of the bodies. In 1960 Pontiac had been the first American automaker to offer optional aluminum wheels. These rims, which were manufactured by Kelsey-Hayes, lowered unsprung weight and improved braking performance. Better yet, they looked terrific.

The Royal Bobcats proved popular; at its peak Royal sold more than 1,000 Bobcats per year. An unknown number of additional cars left the dealership with the full Bobcat treatment, but without Bobcat badging–some people preferred their fast cars to be inconspicuous.

Though Wangers' Royal Bobcat experiment was a local effort rather than a nationally distributed production car, it proved there was a strong market for factory-built performance cars.

At the 1962 Daytona 500 race, Fireball Roberts took the trophy with his Super Duty Catalina. This was the era when stock car racing actually raced stock cars.

CHAPTER 2

DELOREAN'S OUTLAW CAR

Bunkie Knudsen not only fulfilled his assignment from General Motors–make Pontiac profitable or GM would kill it–he exceeded anyone's wildest expectations. Thanks in large part to Knudsen's emphasis on performance and competition and the efforts of Jim Wangers off track and on, Pontiac not only survived, it thrived. By 1961, the five-year mark of Knudsen's tenure, Pontiac had become the number three nameplate in the American auto market, after Chevrolet and Ford.

As a reward for his success, Knudsen was promoted to head Chevrolet, a position generally considered to be the training ground for future General Motors presidents. Pete Estes was promoted to division manager at Pontiac.

GRAND PRIX

The success of the Royal Pontiac performance dealership and of the Royal Bobcat cars indicated there was a strong market for sporty cars. For 1962 Pontiac tested that market by introducing a new model aimed at performance-oriented buyers: the Grand Prix.

The Grand Prix wasn't meant to be an all-out street fighter; rather, it was designed to be a sporty luxury coupe, like Chrysler's original C-300. Based on the Catalina hard-top coupe, Pontiac's stylists gave the new car a European look. John DeLorean, who was by that time the chief engineer at Pontiac, admired the stylish and excellent-handling cars built in Europe, and he wanted the Grand Prix to embody the finer characteristics of European cars. His crew removed all chrome trim from the side panels and gave the car a monochromatic interior with vinyl seat covers. A new grille further distinguished the new Grand Prix from the Catalina.

A 389-cubic-inch engine equipped with a four-barrel carburetor came as standard equipment, though buyers could select the Tri-Power system as an option. A lowered suspension gave the car a firmer ride and better handling in the corners, traits more associated with European cars than with American iron at the time, and aluminum wheels were standard equipment.

Even in base form, the new car was one of the most powerful, most luxurious, and best handling cars sold in America, but a handful of people figured out a way to turn the car into one of the fastest production cars ever built up until that time. Sixteen people with the

Known within Pontiac as Style Number 67, the 1964 GTO convertible had that year's lowest production total of the three body styles, at 6,644 units.

The face of aggressive styling at Pontiac in 1962, the Grand Prix took the Wide-Track concept to its limit. Gold colored grille was part of Royal Pontiac's Bobcat treatment.

right corporate connections managed to get Grand Prixs equipped with Super Duty 421 race engines.

Unlike the stripped-down Catalina race cars that otherwise housed this potent mill (of which Pontiac built 162 examples), the Super Duty Grand Prixs were full-boat luxury cars, available with power steering, power windows, power bucket seats, and stereo speakers. Even with all this power-robbing and weight-adding equipment, a properly set up Super Duty Grand Prix with the right tires and a set of traction bars could break into the 12-second bracket.

The new Grand Prix was a hit with buyers; Pontiac sold 30,195 units in 1962 and sales jumped to 72,959 units in 1963, after a mild redesign of the exterior. Royal Pontiac brought Pontiac's performance image to the streets of Detroit with their Royal Bobcats. The Grand Prix took that image nationwide. Estes, DeLorean, and the rest of the folks at Pontiac proved they knew how to build a high-performance coupe. The Grand Prix was still too big, too luxurious, and too expensive to sell to the prodigious number of young buyers who were entering the market each year, but it certainly gave them something to lust after.

When an automobile designer worked with a full-sized vehicle like the 1962 Grand Prix, even the grille was oversized. The headlights of the era were used as stylistic elements, but were as effective as a pair of flashlights stuck to the front fenders.

Pontiac debuted the Grand Prix in 1962 to combat the Ford Thunderbird, and it met success. With its clean styling and wide range of powerful engines, some Grand Prixes were the subject of Royal Pontiac's famed Bobcatting process.

In stock form, the 1962 Grand Prix's Tri-Power-equipped 389-cubic-inch V-8 was rated at 318 horsepower. But factor in the speed tricks that Royal Pontiac used to Bobcat an engine, and suddenly the engine's output was north of 350.

If you wanted luxury and a Pontiac in the same package, you went for the 1962 Grand Prix. With its upscale appointments and host of standard features, the Grand Prix was an inviting place to watch the world roll by.

THE GENERAL MOTORS RACING BAN

Just as Bunkie Knudsen's investment in racing to promote Pontiac as a performance brand was starting to bear fruit in the marketplace, General Motors pulled the plug on all of its divisions' racing efforts. In 1963, General Motors instituted a total ban on factory racing involvement. Ed Cole, the father of Chevrolet's OHV V-8 engine and by that time a vice president at General Motors corporate headquarters, decided to halt all corporate racing activities, both direct and indirect. In late 1962, GM announced that the company would cease all support of racing for 1963.

Cole had a reason for this madness. Unlike his counterparts at other companies, Cole wasn't hell-bent on promoting a nanny state in which government and the corporate world contrived to protect automotive enthusiasts from themselves. Rather, he instituted the total racing ban in an attempt to keep the heavy hand of the nanny state off of GM's neck; by the early 1960s, GM had the federal government breathing down its corporate neck.

"This wasn't due to safety concerns or emission problems," Jim Wangers writes in *Glory Days*. "That would come later in the decade. The heat was from the Justice Department, who had determined that GM was getting too large a share of the U.S. car market." The real problem, as the Justice Department saw it, was that General Motors had come dangerously close to breaking the Sherman Antitrust Act of 1890, the federal antitrust law designed to prevent one company from monopolizing an entire industry.

Today, when General Motors' share of the U.S. auto market is less than 20 percent and Toyota has surpassed GM as the world's largest auto manufacturer, it seems ludicrous to imagine a U.S. auto manufacturer taking

Pontiac stylists incorporated a number of features to emphasize the lower, longer stance that Wide-Track stood for, including horizontal ribbing between the taillights and rear bumpers that wrapped around the lens elements. The result was a radical departure from the visual excess of just a handful of years prior.

The full-width ribbing between the taillights was a Grand Prix exclusive. Vestigial tail fins were shrinking, and by the time the Grand Prix debuted in 1962, they were almost gone.

moves to keep its share of the auto market from growing, but these were very different times. Imports from Europe comprised only a small percentage of the overall market and imports from Asia were virtually nonexistent. Imports were so rare that the only example many people living in the American Midwest had ever seen was the Volkswagen Beetle.

"You have to understand," Wangers says, "in the late '50s, early '60s, GM was in danger of getting between 57 and 60 percent of the new car market. The Justice Department said they were watching GM, and if GM ever got to 60 percent of the market or more, they'd move in and break up the company. They'd done it before with Standard Oil, so we knew they were serious. General Motors took . . . actions to slow down market penetration. That's why [Cole] issued the edict to ban racing in 1962."

DEATH OF THE SUPER DUTY GROUP

Since the Super Duty Group existed solely to make Pontiac successful in racing, the racing ban heralded the group's demise, as noted in the following memo:

> *ALL ZONE CAR DISTRIBUTORS*
> *EFFECTIVE TODAY JANUARY 24, 1963, 389 AND*
> *421 SUPER DUTY ENGINES ARE CANCELLED AND*
> *NO FURTHER ORDERS WILL BE ACCEPTED. (421 H.O.*
> *ENGINES ARE STILL AVAILABLE.)*
> *SUGGEST YOU ADVISE DEALERS WHO NORMALLY*
> *HANDLE THIS TYPE OF BUSINESS VERBALLY.*

Unlike the 1957 AMA racing ban, the GM corporate ban had teeth. A former manager of GM's Chevrolet division, and its chief engineer before that, Cole knew all

With its air-cooled engine mounted in the rear, the Corvair didn't need a conventional grille. In fact, the front portion of the vehicle was a roomy trunk.

With the optional turbo engine, the buyer of a 1963 Corvair enjoyed surprisingly comprehensive instrumentation. The layout was easy to read through the thin-rimmed steering wheel.

the tricks people such as Bunkie Knudsen and Pete Estes used to circumvent the AMA racing ban of 1957, and he was determined to stop them.

When General Motors announced the ban late in 1962, Pontiac had already delivered 88 1963 model-year Super Duty cars to drag-racing and NASCAR teams. Because these cars would not be offered as production cars in 1963, they didn't qualify for the NHRA's Super Stock class, so the NHRA created the F/X (Factory Experimental) class, in which highly modified cars powered by low-production engines could compete.

This eventually morphed into the Funny Car class.

MARKETING TO A NEW MARKET

The timing of the ban couldn't have been worse for Pontiac. The division had built a reputation for performance, and without the ability to showcase its cars in stock car and drag racing, Pontiac lost its primary tool for reaching the exploding youth market. Now it

was going to have to maintain its reputation as the performance company with that important demographic group solely on the merits of its production cars.

Pontiac hadn't had much luck building cars for the youth market up until that point. Its popular full-size cars were some of the fastest cars on the road, particularly the hot Catalinas and Grand Prixs, but these were big cars and, in the case of the Grand Prix, expensive big cars. Younger buyers gravitated toward smaller, sportier, less-expensive cars. Pontiac's track record for building midsize cars was not good at that time. The division's first attempt at building a small car for the youth market–the Tempest–had more or less been a failure.

Introduced in 1961, the Tempest was developed jointly with Buick and Oldsmobile as part of GM's X-body program. Like the Buick and Oldsmobile versions, the Tempest started life as a front-engined derivative of Chevrolet's peculiar rear-engined Corvair. The X-bodies shared the Corvair's basic unibody chassis, stretched 4 inches to attain a stature

Aimed at the enthusiast market, the optional 150-horsepower turbocharged flat-six-cylinder engine of the 1963 Corvair Spyder used a draw-through forced induction system. Turbocharging for street use was in its infancy, and turbo lag was a constant problem. The owner of this Corvair added braided stainless steel fluid lines to protect his investment. In an air-cooled engine, proper lubrication is essential to keeping temperatures down.

The turbocharged Corvair used discrete badges to inform others about the special powerplant. Vents in the engine cover allowed cooling air to circulate around the aluminum engine. Inset: The aluminum grate below the rear bumper aided in directing engine-cooling air to the rear-mounted engine. Simple bumpers kept the cost down, critical in Corvair's intended demographics.

The 1963 Tempest Le Mans Coupe had a transaxle and independent rear suspension in an effort to create a 50/50 weight distribution. The compact body used the split grille motif like the entire Pontiac line. As befitting an economy car, the 1963 Tempest Le Mans Coupe used a minimum of brightwork and neat, restrained body lines. More than one driver was caught unawares when a V-8-powered 1963 Tempest Le Mans coupe whipped by, especially in a turn. With a transaxle rear suspension and near-perfect weight distribution, the little Pontiac could really hustle around a corner.

more fitting for upscale nameplates like Pontiac, Buick, and Oldsmobile. The engines would be mounted in the front instead of the rear, as in the Corvair, and the Pontiac, Buick, and Oldsmobile cars would not use Chevrolet's opposed, air-cooled, six-cylinder engines. The use of traditional in-line and V engines necessitated a taller front profile than that found on the rear-engined Corvair, with a higher hood and front fenders. Because of this, GM's other X-bodies bore little resemblance to the Corvair.

Bunkie Knudsen, still heading Pontiac at that time, didn't want to produce a cookie-cutter version of the small cars being introduced by sister divisions Oldsmobile and Buick, so he had his engineers develop innovative technology to distinguish his division's version of the X-body platform. Pontiac engineers created a new four-cylinder engine by splitting its 389-cubic-inch V-8 in half. Displacing 195 cubic inches, huge for a four-cylinder, the engine produced ample horsepower and torque: 166 horsepower when equipped with a four-barrel carburetor. Unfortunately, it also produced excessive vibration. Modern large-displacement four-cylinder engines have balance shafts to quell engine vibration, but such technology wasn't available to Pontiac designers at that time.

Like the car itself, Pontiac's 1964 GTO advertising campaign was stylish and minimalistic. *David Newhardt collection*

The 1964 GTO had a track of 54.0 inches and an overall width of 73.3 inches. The standard US Royal Super Safety 800 "Tiger Paw" red stripe, nylon cord bias-ply tires measured 7.50x14 inches.

Instead, they resorted to an innovative system nicknamed the "rope-drive" because it used a flexible driveshaft woven from strands of high-tensile steel like a rope. This flexible driveshaft, which connected the rear engine housing to a transaxle transmission between the rear wheels, absorbed the engine's thunderous vibration remarkably well, keeping it from intruding on the passenger compartment.

With the high-tech Tempest, the reach of Pontiac's engineers exceeded their technological grasp. Even though the passengers were isolated from the vibration, it was still there, pounding the engine's nylon timing gears back into raw petroleum. Worse yet, the rear-mounted transaxle wasn't strong enough to handle the power output of the oversized four-banger engine. In

his autobiography, *On a Clear Day You Can See General Motors: John Z. DeLorean's Look Inside the Automotive Giant*, DeLorean describes the experience of driving the rope-drive Tempest: "The car rattled so loudly that it sounded like it was carrying half a trunk full of rolling rocks."

The system could be made to work—in a clandestine violation of the GM racing ban, Pontiac mounted Super Duty 421 engines in several Tempests and raced them in the F/X class, complete with rope-drive driveshafts and transaxle transmissions. With some development work the Tempest design had potential, but in stock form the fragile transmissions and timing-gear wear caused by the engine vibration doomed the high-tech Pontiac in the marketplace.

Covering a big country requires big power, and the 1964 GTO had it in spades. Pontiac took a serious gamble releasing the GTO, not knowing if buyers would step up. Fortunately, the risk paid off.

Maintaining the familial split grille, the 1964 GTO utilized T3 headlights, ideal for being seen, but less than stellar at illuminating the road.

DeLorean, who had been promoted to chief engineer when Estes took over as Pontiac's division manager and was on the fast track to become division manager himself after Estes' inevitable promotion to Chevrolet division, worried about the effect the GM racing ban would have on Pontiac's image with this emerging baby-boom market demographic. Without racing as a venue for showcasing Pontiac performance, DeLorean decided that Pontiac should build a high-performance passenger car that would take Pontiac's high-performance reputation to the street. This would be a car more like the Royal Bobcat Catalina than the well-appointed and expensive Grand Prix, a bare-knuckles street fighter that even young people could afford.

GRAN TURISMO OMOLOGATO

For 1964, Pontiac planned to replace the Tempest with a car based on GM's upcoming A-body platform. The A-body platform, which also included the Chevrolet Chevelle, the Oldsmobile F-85 Cutlass, and Buick Skylark, was an intermediate-size car with a conventional body-on-frame design that was as traditional as the unit-construction X-body cars had been innovative. The basic platform featured a stout box-section frame, which might have seemed like a move backwards from the advanced unit-body construction of the original Tempest, but it resulted in a car strong enough to pull a plow.

With this car, Pontiac's marketing team faced a two-fold challenge. Not only did they need to overcome the negative publicity generated by the failure of the rope-drive Tempest, they also needed to discover an entirely new method for reaching the youth market. Automobile enthusiasts were just beginning to view Pontiac as GM's performance division. The corporate racing ban seemed like a death sentence for Pontiac, but Jim Wangers saw it as an opportunity.

"Pontiac had carefully planned the image of its new cars," Wangers says. "They were quick on the street, but we knew that racing performance wasn't the only way to sell these cars. When that stage [racing] was abolished, we needed to keep our cars in the performance limelight."

Wangers regularly met with DeLorean to discuss this subject. DeLorean was particularly concerned with the marketing of the second-generation Tempest. In his book *Glory Days*, Wangers describes how DeLorean and his two favorite staff engineers, Bill Collins and Russ Gee, came up with an inspired way to promote the new Tempest and keep Pontiac cars in the performance limelight:

Delorean planned regular "What If?" sessions at the GM proving grounds in Milford, Michigan, on Saturday mornings. . . . It was very early spring, 1963. A prototype 1964 Tempest Coupe equipped with a 326-cubic-inch engine was on a lift.

DeLorean, Collins, and Gee were under the car, discussing the chassis. Collins casually mentioned, "You know, John, with the engine mounts being the same [a result of Pontiac's early decision to develop one family of engines rather than a "big-block" family and a "small-block" family], it would take us about 20 minutes to slip a 389 into this thing. We'll probably need some heavier springs in the front end, but the engine will fit right in."

John looked at him, caught an approving nod from Gee, and without uttering another word they were all in agreement.

One week later the group at the Saturday morning session was greeted by a prototype '64 Tempest coupe with a 389 engine in it.

The first prototype had a four-barrel carburetor instead of Pontiac's popular Tri-Power setup, but it had the prerequisite four-speed transmission with a heavy-duty clutch and a beefed-up suspension. It took one drive in the prototype DeLorean, Collins, and Gee had created to realize that this was the car that would meet the needs of the new baby-boom market: a sporty, intermediate-size car with big V-8 power. Everyone who drove the car came away impressed with the hot new Pontiac. DeLorean liked the car so much that he used the development mule, a beat-up Tempest painted in a nondescript beige Pontiac called Sahara Sand, as his daily driver. DeLorean could have had his pick of any car that Pontiac built, but he didn't find any of them as exciting to drive as the ratty little Tempest with the big engine.

Riding on a 115-inch wheelbase, the 1964 GTO had an overall length of 203 inches, short enough to fit in almost any garage. The tidy design of the GTO was evident in profile.

This was more than the beginning of a new model; this was the beginning of an entirely new automotive genre. That Saturday morning in Michigan marked the moment of the muscle car's birth. DeLorean named the car "GTO," which stood for Gran Turismo Omologato, Italian for "Grand Touring Homologated." The "Grand Touring" part of the name was self-explanatory; "homologated" means to make eligible for racing, which usually consists of building enough passenger cars to qualify a vehicle for a certain racing class. Ferrari also built a car called the GTO, but didn't own the name. The Federation Internationale Automobile

A low-mileage survivor, this 1964 GTO wears its original spark plug wires and patina well. The 389-cubic-inch V-8 didn't have any trouble fitting into the engine compartment, a fact realized at Pontiac Engineering.

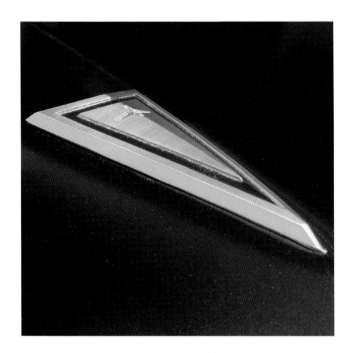

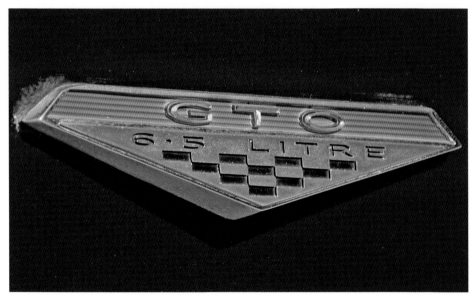

Above: The front end of the 1964 GTO was somewhat flush, as the Tempest, now a midsized vehicle, wasn't intended to possess the kind of visual flash found on the Catalina and Grand Prix.

Above left: In a nod to Pontiac's heritage, the hood ornament was an arrowhead.

Left: The 1964 GTO was the first American vehicle that denoted its engine displacement in liters. Prior to the GTO, all Yank cars used cubic-inch callouts to inform potential streetlight drag competitors.

(FIA), the sanctioning body for most European auto racing, owned the name. Pontiac had no affiliation with the FIA and had no intention of homologating the car for any racing class. Ultimately the car was built in such high quantities that it qualified for the type of racing that mattered most to young American enthusiasts: drag racing.

CORPORATE RENEGADES

Conceiving, naming, and developing the GTO proved to be the easy part. The hard part was getting the car approved by the fun police at General Motors, who were more concerned with staying under the Justice Department's radar than creating the perfect car for the baby-boom generation. In addition to banning

Above: An engine-turned instrument panel face surrounded the GTO's gauges and provided the interior with a bit of flash. The ball atop the standard Hurst shifter fell easily to hand during power shifts.

Right: A hint of a tail fin graced the rear of the 1964 GTO. Total production of the GTO during the 1964 model year was 32,450 vehicles.

Opposite: At a quick glance, the debut year of the GTO could be overlooked, as the styling was subdued. Yet this was usually the angle most saw the car from when they'd challenge it at a stoplight. The 389-cubic-inch engine could effortlessly overpower the narrow bias-ply tires.

The Cordova Top, a fancy name for a vinyl top, cost $75.32. Chromed dual-exhaust tips were standard with the GTO option.

corporate involvement in racing, the fun police had instituted a policy limiting GM cars to 10 pounds per cubic inch. According to that formula, the largest powerplant DeLorean could mount in the 3,400-pound Tempest's engine bay would displace 340 cubic inches.

Pete Estes, who had been promoted to division manager at Pontiac by the time the racing ban was announced, believed in the GTO. To make it a reality, he needed to find a creative loophole to help dislodge the stick from GM's corporate ass. Estes knew that the committee that oversaw such minutia as displacement-to-weight ratios only scrutinized new models and didn't inspect option packages, so Pontiac made the GTO an option package for the two-door LeMans, an upscale version of the Tempest that was to be Pontiac's counterpart to Chevrolet's Malibu, which was an upscale version of the Chevelle.

The list price for a 1964 LeMans Sport Coupe was $2,491, and then the buyer had to pony up another $295.90 for the W62 GTO Group option. It was worth every penny.

Above: Being a mass-produced automobile, the panel alignment could be a challenge. But most buyers of the 1964 GTO were less concerned with cut lines and more interested in the big engine under the hood.

Above right: Clean, simple, and to the point. The Hurst shifter was a point of pride from the GTO's first day, and the ability to consistently grab a gear under duress meant everything to an enthusiast. As the ball on top of the shifter aged, it developed tiny surface cracks, assuming a vintage patina.

Right: Wheel covers with "knock-off" lugs strongly suggested a sporty European flair. Federal regulations would see this type of wheel cover disappear after model year 1966, as some people thought the lugs were a threat to pedestrians. Sure.

In the 1960s, bumpers tended to become design elements rather than a way to thwart body damage in a parking lot. This was an era when stylists ruled, and engineering would find a way to put the eye candy on the road.

The biggest-selling model in the GTO's debut year was the graceful hardtop coupe, with 18,422 built. When equipped with a manual transmission, this model tipped the scale at 3,447 pounds.

To further ensure that the GTO would pass GM's corporate muster, Estes and DeLorean wanted to pre-sell 5,000 units before GM management found out about the car's existence, but to do this, Estes would have to quell a revolt headed by sales manager Frank Bridge. Estes had to convince Bridge that there was a youth market that would buy the GTO. Bridge believed the car wouldn't sell and would end up clogging up Pontiac dealership lots just as the ill-fated X-body Tempest had done. In *Glory Days*, Jim Wangers describes a meeting that he attended

with Estes, DeLorean, and Bridge in which Bridge gave his unvarnished opinion of the GTO: ". . . Bridge made it very clear that he didn't want it. 'Frankly,' he stated, 'this thing is going to be a real pain in the ass.'"

The 1963 line of full-size Pontiacs had been the division's most successful cars ever, and Bridge believed that trying to sell GTOs to teenagers would distract salesmen from the profitable work of selling full-size models. The failure of the Tempest had convinced him that there was no future in smaller cars.

He knew how to operate an efficient dealer network, but Bridge really knew nothing about the auto market. He didn't understand how much more appealing the youth market would find the smoking hot GTO when compared to the unwanted Tempest, and at the meeting he dug in his heels and fought the GTO like a pit bull in the ring. The meeting degenerated into a contentious confrontation between Bridge and DeLorean that appeared to be going nowhere until Estes stepped in and saved the GTO. Wangers describes the meeting in *Glory Days*:

DeLorean was pretty good at corporate politics, and after all this was his car. He wanted Bridge to commit to 5,000 so the car could be pre-sold to the dealers before the Corporation found out about it. The more Bridge protested, the angrier DeLorean got. Estes, who had a talent for handling these kinds of problems, finally turned to Bridge and said, masterfully, "Come on, Frank, you know you and your boys can sell 5,000 of anything."

From its bluff, no-nonsense front end to the straight flanks, the 1964 GTO exuded a performance attitude. The original muscle car could reach 60 miles per hour in just 7.7 seconds.

Is there a better way to work on your sunburn than in a GTO convertible? Even though it lacked a rigid top, it weighed a touch more than the closed cars, with a scale reading of 3,577 pounds for a manual transmission-equipped car.

Bridge smiled, almost as if embarrassed. Estes had hit him right in the middle of his ego.

"All right," Bridge said. "I'll put out a memo, and we'll turn it over to the Zones. We'll let the District Managers go out and see what kind of action they can drum up. If they can take 5,000 orders, I'll commit to it. But I don't want any more, and I bet they won't even sell 500."

Bridge, of course, couldn't have been more wrong, and he got 5,000 orders for the car within days. This made it all but impossible for GM management to kill the GTO without looking like the world's biggest collection of incompetents in front of its dealer network. The Pontiac team had slipped the GTO in under General Motors' corporate radar, but the car wouldn't remain invisible for very long.

SERIOUS HARDWARE

Pontiac rolled out the GTO in late 1963 with minimal fanfare. Officially listed as "W62 GTO Package," the car started as a basic LeMans, which had a 115-inch wheelbase and weighed 3,310 pounds. Ordering the W62 GTO Package transformed the LeMans into a GTO.

The revolutionary nature of the car wasn't immediately obvious. A casual glance at a 1964 GTO revealed a car that looked much like a LeMans. The only obvious visual clues that a car was a GTO were a pair of nonfunctional hood scoops, "GTO" lettering on a blacked-out grille, rear quarter panels, and right side of the rear trunk lid, and a "GTO" emblem on the front fenders. DeLorean's love of European sports cars influenced the understated styling of the new Pontiac and that European connection was strengthened by the fender emblem, which listed the engine's displacement as "6.5 LITRES" rather than announcing the engine's cubic-inch displacement. This was the first time an American car had ever announced its displacement using the metric system.

That "6.5 LITRES" to which the GTO badge referred–the high-output 389-cubic-inch engine–was the primary piece of equipment distinguishing the LeMans from the GTO. Generating 325 horsepower at 4,800 rpm and 428 lb-ft of torque at 3,200 rpm, the standard GTO engine was the most massive and powerful V-8 ever mounted in a midsize car up until that point. A Carter four-barrel carburetor pumped its fuel charge through a

dual-plane intake manifold into high-compression heads pilfered from the division's high-output 421-cubic-inch engine. That fuel charge needed to be of the high-octane variety to placate the 10.75:1 compression ratio without inducing detonation. Spent exhaust gasses exited through a dual-exhaust system. Inside the engine, hardened cast Arma Steel rods connected the flat-top aluminum pistons to the cast pearlitic malleable iron crankshaft.

Serious speed freaks replaced the stock floor-shifted three-speed manual transmission with one of two optional four-speed units. The wide-ratio M20 four-speed transmission was used on cars with gear ratios up to 3.55:1. Pontiac specified the M21 close-ratio four-speed transmission when the stout 3.90:1 gear set resided in the 10-bolt rear differential housing. Stump-pulling ratios of 4.11:1 and 4.33:1 were available as dealer-installed options. Of course, any self-respecting hot rodder replaced the standard one-leg rear end with the Safe-T-Track locking differential. By December 1963, Pontiac made available the $112.51 Tri-Power option, which added a trio of Rochester two-barrel carburetors and bumped power output to 348 ponies. Torque output remained the same as with the four-barrel engine, though the Tri-Power engine didn't achieve its 428 lb-ft of torque until 3,600 rpm.

Other performance options included a heavy-duty radiator, quick-ratio (20:1) manual steering box, transistorized ignition, heavy-duty alternator and battery, metallic brake linings, and heavy-duty springs and shocks. Buyers of post or hardtop body styles could also order the heavy-duty frame with frame-reinforcing crossmembers used on the convertible models.

THE HURST CONNECTION

With the GTO, Pontiac made a break with GM tradition and dropped the awful Inland shift linkage–the "spaghetti" that had hampered the Royal Pontiac drag cars–and gave the car an infinitely better Hurst shifter set up. Jim Wangers had switched to Hurst shifters in his drag racers in 1962, and in the process developed a friendship with George Hurst.

Hurst shifters worked so well in Wangers' drag racers that he convinced DeLorean to meet with Hurst about the possibility of Hurst supplying shifters to Pontiac. DeLorean recognized the quality of Hurst's engineering and appreciated the marked improvement Hurst shifters

While the hood scoops on the 1964 GTO were just for show, it wouldn't be long before the engineers at Pontiac created the Ram Air induction system, feeding the engine with cool ambient air.

and linkage made in a car's performance. He specified Hurst shifters on all manually shifted Pontiacs.

Even though 1964 GTOs were equipped with Hurst shifters, in 1964 the shifters weren't labeled with the "Hurst" logo. That was because GM's corporate policy prohibited suppliers from putting their names on any factory-mounted parts.

By this time Hurst had developed a reputation for quality and performance. Wangers saw a marketing opportunity in branding Pontiac shifters with the "Hurst" logo, then capitalizing on the Pontiac-Hurst partnership in Pontiac's advertising. He convinced Estes that this would be a good marketing tool and Estes agreed. Beginning with the 1965 model year, all manually shifted Pontiacs featured the Hurst logo prominently displayed on their shift levers.

When properly set up, the GTO offered solid all-around performance, let down only by the standard 9.5-inch drum brakes and stock tires. The tires were especially problematic on cars equipped with the M21 transmission option. They were just too skinny to handle all the torque the drivetrain produced. "You could launch the GTO from a standing start and burn rubber to infinity," Wangers writes in *Glory Days*.

SLOW START

Pontiac offered the GTO in three body styles: a two-door post coupe, a two-door hardtop, and a convertible. The W62 GTO Package option added $295.90 to the price of a LeMans. This meant that the price of a base coupe started at $2,776, the hardtop cost $2,852, and the convertible cost $3,081. This made the GTO a car just about anyone with a job could afford. Buyers could raise that price dramatically by liberally checking off the boxes on Pontiac's extensive list of options, such as a push-button AM/FM radio with electric antenna, Separa-Phonic or Verba-Phonic rear speaker, dual-exhaust extensions (often called "exhaust splitters"), tilt steering wheel (which required the buyer to order the optional power steering), power brakes, Rally gauge cluster, Custom Sports steering wheel, rear-window defogger, power windows, power bucket driver's seat, Tri-Comfort air conditioning, center console, Rally wheels, and a two-speed automatic transmission. When fully optioned, the price could climb to $4,000.

When outfitted with all the options the GTO was really more of a luxury touring car, sort of a three-quarter-size Grand Prix, but even the base version was a

It's hard to believe today, but this was considered a midsized vehicle. Note the size of the trunk; it could haul plenty of your friends through a drive-in entrance.

With clean body lines showing a minimum of ornamentation, the 1964 GTO was visually all business, and when the driver slammed the gas pedal to the floor, it could back up its claims.

built race cars of the period like the Super Stock Dodges with their 426 Max Wedge and later 426 Hemi engines, or the Z-11 Impalas or Ford Thunderbolts. These were temperamental drag racers and technically weren't even legal to drive on public highways. They were prohibitively expensive, difficult to maintain, and built in such low volumes that most people outside of the drag racing community never even saw one. And these cars ran in different classes than those in which the GTO competed, so the new Pontiac seldom went head-to-head with these monsters. The GTO did extremely well when competing against similar cars in the NHRA's B/Stock classes.

The GTO's real competition consisted of cars like Ford's Mustang, which only had a 289-cubic-inch engine as its top choice, Chevrolet's Chevelle SS, which only offered engines ranging up to 327 cubic inches, and Plymouth's Barracuda, which only offered a 270-cubic-inch V-8 option. When properly set up and driven by a talented driver, any of them could give the GTO a run for its money, but in the hands of an average driver as delivered by the factory, the GTO was the hottest game in town for 1964.

relatively luxurious car compared to the offerings from the competition, featuring such standard equipment as door-to-door carpeting, which was an option on most intermediate cars of the era, and a turned aluminum dash appliqué that gave the interior of the car a futuristic, high-tech ambiance.

The optional Rally gauge package broke new ground for an American car. Most cars of the period filled the dash with a sweeping speedometer and mounted any optional gauges in pods and clusters in out-of-the-way hard-to-see places. The Rally gauges placed the gauges in four round pods right in front of the driver, where he could read them at a glance. In 1964 the tachometer was located in the far right pod where it was difficult to read, but in 1965 it was moved to a more logical and easier to read location in the right center pod, next to the speedometer, which was in the left center pod.

The driver needed to keep an eye on the tach because the GTO was one of the fastest production cars built in 1964. With its 389 cubic inches of displacement and hydraulic lifters, it couldn't compete with the purpose-

With one hand on the rim of the four-spoke steering wheel and the other resting on top of the shifter, a driver could spend some quality time exhibiting anti social behavior. No gewgaws, just a simple machine designed to go fast.

CAR and DRIVER

MARCH 1964 • 50 CENTS

Tempest GTO: 0-to-100 in 11.8 sec
Who Killed Studebaker? – Page 75
Rover 2000 Road Research Report

CAR and DRIVER ROAD TEST

PONTIAC TEMPEST GTO

Ferrari never built enough GTOs to earn
the name anyway—just to be on the
safe side though, Pontiac built a faster one

Most knowledgeable enthusiasts reacted negatively when
Pontiac announced that their new Tempest sports model
was to be called the GTO. They felt, as we did, that Pontiac
was swiping a name to which it had no right. Like Le Mans,
Grand Prix, Monza, Spyder and 2+2, this was another of
those hard-to-digest bits of puffery from the Detroit/Madison
Avenue axis. Our first look at the car made us feel a little better, because it *is* handsome, and then we got a call from corre-
spondent Roger Proulx, raving about the car's acceleration
and handling, so we arranged to test a Pontiac Tempest GTO.

This was the most exhaustive and thorough road test we

CONTINUED 25

performance that, to us, was absolutely breathtaking. The Tempest GTO is better. First of all, its smaller outside dimensions make it a lot more fun to drive; and, second, it goes faster.

Our test car was equipped with the 389-cubic-inch, 348 horsepower, V-8 engine with hydraulic valve lifters and a compression ratio of 10.4 to one. It had the new GM "Muncie" four-speed transmission and Pontiac's Saf-T-Trak limited-slip differential. The rear axle ratio was 3.90 to one, and the brakes had metallic linings. The car had standard Tempest GTO suspension (slightly stiffer valving in the shocks) and manual steering with an overall ratio of 20 to 1, substantially faster than the standard manual steering ratio of 26 to 1, but slower than the power steering's 17 to 1. We preferred the power steering—not because the manual set-up was too stiff, but because it still wasn't quite fast enough.

A word of caution here: Pontiac is forced by the realities of commerce to build cars for little old ladies and GM executives as well as enthusiasts. It is quite possible to go to your dealer's for a demonstration drive and find yourself in a GTO of infinite dullness—an automatic-transmission-, power-operated-seat-, tinted-window-car with little to distinguish it from a Chevelle, a Buick Special, an Olds F85, or any other semivisible American car. The GTO that delights the executive from the fourteenth floor of Detroit's General Motors Building is *not* going to be the rabid enthusiast's dish of tea. To buy a car like our test car you should either get hold of a catalog and memorize the options you want, or seek out a live-wire dealership like Royal Pontiac in Royal Oak, Michigan, the firm that loaned us our GTO.

Royal is run by a man named Ace Wilson, who must be what regional sales managers ask Santa Claus to bring them for Christmas. His dealership is big and bright, with clean

modern architecture and a whole staff of knowledgeable salesmen and mechanics. Royal *is* Pontiac performance headquarters, and a Royal license plate frame on your GTO or Grand Prix is enough to send teenagers into orbit anywhere in the United States. Royal even has its own line of accessories and speed equipment, certain combinations of which give the proud GTO or Catalina owner the right to call his car a Royal Bobcat, and to fit it with small black and white emblems to that effect.

Our test cars were Bobcats. This means that they were basically stock Tempest GTO's with the following changes:

1. The main jets were changed to .069 in on all three carburetors for maximum acceleration. Normally, the center carburetor runs lean (.066 in) for cruising economy, with rich jets (.073 in) on the outboard carburetors for occasional bursts of speed. The Royal treatment gives a more even mixture distribution at a slight increase in steady-speed gas consumption.

2. A progressive-action throttle linkage is installed to calm the beast down for boulevard use; it's also more accurate than the stock linkage.

3. The distributor is modified to limit centrifugal advance to 7° (14 crankshaft degrees) and initial advance is set at a whopping 20-22° (total advance, 34-36°, is reached at 3600 rpm). This makes a tremendous improvement in low-end response (i.e., below 3600 rpm) but substantially raises the octane requirement.

4. The heat riser is blocked off, a special (thin) head gasket from the Super-Duty 421 engine is installed and still more compression is gained by installing Champion J-10Y plugs without gaskets.

5. Finally, special fiber-insert rocker arm retaining locknuts are installed which permit the hydraulic lifters to function as a solid lifter—operating at 90% bleed-down.

have ever done. We used two nearly-identical cars, the differences being that one car had the shorter-ratio manual steering while the other had power; the manual steering car was also equipped with metallic brake linings. We drove our two cars unmercifully. One was driven from Detroit to New York City, used for ten days by every member of the staff, and then driven from New York to Daytona Beach, Florida, carrying the managing editor, his wife, and three active children. This car—the manual steering, metallic brake version—was driven over 3000 miles. The other car was driven about 500. We ran dozens of acceleration tests on the two cars, plus many, many laps of the Daytona International Raceway's tri-oval and road circuit.

It was our original intention to borrow a Ferrari GTO and to run the two against each other at Bridgehampton's road racing circuit and on the drag strip at Westhampton. We had engaged Walt Hansgen to drive the Pontiac and Bob Grossman to run his own Ferrari. Unfortunately Grossman's Ferrari was tired from a season of racing, and was not considered fast enough to really be a match for our Tempest. We then canvassed all the GTO owners in this country and simply could not get one of those lucky gentlemen and the weather to cooperate simultaneously. As a result, we drove two Ferrari GTO's, but we were never able actually to run the Tempest against either one of them.

Although it would have been great fun and quite interesting to run the Ferrari racing car against Pontiac's similarly-named touring car, our tests showed that there really was no effective basis for comparison—the Pontiac will beat the Ferrari in a drag race, and the Ferrari will go around any American road circuit faster than the stock Tempest GTO. We are positive, however, that a Tempest like ours, with the addition of NASCAR road racing suspension, will take the measure of any Ferrari other than prototype racing cars or the recently announced 250-LM. We should also point out that our test car, with stock suspension, metallic brakes and as-tested 348 bhp engine will lap any U.S. road course faster than *any* Ferrari street machine, including the 400 Superamerica. Not bad for an actual delivered price of 3400 dollars, wot?

It was a shade over ten years ago that events in Detroit took a turn for the better and started the trend that ultimately resulted in the Tempest GTO. At that time, GM announced the Corvette. It was a funny car, hooted and jeered at by enthusiasts and by-passed by the great unwashed in favor of its more understandable competitor, the two-seater Thunderbird.

From those humble beginnings (with the late-fifties prompting of a robust and growing imported car market), came a host of better, more interesting cars from Detroit. The success of the Corvette and the sports-type Corvair Monza led the other GM divisions to build similar cars, particularly in the B-O-P compact lines. Buick and Oldsmobile leaned toward the concept of "Little Thunderbirds," cars with bucket seats and floor-mounted shift levers, but little else of a sporting nature. Pontiac, God love 'em, went the hairy-chested route and came up with our test car, the best American car we have ever driven, and probably one of the five or six best cars in the world for the enthusiast driver.

Obviously, personal preference must come into play here. There are many of our readers who think that a Sprite is the absolute epitome of grand touring, while others feel that no car should have a displacement greater than 1500cc. Add to these the purist who wouldn't drive an American car if his life depended on it, and you have a pretty fair-sized body of opposition. We respect their differing opinions and will defend to the death their right to express them, but we will stand or fall on our enthusiasm for the Tempest GTO.

In 1963 we were a bit stunned by a Mercury Marauder that had 427 cubic inches, 425 horsepower, good handling, and

PONTIAC TEMPEST GTO

Manufacturer: Pontiac Motor Division,
General Motors Corporation,
Pontiac, Michigan
Price as tested: $3377.91

ACCELERATION

Zero to	Seconds
30 mph	1.8
40 mph	2.4
50 mph	3.3
60 mph	4.6
70 mph	6.0
80 mph	7.5
90 mph	9.6
100 mph	11.8
Standing ¼ mile	115 mph in 13.1

PONTIAC TEMPEST GTO

Temperature .... 57°F
Wind velocity .... 22 mph
Altitude above sea level .... 100 ft

In 4 runs, 0-60 mph times varied between 4.4 and 4.9 seconds

Top Speed
115 mph
(observed)

ACCELERATION TIME – SECONDS

ENGINE

Water-cooled V-8, cast iron block, 5 main bearings	
Bore x stroke	4.06 x 3.75 in, 103 x 95.3 mm
Displacement	389 cu in, 6364 cc
Compression ratio	10.75 to one
Carburetion	Three Rochester two-barrel
Valve gear	Pushrod-operated overhead valves, hydraulic lifters
Power (SAE)	348 bhp @ 4900 rpm
Torque	428 lb-ft @ 3600 rpm
Specific power output	0.91 bhp per cu in, 55 bhp per liter
Usable range of engine speeds	800-5600 rpm
Fuel recommended	Super-premium
Mileage	9-12 mpg
Range on 21.5-gallon tank	190-260 miles

DRIVE TRAIN

Clutch	10.4-inch single dry plate
Transmission	4-speed all-synchro

Gear	Ratio	Over-all	mph/1000 rpm	Max mph
Rev	2.26	8.81	-8.7	-49
1st	2.20	8.78	9.0	50
2nd	1.64	6.39	12.2	69
3rd	1.31	5.11	15.0	84
4th	1.00	3.90	19.9	115
Final drive ratio				3.90 to one

CHASSIS

Perimeter frame with torque boxes	
Wheelbase	115 in
Track	F 58, R 58 in
Length	203 in
Width	73.3 in
Height	53.5 in
Ground clearance	6.0 in
Dry weight	3256 lbs
Curb weight	3485 lbs
Test weight	3850 lbs
Weight distribution front/rear %	55/45
Pounds per bhp (test weight)	11.0
Suspension:	F: Ind., unequal-length wishbones and coil springs, anti-roll bar. R: Rigid axle, two upper and two lower trailing arms, coil springs.
Brakes:	9.5-in drums front and rear, metallic linings, 270 sq in swept area
Steering	Recirculating ball (20.1)
Turns lock to lock	4½
Turning circle	41 ft
Tires	7.50 x 14
Revs per mile	773

26

As you can see, these changes are neither extensive nor complicated, and fall more into the area of maximum tuning than that of modification or "hopping up." The net result is an enormously strong engine with the capacity to spin its rear wheels in every gear, in spite of a limited-slip differential! The only penalty we noticed was that the car would knock like twenty-five poltergeists at a seance when anything but Sunoco 260 premium fuel (about 102 octane) was used.

Were we to buy a GTO (and there's a good chance at least one of us will), our selection might go something like this. A GTO is basically a $2480 Tempest Le Mans with a $296 extra-equipment package that includes a floor shift, 389 engine, dual exhaust, stiffer shocks, "exterior identification" and a choice of super-premium tires or whitewalls. The four-speed, all-synchro transmission is $188 extra, and we'd gladly pay $115 to get the hottest (348 bhp) engine. The shorter axle ratios are only available with metallic brakes, HD radiator and limited-slip differential ($75.00 for the lot). Quick steering (20:1) is part of the handling option, though HD shocks and springs alone are only $3.82. The "wood"-rim steering wheel is $39, and from there on in, it's trimming the window with fuzz (like $36 for custom wheel covers). With every conceivable option on a GTO it would be difficult to spend more than $3800. That's a *bargain*.

We find the GTO quite handsome, except for those phony vents that GM Styling's Bill Mitchell insists upon hanging on everything. Unlike the Sting Ray, the GTO has only the ones on the hood, so we can say it could be much, much worse. Our test car was a rich dark blue with black U.S. Royal Red Line tires and very conservative wheel covers. There was nothing to give away the presence of the ferocious beast concealed inside, and yet the car would draw admiring glances wherever it went. Whether it was the car's restrained good looks or the threatening grumble from the four (count

em, four) shiny tail pipe extensions, we never learned.

Once inside, everything seems to be just about where you would have put it in a car of your own design. The optional steering wheel is wood-looking plastic that had us completely conned. To our embarrassment, some smart aleck who'd read the catalog pointed out our mistake and made us feel like General Motors had really taken us. Wood or not, it's handsome as hell and an excellent piece of fakery. The instruments are all well-placed and legible, except for the tachometer, which is terrible—it's too far to the right to be glanced at during a hard run, and, worse, it's the wand type that sweeps horizontally across a four-inch quandrant and is practically impossible to read anyway. The speedometer is just slightly left of center in the panel and it has a typical 270 degree clock-type face. Our choice would be to swap the tach and speedometer locations, substituting a Sun SST (270°) tach for the factory's $53.80 optional tach.

The transmission lever is nicely placed immediately next to the driver's thigh. It has the now famous Hurst linkage which is amazingly short and unerringly accurate. The sports car driver's first tendency is always to try to make the gate wider than it is, and the shift pattern more complicated. After a little time in the car, however, the brutal simplicity of that great tree-trunk of a lever begins to reassure you and you start throwing shifts with the same slam-bang abandon as the drag racing types. Our photographer drove the car and commented that he was used to driving imported cars and he had a hard time getting used to the extreme closeness of the GTO's gate. Kismet.

The so-called bucket seats in the GTO are the same as those in the Corvair Monza or any of the B-O-P compacts. That is to say they are not buckets at all, but actually individual front seats with a modicum of lateral support. We'd like the car better if the seats wrapped around farther and

were more firmly constructed, but that's the breaks. In one way, the softness is a good deal, because anybody who's a middleweight or bigger will compress the seat cushion all the way anyway, and then it becomes quite satisfactory. Fore and aft adjustment on the front seats is excellent provided you have the manual adjustment—the power assisted system limits travel enough to preclude any kind of straight-arm driving technique for would-be heroes. Rear seat room is cramped for three—it is, strictly speaking, a four seater.

Driving this car is an experience no enthusiast should miss. Unfortunately, few Pontiac dealers will have GTO demonstrators with the proper equipment on them, but if you can get your hands on one like we tested, it's almost worth stealing it for a few minutes of Omigod-we're-going-too-fast kind of automotive bliss. One expects the acceleration to be spectacular in first and second, but none of us were ready for the awful slamming-back-in-the-seat we got when we tromped on it at 80 in fourth.

This car does what so many others only talk about—it really does combine brute, blasting performance with balance and stability of a superior nature. The managing editor, for instance, was cruising through a pitch black Florida night on a road that skirted the Atlantic. He was traveling at about ninety when he got into a series of ess-bends marked for 45 mph—he found himself going in at about 75 and coming out at 100, so he choose 95 as a comfortable median and negotiated the entire series, including bumps, camber changes and nasty, narrow little bridges without ever touching the brakes or changing the position of his hands on the steering wheel. The car does not handle particularly well in a 35-mph right-angle turn because of its large size, but as the speed rises the quality of the handling goes up by the square.

Charlie Kolb helped us wring the cars out at Daytona and he liked them so well that he wanted us to promote a team of them for the 2000-kilometer Daytona Continental race in February. Lapping the track at Daytona with Kolb driving was quite interesting because we were able to sit back and examine the car's behavior under really extreme conditions. It was totally forgiving, and always stayed pointed. Its handling starts as understeer at very low speeds, becomes neutral at moderately fast speeds, and gradually—quite pleasantly in fact—becomes oversteer when pressed to its limit. Two staff members managed to spin the car in the same 80-mph corner, and both times the tail came out, stayed out, and led the way off the road. It is, incidentally, a very pleasant car to go off the road in, provided you don't catch a finger in the whirling spokes of the steering wheel.

Obviously, the GTO as we drove it, without the $16.82 heavy-duty suspension option, is not suitable for road racing. It rolls too much and the steering, even with the 20 to 1 ratio manual installed, is too slow. But what a road car! The metallic brake linings pulled the car down from speeds as high as 120-125 over and over again without grabbing or pulling one way or the other. The car would vibrate viciously on the rough banking at 125 mph, but never showed any indication that the suspension was being overtaxed. We used Goodyear Blue Streak Stock Car Specials (7.10-7.60 x 15 rear, 6.70 x 15 front) for the road circuit and the tri-oval, but found them absolutely unable to handle the wheelspin on the acceleration runs.

We didn't like the U.S. Royal Red Line tires on a car this powerful. We would like to have had Dunlop SP's. We prefer belted tires in all high speed cruising situations, and we feel that a tire like the SP, which has proved in rallying that it can hold up and give maximum stability under the wildest power-input and wheelspin conditions, would be just right. An interesting sideline here is that we got more miles per hour in the quarter mile with the Red Lines, while we got better elapsed times with huge drag racing slicks. The times quoted in our data panel were obtained with the standard tires and are spectacular enough, but when we ran the slicks we got down as low as 12.8 seconds at 112 mph. Now that's what we'd call pretty fair acceleration. It was only ten years ago that we were all pretty impressed when a Cadillac Allard cut a 15-second quarter at the Santa Ana Drag Strip. A production Cobra won't go that fast.

So, in winding this up, how do we classify this car relative to other GT cars, and particularly to the car from which it stole its name? The Ferrari GTO is a racing car that costs upwards of $20,000 dollars new. Therefore we are not surprised that it will go around a road racing circuit several seconds faster than our Tempest GTO. What does surprise us is that we found the Tempest GTO a better car, in some respects, than most current production Ferraris. It is not as refined, the quality of the materials and the workmanship is not as good, it feels bigger, and it *is* bigger, but cars are to drive, and when you drive a Tempest GTO with the right options on it, you're driving a real automobile. Can Pontiac help it if they're too dumb to know that a car can't go that fast without a prancing horse decal on the side?   C/D

Above: Nearly 45 years later, Jim Wangers again takes to the street in the 1964 GTO that Royal Pontiac Bobcatted and *Car & Driver* magazine tested. In the 1964 "season" following the tests, this GTO was never beaten in the competitive Woodward Avenue environment.

Right: Cruising the mean streets of Burbank, California, Jim Wangers works the gearbox of the 1964 GTO that was modified before it was loaned to *Car & Driver* magazine for testing. Don't let the stock interior fool you: this was a heavily prepared race car.

Jim Wangers poses with his historic 1964 GTO at the famed Bob's Big Boy in Toluca Lake, California. It was at drive-ins like this, lining Woodward Avenue, that he would line up races. His prowess behind the wheel did wonders in creating the street credibility of the GTO.

It might not be the outskirts of Detroit, but this 1964 GTO looks at home at a West Coast drive-in, looking for a little action. The narrow tires had a tough task transferring the 421's power into traction.

TRYING NOT TO SELL CARS

Pete Estes' outlaw division had slipped the car past GM's corporate arbiters of fun, but just barely. Estes and DeLorean wanted to avoid enraging them further. The corporation had let the rogues at Pontiac have their way, and they were happy to sell the additional 5,000 LeMans coupes to which Bridge's dealers had committed; but they made it clear that this would be a one-time exemption and they supported Bridge's goal of limiting sales to 5,000 units. "'We don't want to see any more,'" Wangers quotes corporate brass in *Glory Days*. "'Remember, just 5,000.'"

Pontiac made a good-faith effort to comply with that ridiculous edict and intentionally deleted the GTO from its full catalog of 1964 models. The division limited initial advertising to black-and-white inserts in enthusiast magazines. In a low-key 1963 press release, Estes proclaimed the GTO "a significant addition to Pontiac's list of individualized Sports Car developments," but in general the car rolled into the market with little fanfare.

Because of the almost complete lack of publicity, initial sales didn't look as though they would break through the 5,000-unit limit GM management had specified. But the GTO was simply too good a car to remain undiscovered. Word-of-mouth publicity proved to be enough to generate strong sales for a car that so perfectly captured the qualities the baby-boom market desired, at a price they could afford. By the time 1964 rolled around, sales had begun to pick up, and within the first six months Pontiac had sold more than 15,000 units.

A test that appeared in the March 1964 issue of *Car & Driver* magazine pitted a Pontiac GTO against a Ferrari GTO, one of the most exclusive and exotic automobiles in the world. The cars didn't actually compete head to head, except in an oil painting commissioned for the magazine's cover, and performance numbers weren't exactly fair, since Jim Wangers now admits he secretly replaced the stock 389-cubic-inch engine in the car used for track testing (Pontiac gave the magazine two cars

Equipped with comfortable bucket seats, a stylish 4-spoke steering wheel, and a beefy shifter, the 1964 GTO was pure muscle car. Fripperies such as air conditioning and power windows didn't help the car go any faster, hence they weren't installed. Neither was any sound-deadening material.

Externally identical to a 389, this engine was actually a Bobcatted 421 that Wangers had installed to boost the performance during magazine tests. He might have forgotten to tell the editors that the engine wasn't completely stock.

While this emblem mounted on a Pontiac denoted that the car was modified to run faster than most, this particular car held a secret. With its Bobcatted 421-cubic-inch engine, it was a big wolf in, if not sheep's clothing, normal wolf's clothing.

for testing) with a tweaked 421-cubic-inch H.O. motor. Wangers, who attended the test, also knew the flawed quarter-mile testing procedure the magazine used was producing numbers bordering on fantasy, but he had no interest in correcting them. Quarter-mile times of 13.1 seconds in the spec box and photos of Pontiac's baby-boom car sitting on the test track next to a mighty Ferrari gave the Pontiac instant credibility. Recognizing that this story compared apples to oranges, the writer asked if, in Pontiac's case, the GTO initials hadn't stood for "Going Too Far Overboard?" No matter; GTO sales exploded upon publication of the article.

OVERWHELMING SUCCESS

People started buying the cars as fast as Pontiac could build them, and Pontiac soon abandoned its pledge to build just 5,000 units. GTO sales for the 1964 model year totaled 32,450 units, of which 8,245 cars were equipped with Tri-Power carburetion. The majority of the cars were hardtops (18,422 units), while 7,384 buyers selected the less stylish (but stiffer, lighter,

The *GeeTeeOoh!* showed what a properly set up GTO could run, when the setting up was done by Royal Pontiac. The performance "tricks" that Royal used to create their vaunted Bobcat treatment were applied to the *GeeTeeOoh!* with good effect.

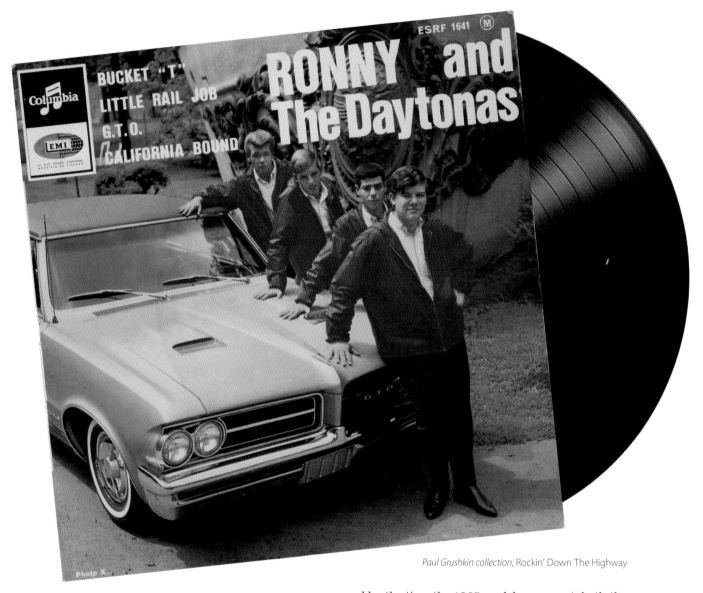

Paul Grushkin collection, Rockin' Down The Highway

and faster) post bodies, and 6,644 buyers selected the ultrastylish convertible.

This was on top of sales of the base Tempest and midlevel LeMans models, and thus represented an unbudgeted financial windfall for General Motors. While a car like the GTO infuriated GM's anti-fun storm troopers, ultimately General Motors was a corporation, and the goal of any corporation is to earn a profit. The GTO option most certainly earned a profit for the Pontiac division, and the revenue it brought to General Motors corporate coffers was enough to get the company to abandon its developmentally disabled edict that the car should disappear after Pontiac sold 5,000 units.

Sales increased throughout the year as more people learned about the existence of the new Pontiac,

and by the time the 1965 models came out, both the public and the enthusiast press were in the grip of GTO fever. Magazines discovered that newsstand sales increased when the GTO was on the cover, and soon even mainstream magazines such as *Esquire* were doing stories about the new muscle car phenomenon. The car even inspired a hit song: "GTO," written by John "Bucky" Wilson and recorded by a group called Ronnie and the Daytonas. The record rose to number 4 on the top-40 charts and sold more than 1 million copies. This song came out around the same time as the *Car & Driver* article hit the stands and probably sold more cars than that article. Given the popularity of the GTO, Pontiac could easily have sold more than 32,450 units, but the division was limited to that number by the availability of 389 engines.

Pontiac built six preproduction pilot 1965 GTOs to check the body dies, using thin .036 steel on the body with the exception of the doors and trunk lid. Built without any sound-deadening material, this GTO weighs 300 pounds less than a regular production GTO. Ordered through Dick Jesse at Royal Pontiac, this factory lightweight 1965 GTO was purchased by Van Seymore, a GM employee. The wheels under the car are four of the 25 numbered prototype wheels built. Inside the 10-bolt differential is a set of 4.88:1 gears, ideal for leaping off the line.

It didn't take long for serious street racers to realize that the Sport Coupe model, also know as a "post" car because of the fitment of a B-pillar, was the lightest of the three GTO versions offered in 1965. Another benefit was structural rigidity, which the Sport Coupe had in spades.

ROYAL BOBCAT PACKAGE

Pontiac performance grew from a local product provided to Detroit residents by Royal Pontiac to a phenomenon available at Pontiac dealerships nationwide, but Royal Pontiac and the Royal Bobcat name still had cachet in the performance world, and Royal Pontiac continued to serve as a test bed for marketing Pontiac's high-performance equipment.

The GTO proved a terrific vehicle for Royal's experimentation. Milt Schornack, the head tuner at Royal, and his crew developed a Royal Bobcat package for GTOs that could be installed by Royal at its Michigan shop or shipped to buyers nationwide. This package consisted of all the go-fast parts that had always been part of the Royal Bobcat Tune Up package: thinner head gaskets to bump the compression ratio, progressive linkage for the Tri-Power carburetors, bigger jets for the carbs, a recurved ignition advance, and blocked intake heat-riser gaskets, along with all the mounting hardware and detailed installation instructions. Royal had developed some new parts for the Tune Up package, too, like special fiber lock nuts that reduced lifter pump-up and allowed the engine

to rev another 500 rpm before valve float set in, as well as what may have been the most important part of the package: a Royal Bobcat decal that GTO owners could apply to the C pillars of their cars. In more than a few instances this sticker, which could be ordered through the mail for the $3.00 it cost to join the Royal Race Team, found its way onto countless GTOs that otherwise contained no Royal Bobcat equipment.

Schornack worked closely with Pontiac when developing the Royal Tune Up equipment for the GTO and in many cases the fruits of his work ended up being offered as optional equipment from the factory on the car. One of the most famous examples of this would be the Ram Air package that Schornack developed and Pontiac began offering as an option late in 1965.

A NEW LOOK

The success of the 1964 GTO enabled Pontiac to further develop the car for the 1965 model year and address the few shortcomings of the original. Now that GM management had grudgingly accepted the existence of the GTO, Pontiac could now develop it openly rather

USE **CAUTION** ON REMOVING
CAP WHEN ENGINE IS **HOT**

If water only is used as coolant CM# 983743
rust inhibitor of equivalent must be used

By installing a pan around the carburetors and fitting foam on the upper edge to seal against the bottom surface of the hood, outside air from the hood scoop was forced into the air cleaners, giving the engine a chance to breathe cooler, denser air.

There's a live one under the hood.

(Have you priced a tiger lately?)

Purrs if you're nice. Snarls when you prod it. Trophy V-8, standard in Pontiac GTO. 389 cubic inches. 335 horsepower. 431 lb-ft of torque. Also standard: bucket seats, heavy-duty suspension, real walnut dash, Hurst floor shifter, dual exhausts, even special tires—redlines! (You don't build a GTO with options, you personalize it.) Want something wilder? Got it: 3-2bbl, 360 hp. Want something tamer? Got that, too—Pontiac Le Mans. Take our 140-hp six or order up the V-8 you like: 250 hp, 285 hp. Try something. Drive a "sporty" car. Then prowl around in a Wide-Track a while. You'll know who's a tiger.

Quick Wide-Track Tigers
Pontiac Le Mans & GTO

Flawless proportions in a performance package. Pontiac built 55,722 hardtop coupes for model year 1965. What we call dog-dish hubcaps were, in fact, the standard hubcap; full wheel covers were optional.

than in the closet, as it had been forced to do with the original outlaw car.

The front end received the stacked headlights that brought the looks of the GTO more in line with the styling of Pontiac's full-size cars, and the twin fake hood scoops gave way to a single fake scoop in the center of the hood. New sleek taillights with chrome strips running their entire length wrapped around the redesigned rear end. These changes necessitated the redesign of the hood, trunk lid, and fenders. While the changes were relatively modest, when taken as a whole they created a sleeker, more modern-looking car.

Pontiac's engineers refined both versions of the engine for 1965, working to improve airflow in the intake manifolds and cylinder heads. Tri-Power cars received new camshafts and those equipped with four-speed manual transmissions used mechanical linkage to actuate the outer carbs, creating a smoother transition to full throttle operation. Royal Pontiac had been setting up Tri-Power carbs this way for years as part of its Royal

Keen street racer eyes would pick up the absence of grille slats and the dog-dish hubcaps as a sign that the GTO's owner cared more for performance than appearance. This factory lightweight pilot car, in fact, doesn't even have power steering or power brakes; it's meant to move very quickly in a straight line, period.

Bobcat Tune Up package. These cars also received a new camshaft to complement the carburetion changes, all of which combined to bump power of the top Tri-Power engine to 360 horsepower at 5,200 rpm. Torque fell slightly to 424 lb-ft at 5,000 rpm. The cost for all this multi-carbureted goodness rose just a tick over $3.00, to a reasonable $115.78. Similar improvements to the base four-barrel engine bumped power to 335 ponies and torque jumped to 431 lb-ft at 3,200 rpm.

Beginning on August 17, 1965, Pontiac sold a dealer-installed Ram Air package that made the fake hood scoop functional. Consisting of a metal pan that mounted under the air cleaners with a foam rubber gasket to create a seal between the pan and the hood, a scoop ornament with Ram Air openings to replace the solid stock ornament, and instructions for cutting holes in the hood and trimming the braces to make room for the system, the Ram Air option cost $29.65 when first released. Original examples go for much more than that today. If a buyer can find one, he or she should plan to add a couple zeroes to the original price. The scoop ornament came unpainted, so owners would have to paint it to match the color of their car.

The optional Rally gauge cluster now contained a complete set of gauges, including gauges for water temperature and oil pressure. The tachometer on early 1965 model year cars didn't have the redline marked, but midway through the year Pontiac added a 5,200 rpm redline mark. The extensive option list grew even longer for 1965, with the addition of aluminum front brake drums, which ran cooler and improved the performance of the GTO's marginal drum brakes, slotted steel Rally wheels, and a Safeguard speedometer that could be programmed to sound a warning when the driver reached a predetermined road speed. A transistorized voltage regulator came as standard equipment on GTOs with air conditioning and was optional on cars without air. Several new "GTO" emblems appeared on the interior of the car, and a new dashboard featured wood veneer.

Prices remained relatively unchanged; the GTO sport coupe cost $2,787.00, the hardtop cost $2,852.00, and the convertible cost $3,093.00, all of which were once again $295.90 more than the equivalent LeMans models without W62 GTO Package. With the release of the more modern-looking 1965 model, enthusiasm for Pontiac's proto-muscle car increased, as did sales. Pontiac sold 75,352 GTOs for the 1965 model year–8,319 post coupes, 55,722 hardtops, and 11,311 convertibles. When it came to carburetion, 20,547 buyers ponied up for the Tri-Power setup, and the vast majority of buyers–56,378–selected manual transmissions. No accurate records exist regarding the number of cars equipped with the Ram Air option.

FROM MILD TO WILD

As GTO sales grew, generating money for Pontiac and ensuring that GM's corporate management wouldn't cut the car from the lineup, Pontiac got braver about advertising and promoting the new car. By the time the 1965 models hit the market, Pontiac's hyperbole machine was in full swing, promoting the GTO in magazines, newspapers, on radio, television, and even at NASCAR racetracks and in popular music. Few American cars have ever benefited from the level of promotion that the

Left: Pontiac used discrete badging on the 1965 GTO to identify the car. The idea was to let the vehicle's performance set it apart. It didn't disappoint.

Opposite: Foam air cleaner elements sit atop the three two-barrel Rochester carburetors on a 1965 GTO's 389-cubic-inch V-8. The optional Tri-Power setup helped to develop 360 horsepower, up from the standard single Carter four-barrel carburetor-equipped engine, which was rated at 335 horsepower.

You want serious? This 1965 GTO was originally ordered without a radio or a heater. The first buyer didn't have any need for such heavy fripperies. Remember, lightness is speed. Starting with the 1964 GTO, Hurst shifters were standard equipment.

GTO received. This was in part because DeLorean had invested a lot of ego energy into the GTO since it was his invention, and in part it was because Jim Wangers was a promotional machine.

The crew at Pontiac still worried that the bliss ninnies running GM might pull the plug on the car, so the initial television ads for the GTO were conservative to a fault, emphasizing everything about the car but performance. Pontiac management figured that said

bliss ninnies most likely didn't read the enthusiast magazines or the magazine ads touting the GTO's power and handling. But they knew that GM's top executives watched a lot of television, so Pontiac made extremely conservative television ads for the GTO.

The first ad, which aired in 1965, played on Pontiac's ad theme of "Wide-Track Tigers" by showing a tiger jumping out from under the hood of a GTO. While this took place, the narrator (actor William Conrad) said,

Buyers wanting to tan as well as smoke the competition were inclined to buy the convertible GTO in 1965. It was a popular body style, to the tune of 11,311 sold. Pricing started at $2,726.

"Some sporting cars are only pussycats. Pontiac's GTO is all tiger." That was about as spicy as the early ads got. The rest were all low-key, emphasizing the fun and practical sides of the car. For example, one ad showed a woman running a GTO through the gears at a normal driving pace. She was happy as a clam and obviously having fun, but judging from her decidedly unsporting driving style she was clearly on her way to the grocery store or beach and not engaging in any kind of street-racing activity.

As GTO sales continued to climb, securing the car's place in the Pontiac lineup, the division began airing more daring television ads, until the ads showed GTOs being driven in a manner that bordered on irresponsible, with tires squealing, engines revving, and dust flying. In one extreme example, a GTO is shown jumping a gully. In reality the car landed so hard it broke its control arms, but that bit of footage ended up on the cutting room floor.

George Hurst marketed his very heavy-duty wheel as "The Dazzler." With a forged aluminum center section riveted and welded to a steel wheel, they were just about unbreakable. Unfortunately, they were also heavy and expensive.

Two of these Riverside 500 Pace Cars were built. One went to race winner Dan Gurney, and this example was given to a lucky ticket holder. The "splitter" exhaust tips were a $21.30 option on production cars.

HURST MOTOR TREND RIVERSIDE 500 PACE CAR

Wangers teamed up with George Hurst to accomplish some of the most ambitious GTO promotional projects. One such project was the 1965 Hurst Motor Trend Riverside 500 Pace Car. Over the 11 years in which Pontiac produced the original GTO, this was the only GTO NASCAR pace car that the division produced, a somewhat surprising fact, given the car's popularity.

The pace car was created as much to promote George Hurst's new custom mag wheel as it was to promote the GTO. Hurst was disappointed with the stamped steel wheels offered by the factories. These were prone to failure, so Hurst developed a wheel that featured a revolutionary forged aluminum center, riveted to a sturdy steel rim. The wheel was strong, durable, and good looking. Pontiac management and Hurst discussed the possibility of making the Hurst wheel a factory option for the GTO, but it was too expensive to produce and in addition to being strong, it was heavy. Pontiac engineers

Though the 1965 GTO was considered a midsized car, the huge trunk could swallow the retractable top and still have enough space for a real vacation. The full-width brightwork emphasized the Wide-Track stance.

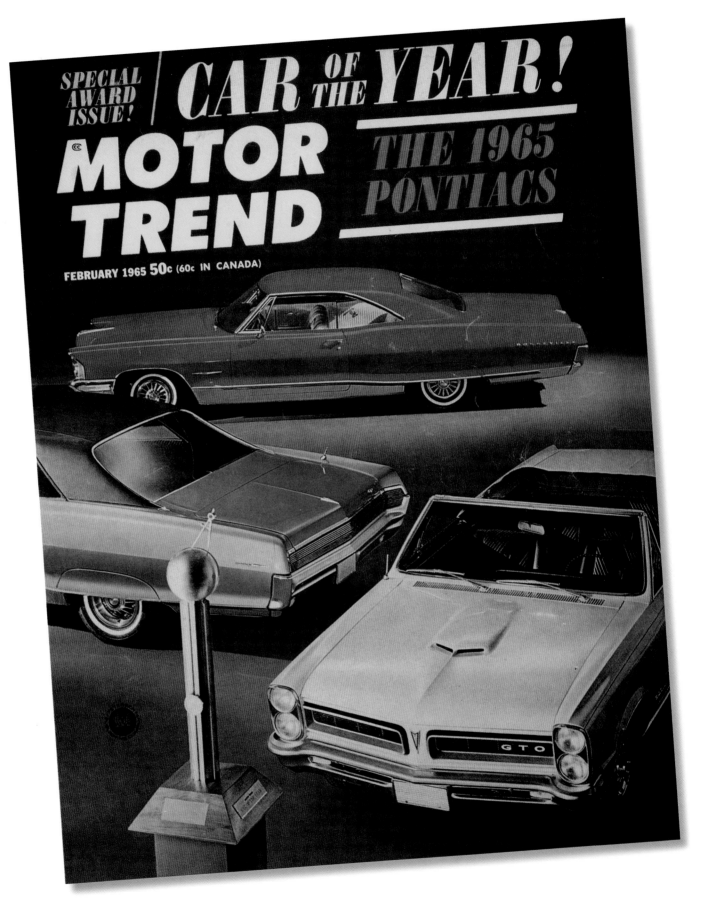

A driver could set the redline on the face of the tachometer by grasping the small knurled knob in the center of the gauge face and rotating it to the desired position. It wasn't really necessary to wind up the GTO's 389-cubic-inch V-8, as most of the torque was produced in the lower portion of the tach. **Opposite:** For the first time in the magazine's history, *Motor Trend* presented its coveted Car of the Year Award to an entire manufacturers division, rather than a single model. Engineering excellence was highlighted as a prime reason Pontiac earned the prestigious award.

feared the unsprung weight of the wheels would detract from the ride and handling of the GTO.

Hurst needed a way to promote his new wheel and conspired with Wangers to tie that promotion in with the Riverside 500 race and the Pontiac GTO. Their plan was to make the GTO the Official Pace Car of the race and get it sponsored by Hurst Performance Products and *Motor Trend* magazine, the title sponsor of Riverside Raceway.

Pontiac built two 1965 GTO convertible pace cars (pace cars are always built in pairs so there is a backup in case one breaks down). Hurst modified them with sets of his new wheels and pace car lettering. The plan was to give them both away at the race; one car would go to the race-winning driver and one car would be given to a ticket holder drawn at random on race day.

George Hurst ordered the cars with 360-horsepower Tri-Power engines, four-speed transmissions, Rally gauges, center consoles, power tops, power antennae, Rally clocks, AM radios, power steering, power brakes, and many other options.

Specially modified at Pontiac Engineering for its pace car duties, the first car was rushed through production and originally invoiced to Majestic Pontiac of Los Angeles on December 27, 1964. On December 31, 1964, the original warranty Protect-O-Plate was made out to *Motor Trend*. On January 4, 1965, the original

application for title was filled out to George Hurst, in care of Hurst Campbell and Company.

Hurst took the car and fitted the very first set of Hurst mag wheels ever installed on a GTO. The car was lettered with the verbose moniker: "Official Pace Car–Motor Trend Riverside '500,' Equipped & Awarded by HURST."

On January 17, 1965, one of the white GTO convertibles paced the *Motor Trend* Riverside 500 NASCAR race. Dan Gurney won the race and was awarded the pace car, which reportedly was destroyed in an accident a short time later. The other car was awarded to a young man from Hollywood, California.

THE HURST GEETO TIGER

Wangers and Hurst again teamed up for a GTO promotion later in the year, resulting in one of the most unique GTOs ever built: the Hurst GeeTO Tiger. With the help of Petersen Publishing, publisher of *Hot Rod* magazine, Hurst and Wangers started a contest based on a special album recorded by the Tigers, a band created just for the record, much like Ronnie and the Daytonas, entitled *GeeTO TIGER*.

Overleaf: Unlike so many muscle cars, the Hurst *GeeTO* contest car was well cared for. Possibly the owners realized what a piece of history was in the garage.

It's been said that the mark of a good designer is knowing when to lift the pen. The stylists that penned the 1965 GTO knew when to lift the pen. Period muscle cars just look right when shod with bias-ply tires.

An inviting blend of creature comforts and raw performance greeted the driver of the Hurst GeeTO. Power windows spared the occupants from the chore of actually winding a window up or down.

The public had begun referring to the GTO as "the Goat," and even though that name was given with great affection, Pontiac was trying to give the car a hip nickname without the negative connotations of "Goat." Wangers personally had no problem with the name. It was what enthusiasts called the car and would continue to call the car, so why fight it? He even tried to build an ad campaign around the name with an ad called "A Boy and His Goat," but that proposal went down in flames. In his book *GTO: 1964–1967*, Wangers described the results of the presentation of the "Goat" proposal:

> *The corporate committee rejected the ad based on its perception of what the word goat defined. "The guys downtown told us a goat is the butt of a joke or the butt end of a mistake," Wangers commented. "And they said they certainly understood it enough to know they wouldn't approve it."*

Thus Wangers and the other people working on marketing and advertising the GTO had to develop a nickname to replace "Goat." "Gee-toe" was one the company thought would work.

The grand prize for the Pontiac/Hurst/Petersen Publishing contest was a 1965 GTO named the "GeeTO Tiger." Specially equipped with 28 factory options, including Tri-Power carburetion, close-ratio four-speed with a Safe-T-Track locking differential, suspension package, power steering, and power brakes, plus special gold Hurst mag wheels, a special Hurst Gold paint job, a gold-plated Hurst shifter, and all the best parts available from Pontiac, it was the ultimate promotional vehicle.

Pontiac promoted the hell out of the GeeTO Tiger in 1965 with full-page ads and editorial coverage in every automotive magazine. Both Hurst and Pontiac advertised the car. Pontiac featured the record in many of its ads, and in total, more than 450,000 *GeeTO TIGER* records were distributed, each with instructions on how to enter the "Win a Tiger!" contest in which the GeeTO Tiger was the grand prize.

To win the contest, you had to listen to the song "GeeTO Tiger" and count the number of times the word "tiger" was sung. You were then instructed to submit this number, along with a 25-word or less paragraph

The center carburetor was the only one incorporating a choke. The front and rear carbs were activated by mechanical linkage. The 1965 Hurst GeeTO was equipped with the rare transistorized ignition.

Above: George Hurst was enamored with gold paint, and few of his products wore it as well as the contest winning GTO. Hurst went on to invent the Jaws of Life emergency rescue equipment.

Left: Pontiac stylists ruled the roost in the mid-1960s, allowing aggressive looking cars to prowl the road. The GTO is an interesting example showing how Pontiac designers incorporated the split grille.

entitled: "Why I'd Like to Win the Original GeeTO TIGER," along with your name and address. The deadline for entering was midnight July 31, 1965. After seeing an ad for the contest in *Hot Rod* magazine, Alex Lampone, a 19-year-old from West Allis, Wisconsin, submitted the following entry:

Dear Sirs: The word "Tiger" is sung 42 times in the record entitled "GeeTO Tiger." Below is my entry as to why I would like to win the original "GeeTO Tiger": Prowling around in a custom Tiger like the "GeeTO." I'd be as sure as a Hurst shift to make a hit with all the "cats."

Strong, angular lines were a visual representation of the performance lurking beneath the broad hood. Stacked headlights made their debut on the GTO in 1965.

The taillights wrapped around the sides of the bodywork, giving the 1965 GTO early side marker lamps. General Motor's design czar was Bill Mitchell, and he insisted on clean, modern shapes. The GTO is one of the best.

Lampone had counted the correct number of times the word "tiger" was sung, and the judges–including George Hurst, Dick Day (*Car Craft* magazine), and Wally Parks (of the National Hot Rod Association)–liked his reason for wanting the car more than any other entrant's. Within weeks, young Alex Lampone was the personal guest of George Hurst at the NHRA National Drags in Indianapolis. George Hurst gave the keys to the GeeTO Tiger to Lampone at a formal dinner. *Hot Rod* magazine chronicled the event.

All the promotion of and excitement generated by the GTO paid off in more than just increased GTO sales; the GTO lifted sales of all Pontiac models by generating foot traffic at Pontiac dealerships. People who came to the shops to see the new GTO often purchased

Catalinas, Bonnevilles, and Grand Prixs, and in 1965 Pontiac had its best overall sales yet. It helped that the rest of the lineup consisted of exceptional cars. *Motor Trend* magazine awarded its Car of the Year trophy to the entire lineup of Pontiac cars, but ultimately the GTO was the engine driving Pontiac sales success.

Pontiac's managerial team had rolled the dice and won. Thanks in large part to the success of the GTO, Pete Estes received his expected promotion to Chevrolet in June 1965 and DeLorean took over as Pontiac division manager. Just 40 years old, DeLorean became the youngest division manager in GM history. Had the car failed, as Frank Bridge had predicted, Estes and DeLorean would have found that their careers with General Motors would have effectively been over.

CHAPTER 3

COPING WITH SUCCESS

J ohn DeLorean took the helm at Pontiac just as the company was about to launch its strongest product-line yet. Year after year Pontiac had set new sales records, and by the time the 1966 model year rolled around, it had cemented its position as the number three nameplate in America.

This was about as high as any car manufacturer other than Ford or Chevrolet could hope to climb in the hierarchy of the U.S. auto industry. Chevrolet and Ford held such enormous shares of the U.S. auto market that no other brand could hope to approach their sales numbers, so the only realistic battle to be fought was for third place. By 1966 Pontiac had such a firm grasp on third place that competitors like Plymouth and Oldsmobile had as little chance of overtaking Pontiac as Pontiac had of overtaking Chevrolet or Ford.

Pontiac had gone from being a moribund GM division headed for extinction to becoming the automotive success story of the decade, and in 1966 it looked like the division would continue the string of record-breaking years. The entire product lineup was stronger than ever, and it was headed by a completely restyled GTO.

ROLLING COKE BOTTLES

For 1966 General Motors redesigned its entire line of intermediate A-body cars, including the GTO, which became a separate model rather than an option package for the LeMans. Instead of the slab-sided body of the original A-cars, the 1966 models featured voluptuous bodywork with curved side glass that gave the car a more rounded organic shape.

The body shape featured what was referred to as "Coke-bottle" styling. Cars earned this nickname by having body panels with arcs over the wheel wells, making them resemble bottles of Coca-Cola laid on their sides. Chevrolet introduced this style to the American auto market with its 1963 Corvette and took it to its extreme with the 1968 Corvette. General Motors applied Coke-bottle styling to all of its A-body cars for 1966.

The redesigned GTO enhanced its curvaceous new shape by adding a sleek new roofline with a raked C pillar, giving the car what was then referred to as a "fastback" profile. This profile was enhanced by placing the rear window in what designers called a tunnel; that is, instead of following the roofline, the rear window

Pontiac used a stacked headlight configuration to give the 1967 GTO an even wider look than normal. Most Pontiacs of the era shared a familial front end treatment, enabling anyone to recognize a Pontiac at long range.

An aluminum air cleaner housing sat on top of the Rochester Quadrajet four-barrel carburetor as fitted on the 400-cubic-inch V-8 in the 1967 GTO. Chromed valve covers were standard; in these pre-emission days, you could actually see the engine.

was more upright, with the C pillars extending past the window toward the rear of the car, creating buttresses on either side of the window. This hindered rearward visibility, caused water to collect at the base of the window, and was aerodynamically awful, but it looked cool as hell.

To emphasize that the GTO was a separate model rather than a gussied-up LeMans, Pontiac gave the GTO styling that differed markedly from the styling of the LeMans. The front end of the GTO took its cues from the sporty Grand Prix, which featured recessed split plastic egg-crate grilles. When applied to the GTO, the left grille featured "GTO" lettering on its outer edge. Turn signals moved up from the bumpers into the blacked-out grilles.

Other than the bold new bodywork, the car was changed little for 1966. The wood appliqué on the dash was now real walnut on all cars (in 1965 some cars had been fitted with real wood appliqués on the dash and some had been fitted with fake wood). The bucket seats were redesigned, but mechanically the car was virtually identical to the 1965 car.

For 1966 Pontiac offered optional red plastic fender liners. Constructed of heavy-gauge plastic, these liners saved weight and protected the suspension components from dirt and road salt.

The engine options were virtually unchanged; the four-barrel engine still generated 335 horsepower, and though the Tri-Power system had been modified slightly–the middle carburetor was enlarged to improve flow–the Tri-Power engine still generated 360 horsepower. In a harbinger of things to come, the heads were redesigned to accept the Air Injection Reactor Control System, a smog-reducing air pump fitted to cars sold in California.

Otherwise everything remained much as it had been in 1965: The tires were still too small to cope with that power and the brakes were still inadequate, though the optional aluminum drums and metallic brake linings were still available to marginally improve braking performance. And the GTO was still the coolest car sold in America.

The Ram Air option, often referred to as the "XS Package," was again available, and Pontiac sold approximately 300 kits through dealers. An additional 25 to 35 Ram Air kits were installed at the factory late in the model year. In addition to the Ram Air hood scoop hardware, the 1966 Ram Air cars were equipped with a hotter cam and heavy-duty valve springs to take advantage

When a hood-mounted tachometer was ordered, the instrument panel held ancillary gauges. Slamming the hood had a detrimental effect on the accuracy of the tach.

of the improved breathing. The cam and valve springs were available through Pontiac's parts department for those buyers who purchased their Ram Air kits from the dealers and installed the kits themselves.

THWARTED

DeLorean wanted the GTO to compete not just with the other intermediate-size cars but also with the best sedans and coupes built in Europe. To do this he would have to improve handling. The primary shortcomings of the GTO when it came to handling were its tires and its brakes.

Solving the GTO's tire problem should have been a relatively easy fix: All it required was better ones. What the car really needed was a set of Michelin radials, which were original equipment on many European cars. Mounting these tires led to tremendous improvements in ride, handling, and traction. DeLorean began negotiations

The "Coke-bottle" side contours are clearly visible as this 1966 GTO waits for its turn at the starting line. The standard 7.75x14-inch tire didn't put a lot of rubber on the road, a fact that the 389-cubic-inch engine could use to generate impressive clouds of tire smoke.

with Michelin to have the French firm provide its advanced radial tires as original equipment on the GTO, but when the American tire manufacturers found out about this they exerted pressure on General Motors to force Pontiac to stick with American-made tires. The pressure succeeded, and the GTO would continue to wallow around on inferior bias-ply tires.

Pontiac tried to address the inadequacies of the GTO's weak 9.5-inch drum brakes by developing an advanced combination wheel-brake in which the brake disc was an integrated part of the wheel itself. These were based on the aluminum eight-lug wheels the company offered on its full-size cars. This brake-wheel combination featured an advanced cooling fin system for the brakes that would have improved brake performance, but the wheels, which were to be made of cast iron rather than aluminum, were too heavy and too expensive to put into production.

THE MONKEEMOBILE

Pontiac's advertising team consisted of some of the most resourceful and creative people the auto industry has ever produced, and they were always looking for ways to spread the gospel of Pontiac performance. Pontiac pioneered the art of product placement in film and television. John Malone, Pontiac's advertising manager at the time, was

Opposite: For the 1966 model year, Pontiac fitted the GTO with a thin-slit taillight treatment. The chrome trim around the rear light panel echoed the shape of the front grilles.

Above: Automotive customizer Dean Jeffries stands by one of two *Monkeemobiles* that he built for the hit 1966 TV show. The cars were based loosely on the GTO, with a third row of seats where the trunk used to be. *Dean Jeffries collection*

Right: Using two GTOs to create a single *Monkeemobile*, Dean Jeffries preformed radical body modifications to create a visually striking vehicle. Universal Studios, producing the TV show, wanted the *Monkeemobile* to be over the top. They got that. *Dean Jeffries collection*

a fan of both mediums and he recognized the value of placing Pontiac cars in movies and television programs.

One of the earliest examples of product placement came when Malone engineered a deal in which Pontiac cars would be featured in the television program *Naked City*. Both the cops and the bad guys in this New York City–based crime drama drove Pontiacs, pushing their wide track chassis to the absolute limit in the chase scenes. In *Surfside 6* actor Troy Donahue, who played an undercover Miami cop living on a houseboat, chased the bad guys in Pontiacs.

It wasn't a tough sell to convince producers to feature Pontiac's popular GTO in their films and television shows. *My Three Sons* star Fred MacMurray taught at least one of his three sons to drive in a GTO, and in *I Dream of Jeannie* Larry Hagman's character, Major Tony Nelson, drove a GTO whenever the Jeannie character, played by Barbara Eden, wasn't making him or the GTO disappear.

Perhaps the most controversial GTO product placement appeared in the whimsical 1960s sitcom *The Monkees*. The Monkees became wildly popular as both a television show and a musical group, thanks to a series of classic pop songs that in reality were recorded by studio musicians. Regardless, these were excellent pop songs and can still be heard on classic rock stations today.

Above: Customizer Dean Jeffries used his left hand to show how he planned to have the lengthened nose of the *Monkeemobile* utilize the stock GTO grille inserts. From the front, the finished *Monkeemobile* was somewhat recognizable as a GTO, but aft of the nose, it was pure fantasy car. *Dean Jeffries collection*

Left: The stars of *The Monkees* TV show pose with "their" *Monkeemobile*. Dean Jeffries built the two vehicles in one month under heavy pressure from Universal Studio to have a car ready when filming started. *Dean Jeffries collection*

Parked above his shop on Mullholland Drive, Dean Jeffries shows off his handiwork. The functional 6-71 supercharger helped the engine to overpower the chassis, so the blower was replaced with a dummy casing, maintaining the look but covering a four-barrel carburetor. *Dean Jeffries collection*

In 1966 Pontiac scored a product-placement coup when a GTO was chosen to be the Monkees' car, but to the dismay of many people at Pontiac, the car on the show was so highly customized that it bore little resemblance to the stock GTO. Pontiac wanted the GTO emblems to remain on the car, but the show's producers felt that this might deter other automakers from advertising on the show, so all the identifying badges were removed.

The *Monkeemobile* came into being when Universal Studios contracted customizer Dean Jeffries to build a customized car for use on the *Monkees* TV show, which at that point had yet to begin production. The specific model of car had not yet been chosen. Jeffries mentioned this assignment to George Toteff, the CEO of Model Products Corporation (MPC). Toteff told his friend Jim Wangers about the situation.

Wangers jumped on the opportunity to promote Pontiac cars on such a high-profile television program and negotiated a deal with the show's producers. Pontiac would provide cars for the personal use of the stars and producers, a perk the cast of the show–Micky Dolenz, Mike Nesmith, Peter Tork, and David Jones–appreciated, since it meant they always had brand-new GTOs to drive, as well as a pair of cars to be modified for use on-screen. Wangers ordered a pair of 1966 GTO convertibles equipped with four-barrel carbs and automatic transmissions and sent them to Jeffries to be converted into *Monkeemobiles*.

Pontiac granted Toteff the exclusive rights to produce and sell a model kit of the car. The show became a huge hit and MPC sold seven million *Monkeemobile* kits, making it the second-best-selling model kit of all time, after *The Dukes of Hazzard* "General Lee" 1969 Dodge Charger.

Jeffries was ordered to customize the cars pretty heavily, and Wangers knew that GM management might not be pleased with what Hollywood would do with the cars. The last thing they wanted was a car that would be the object of ridicule, but what Jeffries came up with was much more radical than Wangers had anticipated.

GTO customers wanting something different could order a special solid color for $83.20, such as this Iris Mist example. Redline tires were standard in 1966; buyers wanting four-ply whitewall tires lightened up their wallets by $17.78.

Hurst wheels could take any treatment the driver could dish out, but the high cost kept them off most GTOs. Pontiac continued to call out the engine displacement in liters for 1966.

The front end was recognizable as a GTO, but the rest of the car appeared to be an overgrown dune buggy. Jeffries added a very tall split windshield, a T-bucket-type convertible top, large fender flares, exaggerated taillamps, and even a parachute. He mounted a third row of seats over the area that had previously been the trunk lid. The show's producers ordered a flamboyant car, and that's just what Jeffries built.

Jeffries also made mechanical modifications. On the first car he modified, he mounted a supercharger on the engine and weighted the rear end so the car could pop wheelies. With the blower in place the car generated too much power for the suspension and was a difficult car to drive, so he installed a dummy blower in its place.

Jeffries built the two cars within the span of one month, working around the clock to finish the project in time. Wangers warned Pontiac General Manager John DeLorean that the cars were not at all what Pontiac was expecting, but there wasn't time to build new vehicles. They decided to bite the bullet and let the producers use

Red plastic inner fender liners were essentially an appearance option. Made of thin plastic, they fit snugly against the steel inner fenders. A set of four factory installed liners, option code T46, cost $26.33.

When a buyer ordered the pricey aftermarket Hurst wheels, this badge was fitted to the trunk lid. It was intended to let vehicles in the GTO's wake realize what just passed them.

For the 1966 GTO model year, Pontiac offered an optional walnut shift knob ($3.69) that used the vehicle emblem as well as showing the shift pattern. The D55 center console was a $47.13 option with bucket seats.

the cars as Jeffries had built them. If GM's corporate watchdogs came down on the division, DeLorean and Wangers would take the blame.

"BEAT THE TIGER"

One factor limiting Pontiac's ability to promote the performance of its GTO came not from outside sources or GM corporate management but from within the car itself. The GTO offered buyers terrific value when it came to performance obtained per dollar spent, but the car simply wasn't competitive in any of the NHRA's top Stock Car classes. The car was plenty fast, but the cars from the competition were faster. With minimal modification the GTO could break into the 12-second bracket, which, while fast, wasn't fast enough for the NHRA Super Stock class.

In an attempt to boost the car's on-track performance image, Wangers built a pair of very special GTOs. Both were painted Hurst Gold (now renamed Tiger Gold) and were virtually identical, except that one was

finished with a white panel along its midsection and the other car had a black panel.

These cars, called the GeeTO Tigers, the same as the contest car from the previous year, received blueprinted 421 H.O. Tri-Power engines at Royal Pontiac's shop. With M21 close-ratio transmissions, 3.90:1 gears in the Safe-T-Track rear ends, and cheater slicks (extra soft tires with the minimum amount of tread allowed for road tires, leaving most of the contact patch of the tire free of tread so that they were practically slicks), these cars could win races. With the stock 389 the GTO didn't have the snort to run with a race-tuned Chrysler 426 Hemi or even sister division Chevrolet's Chevelle SS396. With the big 421 engine, the GTO achieved its true potential at the drag strip.

The GeeTO Tigers weren't built for racing. They wouldn't qualify for any of the NHRA's stock classes because the 421 wasn't a regular production option for the GTO, and it wouldn't become one anytime soon.

As many owners found out, the front bumper did little to protect the nose of the car. But it sure looked good, and in 1966, that's what was important.

GTO stands for *Gran Turismo Omologato.* You've probably heard of it. A Pontiac in a saber-toothed tiger skin. The deceptively beautiful body comes in convertible, sports coupe, and hardtop configurations. With pinstriping. On a heavy-duty suspension system that thinks it's married to the ground. Bucket seats and carpeting. Wood-grained dash. Redlines or whitewalls at no extra cost. Chromed 335-hp 4-barrel under the hood. Fully-synchronized 3-speed on the column. Or order a heavy-duty all-synchro 3-speed or 4-speed with Hurst floor shifter. Or 2-speed auto. Or the 360-hp 3 2-BBL. There's a catalog full of options. See if you can get your Pontiac dealer to cough one up. That's the GTO/2+2 performance catalog. You'll recognize it. It vibrates.

Speak softly and carry a GTO

Pontiac had broken GM's rules when it snuck the GTO into its lineup, but the corporate suits weren't going to allow such a thing to happen again. To keep the GTO from going off the corporate reservation completely, they expanded the boundaries of the reservation. They rewrote the rules limiting midsize car engines to 400 cubic inches. (Buick squeaked past this by installing a 401-cubic-inch engine in its Gran Sport, which was that division's version of an A-body muscle car, but they had designed the car before the new rule was instituted, so GM grandfathered in the Gran Sport's outlaw cubic inch.)

Rather than racing, Wangers built the 1966 GeeTO Tigers to run in a series of demonstrations held at drag strips around the country during the 1966 drag racing season. In these spectacles one car would be driven by the Mystery Tiger, who would be played by a veteran drag racer in a tiger suit, and the other would be driven by

In the mid-1960s, American automobiles were painted colors that had names with presence, like this 1966 GTO in Montero Red. The painted white roof, a two-tone option, cost $31.07.

When the 1966 GTO rolled out, sharp-eyed enthusiasts might have noticed that the new car was 1 inch wider than the '65 model. Inset: It wasn't until early 1966 that Pontiac released the Ram Air option. Tests showed that the center of the hood wasn't the best place to mount a functional scoop, but styling ruled the roost, and engineering didn't have the clout to have the scoop repositioned.

a member of the audience chosen at random. Spectators would be given a numbered ticket when they entered the race and ten winners would be chosen. Once they proved they had valid driver's licenses and could shift a manual transmission, they could pick one of the GeeTO Tigers and race against the Mystery Tiger, who would drive the other car.

The Mystery Tiger, played by a number of different drivers throughout the year, put on quite a show, hamming it up and playing to the crowd. When it came time to race, they made sure that at least three out of ten guest drivers beat the Mystery Tiger. To keep the guest drivers safe, the cars were set up with retarded timing and throttle stops, as well as over-inflated tires so that the drivers would burn off a lot of speed in tire spin on take off, but the cars were still faster than any stock GTO, easily turning in 13-second quarter-mile times, and everyone who participated had a blast.

After the last race, the Mystery Tiger would go up to the announcer's booth and challenge the fastest

With the Stereo Magic close at hand, the occupants of this 1966 GTO were ready for an exciting night on the town.

GTOs sold in California in 1966 were required to have a special emission control system, known as the Air Injector Exhaust Control. This mandatory option for Golden State residents, K19, cost $44.76.

Pontiac's versions of the 1966 A-body platform were the Tempest and the GTO. Buick also built Skylarks with this body shell.

B/Stock car of the day to a match race. The team would adjust the timing, lower the air pressure in the tires, and remove the throttle stops. When set up like this, the GeeTO Tigers dipped into the low 12-second range and could outrun just about any stock-class car of the day, so the events always culminated with the GeeTO Tigers being the fastest cars at the events.

Since these cars didn't meet the NHRA's requirements for B/Stock classes, they couldn't compete in sanctioned events; but they were show cars, not race cars, and the match races were exhibitions put on for entertainment purposes, not competitive events. There were no tech inspections or challenges from other competitors. The main thing was that the events made the GTO look like the fastest car on the road.

The GeeTO Mystery Tiger program was a huge success, culminating with a performance at the NHRA Nationals, held in Indianapolis that year. Wangers cooked up a promotion in which the Mystery Tiger would be unmasked at the event. No one would know who the actual drivers had been since they hadn't hired any big-name racers to play the role of the Mystery Tiger, but Wangers wanted a celebrity to play the role at the unmasking so for the Nationals he got his friend George Hurst to play the Mystery Tiger role. Hurst, who was a gifted driver as well as a brilliant engineer, was a popular figure in the drag-racing world and the crowd went nuts when he turned out to be the Mystery Tiger. The Nationals event was a terrific success that culminated a tremendously successful promotion for the GTO.

The tiger scores again!

change its stripes for '66?

Wide-Track Pontiac/'66

The Ram Air option became available in early 1966, and it gave the GTO additional street credibility. With 360 horsepower, it could play with the big boys.

RECORD YEAR

Wangers and his crew performed the GeeTO Mystery Tiger show at events in 32 different cities, in front of more than 150,000 spectators. In the process they helped sell a lot of GTOs.

Not that Pontiac needed much help selling GTOs. For the 1966 model year the division sold an astounding 96,946 GTOs. It sold 10,363 examples of the $2,783 post model, 73,785 examples of the $2,847 hardtop, and 12,798 examples of the $3,082 convertible. Most buyers stuck with the standard four-barrel engine, but 19,045 buyers upgraded to the Tri-Power engine. A surprising number of buyers–35,667–bought the optional automatic transmission, an antiquated two-speed unit that was poorly suited to the engine's performance characteristics.

The base car was still a bargain, offering more performance per dollar spent than just about any car on the market, but as the option list grew longer and the price of the options crept higher, the price of a loaded GTO skyrocketed, with well-equipped examples nearing the $5,000 mark.

The year 1966 marked the zenith of GTO sales, but that year was the last that Pontiac had the muscle car market virtually to itself; over the next few years the car would face increasing competition from its sister divisions at GM, from the potent muscle cars that Chrysler was developing, and from Ford. Even lowly American Motors would get into the muscle car market.

Other darker forces besides increased competition would soon play a role in diminishing GTO sales. Some of

In 1966, it didn't get much better than this under a hood. The optional L71 Ram Air package was released for sale on February 28, 1966, costing $113.33. Today it looks like a real bargain.

Arnie Beswick not only drove his winning Pontiacs, he turned wrenches on them as well. While his day job was as an actual farmer, his passion was on the drag strip.

them were simple demographics: The same youth market that drove the car's initial sales success were starting to get older and would soon have kids of their own. When they started raising families they would have to trade their GTOs for Safari wagons so they could haul their kids to football practice.

Government-mandated pollution regulations would soon cut into the sales of every automaker worldwide by forcing them to invest so much money in developing pollution-control equipment that there would be little money left to develop the cars themselves, especially niche cars such as the GTO. Back then it took at least three years to get a car from concept to production, so in 1967 the manufacturers would be developing the 1970–71 model-year cars and would begin making the changes

needed to meet the new automotive emissions standards that were being proposed for the next decade.

This would prove so costly and time consuming that the product itself would begin to suffer, and quality would soon take a nosedive. The cars GM produced in the mid- to late 1960s represented the zenith for quality in American automobiles. Within a few years the quality of American cars would begin to slide, opening up the door for imports to take an ever-increasing market share.

Insurance rates were rising, too, and it was beginning to get expensive for young drivers to insure fast cars. Add to that an increasingly vocal safety movement that abhorred fast cars and there's little wonder that GTO sales would decline in the latter half of the 1960s.

Left: In it's element, the Farmer's lightweight 1966 GTO Funny Car was a solid performer at drag strips across the country. Beswick himself was a Midwesterner, living in Morrison, Illinois, surrounded by crop fields.

Below left: Arnie "The Farmer" Beswick's 1966 GTO S/FX Funny Car prepares to roll toward the starting line. The "Tameless Tiger" was one of a string of Pontiac's that Beswick campaigned.

Below: With a gutted interior and repositioned driver's seat, Arnie Beswick set records with his 1966 GTO. Beswick was the first driver to run the quarter-mile in the 9- and 8-second range in a stock bodied car.

IRRESPONSIBLE BEHAVIOR

The beginning of the end came in 1966, when GM's corporate management, or more specifically James Roche, the chairman of General Motors, ordered Pontiac to tone down its advertising, which had continued using the "Wide-Track Tigers" theme to promote Pontiac performance. Never mind that the ad campaign had been wildly successful and propelled Pontiac to multiple years of record sales, Roche felt that Pontiac's focus on performance and the aggressive image represented by the tiger were liabilities for the company. He felt the tiger was just plain undignified.

In some ways this edict sprang from Roche's personal biases, but in general it reflected the opinion of most of GM's top brass. Their growing timidity when it came to marketing performance cars was a direct response to pressure being exerted on the company by a group of activists. In 1965 General Motors found itself under attack from a growing number of safety zealots hell-bent on saving street racers from themselves. This group, led by *Unsafe at Any Speed* author Ralph Nader, rattled the cages of GM's corporate management. More important, the Naderites had the ear of the Federal Trade Commission, which notified the automakers that they should not advertise their high-performance cars in ways that promoted racing or aggressive street driving.

Nader's book, published in 1965, criticized the U.S. auto industry for neglecting safety when it came to designing cars, and it had singled out the Chevrolet Corvair as the prime example illustrating this neglect. The book had been a national bestseller and a public-relations disaster for General Motors. By the time the 1967 model year rolled around, the company was practically prostrating itself before Nader in an attempt to appease his humorless army of safety Nazis.

It seemed that Pontiac's promotional efforts were continually thwarted, regardless of how successful they had been. First the parent corporation killed corporate racing, and then it put the kibosh on Pontiac's highly successful performance-oriented advertising campaigns. Corporate headquarters would soon have more bad news for its performance division.

THE DEATH OF TRI-POWER

One of the first moves GM made in an attempt to mollify Nader's minions (not realizing that this fanatical group wouldn't be mollified until everyone on earth was transported in rainbow-colored foam cocoons powered by fairy dust) was to kill multiple carburetion on every passenger car except Chevrolet's Corvette for the 1967 model year.

This allowed GM to brag that it was de-emphasizing performance, but it took away a cornerstone of Pontiac's performance image at a time when the division was selling cars into an increasingly competitive market. "Tri-Power" had been an important part of the GTO image since almost the beginning, and it had been a defining piece of Pontiac performance for the past decade.

The popular GeeTO Mystery Tiger program would be cancelled for 1967, in part because Pontiac was dropping the Tiger theme, but mostly because Pontiac's insurance company refused to insure the events for another year. Nothing, it seemed, was going Pontiac's way. Its marketing and advertising people would need to find yet another new way to market the GTO.

THE GREAT ONE

In an attempt to create an advertising theme that would be acceptable to Roche and not get Ralph Nader's undies up in a bunch, Pontiac developed a new nickname to use when marketing the GTO: "The Great One." In *GTO: 1964–67*, author Paul Zazarine relates Jim Wangers' description of the genesis of The Great One theme:

> *Wangers' first responsibility was to set the tone for the 1967 GTO introduction. For the public to forget about the Tiger, he needed a theme that would set a new direction for the GTO. "We took liberty with the initials GTO and came up with TGO–The Great One."*

While technically this promoted "TGO" rather than "GTO," no one seemed to care, and The Great One theme succeeded in establishing a new direction for promoting the GTO. The Great One had a sophisticated ring to it, emphasizing the all-around capabilities of the GTO rather than just the car's performance, and it played upon the legendary reputation the GTO had earned in just a few short years.

Better yet, people liked "The Great One" as a nickname. While the name "Goat" continued to hold sway among most automobile enthusiasts, "The Great One"

It took a real knucklehead to run against a 1967 GTO with a discreet Royal Bobcat badge on the fender. This particular car was fitted with a 428-cubic-inch V-8 by the wrenches at Royal Pontiac.

This high-option 1967 GTO was ordered with a Ram Air induction system, air conditioning, power steering, and power drum brakes.

Pontiac moved the GTO side badge to the front of the rocker panel for the 1967 model year. The Royal Bobcat badge on the fender spoke volumes to performance enthusiasts.

For the 1967 model year, GTOs equipped with an automatic transmission were outfitted with a Hurst Dual-Gate shifter. This device allowed a driver to leave the transmission to shift gears, or any gear could be manually engaged. The eight-track player was cutting edge audio entertainment in 1967, and cost a hefty $128.49. Donovan anyone?

caught on and stuck over time, unlike GeeTO Tiger, which never really transcended advertising copy to become a term that people actually used to describe the car.

In an attempt to move the GTO's image upscale, Pontiac hired actor Paul E. Richards to appear in its GTO television ads. In the ads, Richards, who was best known for his role as Mendez in the film *Beneath the Planet of the Apes*, walked around the car asking viewers if they had what it took to drive the "ultimate driving machine." "If you don't know what that means," Richards said, "then you're excused. But if, when you see this car, you're seized with an uncontrollable urge to plant yourself behind the wheel and head for wide-open spaces, then we're talking to you."

MAXIMUM DISPLACEMENT

Although Pontiac's marketers lost most of the tools they had relied on to promote the GTO, the car itself hadn't lost any of its performance. Pontiac introduced a revised V-8 engine for 1967 with better-flowing cylinder heads. Widening the bore to 4.12 inches raised total displacement to 400 cubic inches, the maximum capacity a nervous GM management would allow in its intermediate cars at the time. The heads featured narrower valve angles (14

Talk about a moving performance.

GTO—The Great One by Pontiac

You won't be young forever.

The Great One by Pontiac.

versus 20 degrees) and larger intake and exhaust valves. Compression remained the same high 10.75:1 as it had been with the previous 389 engine.

With the Tri-Power carburetion system dead, Pontiac switched to a Rochester four-barrel Quadrajet carburetor. While the old Carter AFB had been adequate for the base GTO, it was too crude for the top engine. The more-modern Quadrajet could flow much more air than the Carter; in fact, it could match the Tri-Power set up. The Quadrajet featured a small primary circuit that enhanced drivability in low-speed operation (and increased fuel mileage at highway cruising speeds, if that mattered to anyone at the time) and a monstrously large secondary with jets that could vary their flow through the

use of what Rochester called "metering rods," graduated rods that slid up and down in the jets varying the size of their apertures. This system allowed smooth, progressive acceleration all the way through the rev range, from a standing start to a full-blast run down the highway. The overall characteristics of the Quadrajet were very much like the characteristics of a well-tuned Tri-Power setup.

As a result of the improved carburetor and increased displacement, horsepower figures remained unchanged, with the standard four-barrel engine producing 335 horsepower at 5,000 rpm and the H.O. engine producing 360 horsepower at 5,100 rpm. Torque figures rose, with the standard four-barrel engine generating a tire-burning 441 lb-ft at 3,400 rpm and the H.O. engine cranking out 438 lb-ft at 3,600 rpm.

The Rally II–styled wheel was a popular GTO option in 1967 for only $72.67. It came in only one size, 14x6 inches.

As most owners of a 1967 GTO convertible will attest, the removable boot meant to cover the convertible stack could present certain, well, challenges in installation. Leaving the cover in the sun to soften did wonders to allow the cover to stretch to fit.

Right: For the 1967 model year, Pontiac's stylists reduced the hint of a tail fin by bringing the thin chrome trim piece above the bumper straight across the trunk lid.

Below: Simple, clean, and purposeful, the interior of the 1967 GTO was better appointed than it needed to be for a muscle car. However, the typical performance customer wanted bells and whistles as well as being able to waste a set of rear tires.

There are few great moments in life.   This is one of them.

There is only one thing more spectacular than owning a GTO. That's driving one. Even if you don't own it.

For a GTO was made to drive. Relentlessly. In fact, the more you drive it, the more eager and responsive it becomes. Like a sleek cat that achieves perfection by being put through a hoop.

A GTO handles itself well because of its 400 cubic inches of powerplant and specially designed suspension. You can order a 255-hp regular-gas version (only with Turbo Hydra-Matic), the standard 335-hp, or the fabulous 360-hp Quadra-Power 400. All come with the GM safety package which includes folding seat back latches and GM's energy absorbing steering column.

When you drive this driving machine, you will understand the ultimate conceit of our calling it The Great One.

The Great One by Pontiac

GM
MARK OF EXCELLENCE
Pontiac Motor Division

Buyers who wanted to keep track of the new engine's revs had an interesting option for 1967: a hood-mounted tachometer. The position wasn't ideal from a performance standpoint. Under certain lighting conditions the tach was difficult for the driver to see, and every time someone dropped the hood it knocked the calibration of the tachometer out of whack. But it did look cool and proved a popular accessory, one that remained on Pontiac's option list throughout the classic muscle car era.

MINIMUM MOTIVATION

One huge change for the 1967 model year was that the standard four-barrel car was no longer the lowest-performing GTO; buyers of what was referred to as the "economy" model got a neutered low-compression (8.6:1) two-barrel version of the new 400-cubic-inch engine that generated just 255 horsepower at 4,400 rpm and 397 lb-ft of torque, also at 4,400 rpm. This was available as a no-cost option on cars equipped with automatic

Pontiac used a mesh grille material to set the 1967 GTO apart from the prior year. The parking lights served double duty as turn signals. The upper headlights were the low beams; the lower mounted T3 lamps were the high beams.

The large trunk allowed Pontiac's engineers to design the convertible top to be virtually flush with the bodywork when folded. The result was a sleek, flowing design.

There isn't a better way to pass a summer day than cruising in a top-down 1967 GTO. The contrasting pinstripe was color keyed to the interior.

transmissions. The engine wasn't offered in cars with manual transmissions.

THE BEAST

Pontiac refined the Ram Air system for 1967. The factory supplied this system in the trunks of Ram Air-equipped GTOs and specified it for use only in dry weather. The fresh-air intake portion of this system consisted of a second insert for the hood scoop, one that lacked the block-off plates of the standard scoop insert. This effectively turned the fake hood scoop into a real one. A driver could remove the standard plate with three speed screws and install the Ram Air system, though he or she was supposed to replace the standard plate in the event of any precipitation.

As before, Ram Air-equipped cars came with hotter camshafts and stronger valve springs. For 1967 the Ram

Air option came with mandatory 4.33:1 gear set in the 10-bolt rear end when equipped with a four-speed. Ram Air cars equipped with the TH-400 automatic transmission received 3.90:1 gearing. Although the Safe-T-Track rear end wasn't specified with the package, it's difficult to imagine that anyone would order such a car with an open rear end. Polished valves filled the intake and exhaust ports in the cylinder heads. This setup made a Ram Air-equipped GTO unpleasant to drive at highway speeds and gave the car a tendency to overheat in hot weather, but it resulted in the quickest GTO yet. This was the hot setup for weekend drag racers.

HIS AND HERS

The manual transmission choices remained unchanged, but buyers who opted for the optional automatic transmission received GM's terrific new heavy-duty

Hurst wheels were strictly aftermarket items in 1967, but the relationship between the Hurst Company and Pontiac was long-standing. Many Pontiacs were used to showcase the latest Hurst products. Pontiac marketing was wise to use the metric system to denote engine displacement. Other American manufacturers were using cubic inches to show the size of their powerplants, and the use of liters set Pontiac apart, besides giving it a whiff of European sportiness.

Unlike the "pony cars" that used a long hood and short deck, the 1967 GTO embraced a more traditional composition with almost equal length hood and trunk. The short overhang in the front and the long overhang in the rear gave the visual impression of motion.

three-speed TH-400. The old two-speed automatic had been aimed at people who couldn't or wouldn't shift themselves; everyone else selected the much more capable four-speed.

But there was another market for automatic transmissions: drag racers. Some of the most successful drag racers of the time were using the excellent automatic transmissions built by Ford and Chrysler, transmissions that far outclassed GM's lousy two-speed slush box in performance and durability. With the advent of the new TH-400 three-speed unit, an automatic transmission became a much more viable choice for performance-oriented GTO customers.

When a buyer ordered a console for a GTO equipped with the new automatic transmission, he or she also received the innovative Hurst Dual Gate shifter. This shifter featured an additional gate to the right of the main gate and a ratcheting mechanism that allowed positive shifts between first, second, and third, while eliminating the possibility of accidentally hitting neutral, which could result in a blown engine during a drag race.

This shifter was often called the "his-and-hers" shifter because a less aggressive driver (presumably the "her") could leave the lever in the left gate and use it as an ordinary automatic transmission, while an aggressive driver (apparently the "his" in "his-and-hers") could shift over to the right gate for serious street racing.

NEW POWER, OLD LOOKS

Though the GTO received the most thorough mechanical makeover yet in 1967, the exterior of the car remained virtually unchanged. A pair of polished aluminum mesh grilles replaced the black plastic versions of the previous

The hood bulge served a purpose, even on cars not equipped with Ram Air. Having the extra clearance under the hood allowed Pontiac's engineering staff to equip the 1967 GTO with an effective air cleaner. The $63.19 hood-mounted tachometer looked better than it worked.

year. Out back the car featured new slotted taillights and the rocker trim became more prominent, extending up over the doors.

The interior of the car received only incremental changes, too, though it did receive a number of genuine improvements when it came to safety, such as an energy-absorbing steering column, a dual-circuit braking system, front seat back locks, standard four-way flashers, and a breakaway non-glare day/night rearview mirror.

Pontiac offered an eight-track stereo tape deck as an option for the first time in 1967. The tape deck resided in a plastic pod mounted below the dash. Though crude by today's digital standards, the eight-track tape was considered state-of-the-art in 1967. Nothing could be cooler than cruising around a college campus in a convertible GTO with the Who's "My Generation" blaring from the eight-track tape deck.

In what was both a safety and a performance upgrade, optional power-assisted, vented front disc brakes finally became available. Supplied by Delco Morraine, these brakes featured four-piston calipers and were available with or without power assist. New F70x14-inch Wide Oval redline tires, which became standard equipment on the GTO in 1967, also qualified as both safety and performance enhancements, since they improved handling and braking as well as providing better traction for quicker acceleration. They

Rarely seen, a column-shift GTO. Via linkage, a three-speed Turbo Hydra-matic automatic transmission took care of getting the power to the driveshaft.

weren't Michelin radials, but they were a step in the right direction.

Those tires could now be mounted on either the original optional Rally wheels (now called Rally I) or stylish new Rally II wheels, which were designed for cars equipped with the optional power front disc brakes.

The red plastic fender liners made their final appearance on the 1967 model GTOs. They looked cool but never caught on with the public, and in the two years they were offered, Pontiac sold just 1,334 of them.

Opposite: No, the passenger seat back isn't broken. It's the $84.26 option A70, the reclining Strato Bucket Seat with the mandatory $52.66 A82 headrests. The convertible top allowed the occupants to savor the sound of the dual exhaust.

Surely there's a race happening somewhere. As the sun sets, this 1967 GTO is ready to hustle up some stoplight action. This was a young man's rite of passage in the 1960s.

MARKETING CHALLENGES

When Pontiac brought out the GTO late in 1963, the car literally had no competition. By 1967 it had to compete with other GM A-body muscle cars: the Chevrolet Chevelle SS396, the Buick Gran Sport, and the Oldsmobile 442, as well as the Plymouth GTX and two Dodges, the Coronet R/T and the Charger.

The new Mopar muscle cars were especially troublesome for the GTO. They were approximately the same size and shape as Pontiac's muscle car, but they offered a couple of engine choices: the 375-horsepower 440-cubic-inch RB engine and the 425-horsepower 426 Hemi. These engines outclassed the GTO's 400-cubic-inch engine on paper, and, at least in the case of the 440, on the street. While the stock 440 was an awesome performer, a stock Hemi was really an unfinished race car and required careful tuning from an experienced mechanic to reach its full potential. Extracting the potential performance from the Hemi was an expensive proposition, and mechanics who knew how to work on the

With its stacked headlights, the 1967 GTO couldn't be mistaken for anything else. The stylish grille openings let plenty of cooling air into the radiator while making a dramatic entrance.

Pontiac built just 7,029 sport coupes in 1967, the lowest production of the three body styles available. With a manual transmission, the "post" cars were five pounds lighter than the hardtop coupe.

complex engine were few and far between. On the street a strong running GTO could beat an as-delivered Hemi, but it couldn't keep up with a 440.

Ford really didn't have a direct competitor; its hot intermediate-size cars were designed to homologate the cars for NASCAR racing rather than to capture a sizable portion of the youth market.

For that market Ford had its hot-selling Mustang, which had become one of the best-selling cars in history. In 1967 the Mustang was redesigned to accommodate larger engines, which put it in the GTO's performance league, at least on paper. In reality the big 390 engine was an underachieving pig; the Mustang wouldn't really become a threat to the GTO until the advent of the Super Cobra Jet 428 in the 1969 model year.

Chevrolet had responded to the Mustang by introducing the Camaro for the 1967 model year. With its top engine options–the 375-horsepower L78–Chevrolet's

pony car had more muscle (and less weight) than Pontiac's muscle car. The L78 engine was also available in the Chevelle SS396, making Chevrolet's A-body muscle car faster than Pontiac's original example of the genre.

The GTO had to compete not only with cars from other brands in 1967 but with a car within Pontiac's own lineup: the Firebird, Pontiac's version of the Camaro. This car, which was also several hundred pounds lighter than the GTO, could be ordered with a Ram Air version of the GTO's 400-cubic-inch engine.

When mounted in the Firebird 400, Pontiac rated both the standard 400 and the Ram Air version at 325 horsepower. In part, this relatively low rating was the result of a half-hearted attempt to detune the engine, a token act that consisted of such easily disabled pieces as a tab on the carburetor linkage that prevented the throttle from opening fully. Simply breaking off the tab unleashed an additional 25 horsepower.

But there was more to this low rating than a token attempt to placate corporate safetycrats. In part, the 325-horsepower rating was fictitious. Pontiac purposely underrated the 400-cubic-inch powerplant to avoid frightening the timid souls running General Motors and their equally mousy counterparts in the insurance industry and to avoid pissing off GTO buyers. A Firebird with a horsepower rating identical to that of a GTO would make it difficult for Pontiac dealers to sell GTOs.

The new Firebird sold extremely well, especially considering it had a mid year introduction. Pontiac sold 82,560 Firebirds in 1967, many of which undoubtedly went to potential GTO customers.

But even with increased competition and the marketing impediments created by General Motors' corporate management, such as forcing Pontiac to tone down its advertising and banning the Tri-Power carburetors, the 1967 GTO sold well. Pontiac sold an impressive 81,722 GTOs for the model year: 7,029 coupes at $2,871 apiece, 65,176 hardtops, each of which set buyers back $2,935 plus the cost of options, and 9,517 convertibles, which cost $3,165 in 1967.

Sales of the Ram Air option grew to 751 units, and 13,827 buyers opted for the optional H.O. engine. Just 2,967 buyers elected to purchase cars with the low-compression two-barrel economy engine, but for the first time the majority of buyers (42,594) chose the automatic transmission over the manual options. This, in part, reflected the availability of the new TH-400, but it also reflected changing trends among American buyers. These trends would radically alter the U.S. auto market a few years down the road.

In a hurry, the driver of a 1967 GTO tended to ignore the hood tachometer, relying instead on their ears and the kick in the backside to determine when to grab the next gear.

By incorporating a B-pillar, the sport coupe increased the vehicle's rigidity. Unlike the hardtop coupe, the door glass on the "post" cars rode in a full frame.

CHAPTER 4

A MATURING CAR
FOR A MATURING AUDIENCE

Pontiac had reason to be excited going into 1968–the division had a completely new GTO. General Motors redesigned all of its A-body intermediate cars for the 1968 model year. This was no mild facelift or reskinning of existing chassis components; this was a top-to-bottom redesign of the cars.

The company's designers took the opportunity to apply the then trendy pony car proportions–long hood, short rear deck, small passenger compartment–to GM's lineup of intermediate cars. Built on shorter wheelbases than previous A-body models (112 inches versus 115 inches), these cars began to blur the distinction between muscle car and pony car. The Mustang had grown in size for 1967, and both the Mustang and the Chevrolet Camaro/Pontiac Firebird twins offered big engines. It was getting difficult to tell a pony car from a muscle car.

The new A-bodies still featured curves over the wheel wells, but by blending the roofline into the rear deck in even more of a fastback style than the previous generation, designers moved away from a design that could reasonably be compared to a bottle of Coca-Cola.

ENDURA BUMPERS

Pontiac produced the most outrageously styled version of the new A-body platform. The 1968 GTO, which was only offered in hardtop and convertible body styles after the 1968 redesign, featured what GM's performance division called an "Endura" bumper, a body-colored, closed-cell, urethane foam bumper bonded to a metal frame. The absence of a chrome bumper gave the GTO's front end a futuristic appearance unlike any car Detroit had ever produced.

These bumpers weren't just cool-looking; they were also dense and resilient. During testing, the foam recovered its shape in 24 hours after being depressed by a 4,000-pound load for 8 hours. To demonstrate the strength of the new Endura bumpers, Pontiac ran a television ad in which actor Paul Richards slugged the front end of the car with a crowbar seven times doing no apparent damage. If anyone watches the commercial closely, they might notice that Richards was breathing heavy while swinging the crowbar. That was because Richards, a heavy smoker, was already suffering from the emphysema that would eventually kill him.

This is the last 1969 GTO Judge convertible built, rolling down the Baltimore, Maryland, assembly line during the last shift on the last day of production, August 4, 1969. With its Ram Air III engine and four-speed manual transmission, it's one of only 74 units so built.

To demonstrate the strength of the new Endura bumpers, Pontiac ran a television ad in which actor Paul Richards slugged the front end of the car with a crowbar seven times doing no apparent damage.

The GTO's new bumper is so fantastic you can't even see it.

It seems that everything our engineers touch turns to great. Last year, they made wipers disappear. This year, the most unique bumper since the invention of the bumper.

In constructing this super-snout, they begin with a sheet of heavy stamped metal. Then, a new micro-cellular urethane foam—a substance that's more than rubber, but not quite plastic—is bonded

to the metal. And finally, the bumper is coated with a special resilient paint.

The result? A bumper that not only is color-keyed to the car, but also resists minor chipping, peeling and corrosion. There are, however, some people who have to kick the bumper before they'll believe it. If you're one of these, go ahead. Kick the bumper. When you find it.

Specs, decals and 5 color pictures are yours for 30¢ (50¢ outside U.S.A.). Send to: '68 Wide-Tracks, P.O. Box 888H, 196 Wide-Track Blvd., Pontiac, Michigan 48056.

Up until the late 1960s, automotive bumpers were little more than design elements, hardly up to the rigors of the real world. When Pontiac debuted its Endura flexible bumper, it used demonstrations like this to show how impact resistant it was. Note the malfunctioning headlight door on what was presumably a new car. *Motor Trend archives*

Early on in the model year Pontiac experienced some production problems regarding fit, matching paint color, and bonding the material to the base metal. As a result, 2,108 1968 GTOs left the factory with chrome bumpers borrowed from the LeMans. These cars had a special option on their order sheets called "Endura bumper delete." Everyone wanted the Endura bumpers and no one ordered that option of his or her own free will. As soon as Pontiac worked out the production problems the chrome bumpers disappeared for good and "Endura bumper delete" disappeared from the option list.

ONE HEADLIGHT

If a customer wanted an even more dramatic-looking front end on his or her GTO, he or she could order optional concealed headlights. These used vacuum-operated doors to cover the headlights when not in use. Many cars offered this feature in the 1960s, and in every case the system

proved troublesome and prone to problems inherent in the design of the vacuum system. A reserve tank held the vacuum, which powered actuators that raised and lowered the doors. Diaphragms in the actuators leaked over time, and cars with one headlight exposed and one covered were not uncommon sights as the cars aged in the 1970s and 1980s. The GTO was no exception.

The rest of the car was as dramatic as its front end. Designed under the direction of Pontiac designer William L. "Bill" Porter, the new car abandoned the boxy shape of the original GTO completely and embraced a look much more akin to the beautiful sports and grand-touring cars being built by some of Europe's finest automakers, such as Ferrari and Aston Martin. The design was filled with clever touches, like shaping the rear side markers like arrowheads.

Mostly people loved the look of the new GTO, though a few of the changes were controversial. In a move that wasn't appreciated by everyone, the metal "GTO" badges were replaced by stylish, modernistic

As the 1960s came to a close, Royal Pontiac was still working its performance magic on street-driven GTOs, including convertibles. One advantage of a ragtop was that the driver was able to enjoy the aggressive exhaust note more easily than in a coupe.

decals. That year marked the end of the line for a much-loved feature on the GTO: the side vent window. This little triangular window at the base of the A pillar, which was especially appreciated by smokers, was remarkably effective at getting controlled airflow in the cab of the car. The 1969 car would receive an optional Power Flow Ventilation system, allowing designers to eliminate the vent window, but the built-in ventilation system was never as effective at cooling the cabin as the side vent windows had been. Plus drivers couldn't toss their cigarette butts out of the vents.

Since the body of the 1968 GTO shared no common dimensions with its predecessors, the interior had to be replaced entirely. A new dash housed the instruments in three pods instead of four, allowing the installation of larger, easier to read speedometers and tachometers. The hood-mounted tach remained available as an option fitted to 5,931 GTOs for the 1968 model year.

Through these service department doors passed the hottest Pontiacs. Currently Fresard Pontiac, this was the home of Royal Pontiac in its heyday.

RAM AIR II

When Pontiac introduced the restyled GTO for 1968, the H.O. version of the 400-cubic-inch engine returned virtually unchanged, except for the intrusion of a little bit more pollution-control equipment. The horsepower rating remained unchanged, though that hardly seems possible since the engine received new freer-flowing intake and exhaust manifolds that undoubtedly added a few horsepower.

But Pontiac was playing nice now; the time had just about come for DeLorean to be promoted to Chevrolet and he was less inclined to anger his corporate masters than he had been just a few years earlier. If GM wanted Pontiac to downplay the performance of its cars, then Pontiac would downplay the performance of its cars. The division was more forthright when rating the power output of the lesser engines.

The freer-flowing manifolds brought the horsepower rating of the standard engine up to 350 horsepower and similar breathing improvements bumped the optional economy two-barrel engine to 265 horsepower.

The big news in the engine compartment of the GTO came about halfway through the model year. Pontiac announced the new Ram Air II engine on March 15, 1968, and cars ordered with the Ram Air option after April 1 would receive the new engine. The first Ram Air II cars began rolling off the assembly line on May 16 of that year.

Like the original Ram Air, the breathing equipment Pontiac supplied came in the car's trunk. This breathing equipment now connected to a pair of hood scoops rather than the single scoop of the 1965–1967 cars. Pontiac moved the new pair of air inlets up higher on the hood of the redesigned GTO, where they could scoop more air into the engine compartment, at least in theory; in reality these scoops were still located too low in the hood to rise out of the boundary area, an area of unstable air that extends about 1.25 inches above the surface of the hood of a moving car. This meant that the fresh air supplied by the Ram Air scoops was marginal at best, though the system did result in under-hood temperatures that averaged 75 degrees lower than cars without the fresh-air system.

The scoop inlets were the least important part of Ram Air II. More important to a driver's right foot were new round-port cylinder heads with polished valves, a wilder camshaft, and freer-flowing exhaust manifolds.

The round ports, which replaced the D-shaped exhaust ports used on other versions of the engine, defined the new design, and Ram Air II and later engines are often referred to as "round-port" engines. The round ports flowed exhaust gasses much more efficiently than did the older D-shaped ports. The new ports were larger overall than the earlier ports, as were the intake ports, requiring 2.11-inch intake and 1.77-inch exhaust valves. These valves were polished and purposely "tuliped"; that is, their valve faces were purposely deformed in a way that increased high-speed airflow.

Streamlined exhaust headers were designed to fit the new round exhaust ports, and the engine featured thicker, stronger $^{11}/_{32}$-inch pushrods, heavy-duty valve springs, forged pistons, Arma Steel connecting rods, and the anvil-like nodular-iron crankshaft that had long made Pontiac bottom ends some of the strongest in the auto industry. The engine also featured four-bolt main bearings, a feature that had appeared on the original Ram Air engine block at the beginning of the 1968 model year.

The Ram Air II featured an even wilder cam than the one used in the original Ram Air engine. The engine could be ordered with either the close-ratio M21 four-speed manual transmission or the TH-400 automatic, and, as with the previous year, the only available rear-end gear ratios were 4.33:1 for four-speed cars and 3.90:1 for automatic cars. Air conditioning was not offered with the Ram Air II. The result of all this fine-tuning was that the 400-cubic-inch Ram Air II engine generated 366 horsepower at 5,400 rpm and 445 lb-ft of torque at 3,800 rpm. This rating was more a reflection of the conservative atmosphere at General Motor's corporate headquarters than an accurate power rating, a fact proven time and time again as Ram Air II GTOs beat cars with much higher horsepower ratings in street races across the country.

continued on page 177

Above: Royal Pontiac developed this graphic emblem to represent the Royal Racing Team mail order program. Nicknamed "Philoh," the decal graced Pontiacs from coast to coast.

Right: This badge was the only way most Royal Bobcat vehicles could be visually identified.

Pontiac unveiled a new look for the GTO in 1968, due to the introduction of a new A-body platform. Though the wheelbase was 3 inches shorter than the prior year, weight was up about 50 pounds. In model year 1968, the convertible style was popular, with 9,980 units sold. But the coupe body generated far larger sales numbers, with 77,704 finding good homes.

For customers wanting a touch more power than provided by the standard engine, Pontiac offered the L74 H.O. package that delivered 360 horsepower and 445 lb-ft of torque. This engine was a bargain at $76.88.

Buyers wanting the sleek hidden headlight feature had to fatten the payment to the dealer by $52.66 for option T83. Verdoro Green was a popular color in 1968.

Wide-Tracking is also taught in these other Pontiac editions: Le Mans, the Five Firebirds, Catalina, Grand Prix, Bonneville, Brougham

etween Wide-Tracking and just plain ordinary driving.

We've got a machine that teaches Wide-Tracking instantaneously. Everything you need to know is wrapped up in that one sleek, inimitable package labeled 1968 Pontiac GTO. You'll find a new 350-hp 400-cubic-inch V-8 inside with new standard Quadra-Power carburetion. (Or you can specify either a 360-hp version or our exclusive Ram Air option.) Turn the key and you've learned lesson one.

Now try it out on the road and note the difference GTO's Wide-Track stance makes in handling and stability. That's lesson number two.

Then step back and admire the lines that put The Great One in a class by itself. With a revolutionary new bumper that dramatically lengthens the visual sweep of the hood. (It's the same shiny color as the car, but it won't chip, fade or corrode.) Vanishing wipers are standard . . . order disappearing headlights for even more of a custom look. If performance, handling and uncompromising beauty aren't enough, check out the new padded safety armrests, front and rear side marker lights and myriad other safety features that make '68 Wide-Tracking more secure than ever before. When you're ready to give up ordinary driving and graduate to Wide-Tracking, turn on a GTO.

GM
MARK OF EXCELLENCE

Wide-Track Pontiac

Pontiac Motor Division

For the 1968 model year, the GTO coupe could be ordered with the $84.26 Cordova Top in one of four colors: white, gold, teal, or black.

"HIS AND HERS" LAST RIDE

Transmission choices remained the same as before. The base transmission was the heavy-duty three-speed manual (which had been sourced from Ford) that almost never actually found its way into the car. The optional four speeds were still the M20 wide-ratio and M21 close-ratio units. People mistakenly assumed that the close-ratio unit was the high-performance setup, and it was, if you hauled your car to the track and only drove on road courses. If you stopped and started, especially if you started quickly enough to light up the rear tires in billowy plumes of smoke and continued to keep your foot in the carburetor until the guy beside you receded in your rearview mirror, you wanted the lower first-gear ratio offered by the wide-ratio gear set.

The optional automatic transmission remained the excellent TH-400, and once again buyers who ordered an automatic car with the optional console received Hurst's Dual-Gate shifter as standard equipment. Pontiac was the first company to offer this shifter, and owners liked it. While many features turn out to be styling gimmicks (like Pontiac's hood-mounted tachometer, for instance), the Dual Gate offered genuine benefits for a driver who drag

Drivers in search of audio excellence looked to option U57, a $133.76, Delco Electronics eight-track tape player to deliver lifelike performances. Technology didn't take long to relegate this option to the dustbin.

Below: Pontiac used a pinched rocker treatment to emphasize the "Coke-bottle" shape in the center of the 1968 GTO. Overall vehicle length decreased 6 inches this year to 200.7 inches.

General Motors introduced a new A-body platform for 1968, and most of the divisions reaped the benefits. Pontiac's vehicle on the A-body was the GTO, while Buick built Skylarks, Chevrolet had the Chevelle, and Oldsmobile the Cutlass.

raced his or her car. For everyone else, it was just plain fun to fool around with.

Even so, 1968 would be the last year the shifter was offered on the GTO. DeLorean would have liked to use the shifter in Pontiac's entire line of sporty cars, but it was just too expensive and its continued use would have eaten into the division's profit margins.

Pontiac improved the handling of its redesigned GTO by increasing the size of the front stabilizer bars to 1 inch and increasing the spring rates to 310 pounds per inch in the front and 122 pounds per inch in the

rear. The front disc brakes were still optional, and again they were available with or without power assist. Even though the new car was shorter than before, it was also heavier, and the "optional" front disc brakes really were more of a required item than an option. The base 9.5-inch drums carried over from the original 1964 GTO were inadequate to the point of being criminally dangerous on the heavier new 1968 car. The front drums were modified halfway through the model year, but this modification was designed to ease servicing the brakes rather than improve performance.

MARKETING MISCREANTS

Even though Pontiac had been ordered to deemphasize performance in its advertising, it continued to try to sneak racing and performance into its promotional efforts. For example, the division's advertising team developed a billboard that showed a couple of young men sitting inside a GTO beneath a sign pointing toward Detroit's Woodward Avenue, which was nationally recognized as the street racing capital of the world. The text of the ad read: "The Great One by Pontiac. Now you know the rest of the story."

GM's corporate management was so afraid of looking irresponsible in front of Nader and his minions that it had gone so far as to order that all cars in the advertisements created by all GM divisions be static; they didn't even want to show a moving car, since that car could be moving in an irresponsible manner.

While technically complying with this edict, the Woodward Avenue ad implied that the car was on its way to engage in reprehensible behavior. The two young men were clearly on their way to Woodward Avenue to go street racing, which is what one did when one went to Woodward Avenue in a GTO.

Pontiac might have gotten away with the ad, had it not put up a version of the billboard near Woodward Avenue, in the exact spot the photo had been taken, and changed the tagline to: "To Woodward Avenue with love from Pontiac."

Buyer preferences had, by 1968, made the automatic transmission the gearbox of choice, with 51,385 vehicles using the Hurst Dual-Gate Shifter to select the gear, while 36,299 GTO owners rowed through the gears.

Shortly after the billboard went up General Motors received an angry letter from the city council of Berkeley, Michigan, a suburb that borders Woodward Avenue. The council was apoplectic because Pontiac was belittling the law of the land by encouraging street racing in an effort to sell cars. As everyone knew, street racing led to carnage, death, flipper babies, and possibly even bestiality. Pontiac was indeed thrusting its middle finger at the law with this ad campaign, and it might have gotten away with it had the division not angered the locals near Woodward Avenue. But it did, and as a result GM ordered Pontiac to remove any Woodward Avenue billboards that were still standing.

A VERY GOOD YEAR

Pontiac's advertising and marketing folks might have been hog-tied when it came to promoting the division's performance cars, but the cars themselves were so good that they didn't need much promoting.

This was especially true of the new GTO. *Motor Trend* magazine picked the GTO as its car of the year and sales rose to 87,684 units, up nearly 6,000 units over the previous year. More important for Pontiac, the division sold more than 340,000 Tempest models, including the GTO versions, putting Pontiac second behind Chevrolet in the intermediate car market and ahead of Ford and every other brand.

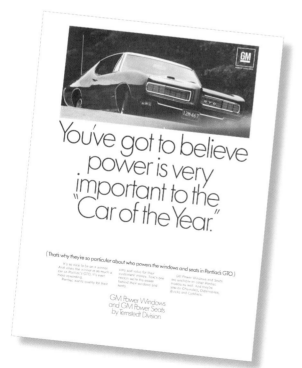

The optional Rally II–styled steel wheel was a popular option, costing only $84.26. Good luck picking up a set today for anywhere near that price.

The price of the GTO had risen rather dramatically for 1968, with the base hardtop selling for $3,078 and the convertible starting at $3,327. As always, the cars could be optioned up to infinity and beyond, and the price rose accordingly. Sales of the single-purpose Ram Air and Ram Air II cars rose to their highest level yet; 848 people bought four-speed versions and 205 purchased automatic-equipped cars. One hundred fourteen thrill seekers purchased convertibles with one of the Ram Air engines. The unpopular two-barrel economy car became slightly less unpopular–3,273 people ordered cars equipped with the neutered engine–but sales of the H.O. cars fell, to a total of 10,464 units, 3,601 of which were equipped with automatic transmissions and 1,227 of which were convertibles.

The bulk of the cars sold were hardtops–77,704–and as in the previous year more cars were sold with automatic transmissions than with manual gearboxes: 51,385 versus 36,299. The breakdown of GTO sales, particularly the move toward automatic transmissions, indicates that the audience was maturing. The car, with its increased emphasis on handling, comfort, and all-around performance rather than just straight-line acceleration, certainly was maturing, and the increased sales indicated the market approved of the direction the GTO was taking.

A SERIOUS CAR FOR CRAZY TIMES

Pontiac continued to refine its sophisticated muscle car for 1969 to meet the tastes of a maturing market. If that market was maturing in the late 1960s, you wouldn't know it from the cars coming from Pontiac's competitors, like the outrageous Dodge Super Bee with its 440 Six Pack engine, the over-the-top Hurst/Olds, and the colorful SC/Rambler from American Motors. These cars (and their advertising campaigns) promoted psychedelic cars to a youth market that seemed to have a cult-like devotion to wretched excess.

Pontiac catered to this new hedonism to a degree, offering 21 colors for 1969, including paint with trippy names like Goldenrod Yellow, Mayfair Maize, Castillian Bronze, and Limelight Green. The body received only the obligatory trim changes. The most noticeable change for 1969 was the removal of the side vent window.

Inside, the dashboard was redesigned with a two-tier placement of the gauges, and there were a few token trim changes. The ignition key moved from the dash to the steering column to accommodate the government-mandated steering lock. Otherwise the exterior and interior were pretty much just as they had been the previous year. But for the egg-crate motif on the new grille and the deletion of the side-vent window and its attendant crank, a casual observer would be hard-pressed to tell a 1969 car from a 1968 car inside or out.

RAM AIR III AND RAM AIR IV

In 1969 the biggest changes occurred under the hood. The two-barrel economy engine remained the same, but the base four-barrel engine got a hotter cam for use with four-barrel transmissions. Even with the steeper cam the power rating remained at 350 horsepower.

The H.O. engine also received a hotter cam for use with four-speed transmissions, though this was changed back to the same cam used in earlier versions of the engine partway through the year. The engine did receive a cable-operated fresh-air hood scoop system that the driver could open or close with a push-pull lever on the dash, depending on weather conditions. The engine also received a new name to go along with its functional hood scoop: Ram Air III.

The Ram Air II engine was replaced with what would become perhaps the most legendary engine in

continued on page 193

SPECIAL ANNUAL AWARDS ISSUE

MOTOR TREND

50¢

FEBRUARY 1968

UT 3'6 SWEDEN KR. 3.95 INKL. OMS

Motor Trend names

TOP '68s

FOR THE FIRST TIME:
Outstanding Cars in Class!
Significant Foreign Cars!
Individual Merit Awards!
Achievement Awards!

AND

CAR OF THE YEAR!

'68 Preview:
Will Petty/Plymouth Repeat?

Each year, beginning in 1956, it has been the responsibility of the editors and technical staff of Motor Trend to weigh the many contributions and new developments inherent in all makes and models from all automotive manufacturers, and to present awards to those who, in the opinion of the staff, deserve to be recognized for their achievements. The awards are presented not only to honor the quest for automotive excellence, but as an inducement for others to look ahead to even greater accomplishments. To those in the automobile business, the Annual Motor Trend Awards are comparable to receiving Oscars in the motion picture industry.

Over the years, Motor Trend readers have responded to the Awards announcements with a degree of interest and enthusiasm that serves to affirm the authority with which the selections are made. During this time, however, a new breed of car buyer has come to demand an entirely new variety of specialized styling and performance capabilities. A vigorous economy has spawned a conglomerate of many market segments, all with their own unique attitudes and expectations. The battle cry of the influential younger—and not-so-young—generation is "involvement," the personal involvement of performance wedded to a complex variety of equipment and design options. At the same time, millions of motorists continue to insist upon progress in economy, safety, function and luxury.

This year, Motor Trend has expanded its Annual Awards Program to fulfill an obligation to its readers to recognize the diversification of automotive interests and the accelerating efforts of industry and individuals on behalf of the motoring public.

In 1968, cars have been evaluated for achievements in the generally acknowledged groups into which they fall by virtue of design/function concept, price, size and other distinguishing characteristics.

In addition to

1 Car of the Year, awards have been presented this year to

2 Cars in Category which, in the opinion of Motor Trend, have achieved outstanding significance in engineering, styling and/or market timing. The winners have been selected from among the product lines of U.S. manufacturers. To qualify, cars must have been introduced to the public by January 10, 1968. Since there are some entirely new cars and major changes in others, group classification has been broadened, where necessary, to permit their inclusion in the most logical judging category.

3 Accessory Achievement Awards, initiated in 1967, again honor those original equipment suppliers or manufacturers whose features and accessories, appearing on 1968 cars, reflect significant achievements in comfort, safety, convenience, performance, economy, engineering or applied research.

4 Foreign Car Awards, presented here for the first time in the history of the Motor Trend Awards Program, recognize cars from overseas for their achievements in engineering design, safety, styling, or a combination of factors related to product excellence. They have been selected from among the product lines of foreign automobile manufacturers without regard to distribution in the U.S.

5 Merit Awards for 1968 were created to recognize the human effort that so frequently goes unrewarded in the formulation of automotive progress. In a departure from customary selection procedure, the nation's automotive press has cooperated in the presentation of Merit Awards. Utilizing ballots provided by Motor Trend, they have cast their votes for outstanding individuals who, in the opinion of the press, have influenced the industry to the ultimate benefit of the public.

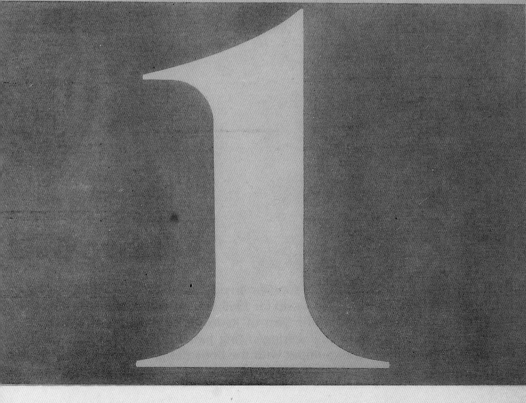

Once again in 1968, the traditional criteria used to select the recipient of Motor Trend's coveted Car of the Year Award has been "that combination of engineering, styling and market timing that when perfectly enjoined creates progress sufficient to set an industry trend." The significance of automotive concept, in addition to pure mechanical achievement, was among the prime considerations and, as in the past, contenders must be introduced to the public by January 10th. This year, following careful evaluation of the 1968 product lines of all domestic manufacturers, the winner of the Car of the Year Award was the unanimous choice of Motor Trend's editorial staff.

Car of the Year

Pontiac GTO

The inertial force that started the supercar trend — Pontiac GTO — holds a distinctive position in the automotive world for 1968. Not only does it continue to establish the class standard in the fifth year of its existence, but it also represents a unique and revolutionary engineering/styling function. Its salient innovation is the integration of a rubber bumper with the body design, rendered in a manner that provides a direction and impetus for the entire industry. Never before has an

42 MOTOR TREND / FEBRUARY 1968

Kollar

Motor Trend's Car of the Year

automobile been so successful in confirming the correlation between safety, styling and performance as the 1968 GTO. With the new combinations of aesthetic unity, unbroken styling lines, decreased body vulnerability, increased impact absorption, and responsive power, handling and controllability, it convincingly proves that optimum design/function criteria for nearly all automotive purposes, can be achieved in one unit.

Pontiac people eat well. Prime rib an inch and a half thick, choice veal with a grapefruit and cheese condiment, filets, grapefruit in V.S.O.P. brandy for dessert . . . all in the company cafeterias. Maybe that's where they developed their technique.

They're all epicureans . . . sophisticated . . . they know that the best way to assess the competence of the chef is by his omelette. Turning a proper omelette takes guts and time and some pretty crafty legerdemain, but once it's done you'll stand two heads higher than the next man.

With most people, their eggs shall always be chickens. Never Benedicted. Not even a mediocre liver omelette. Just chickens. They're members of The Establishment, so they let things develop in their own conventional, natural, inferior way without any attempt to buck the tide with improvements. Then they all disappear in anonymity.

But lots of people are different. John DeLorean, for instance, is Pontiac's general manager and only 42 years old; Jack Humbert, chief stylist, is 40; Josh Madden, plastics expert, appears to be less than that; and they're all just too far removed from that inglorious moment of being dropped into the dregs of oblivion known as corporate retirement programs, to let it dull their acumen.

So they spend their time perfecting that omelette and turning out new ones, because that's where the fulfillment is. The result speaks for itself, and it's considerably more than a plastic-lipped supercar. It's five years of new attempts that have matured into a new-dimension-type automobile that is almost revolutionary without being kooky.

Ever since the GTO brazenly established itself in 1964, it has exuded an undeniable kind of magnetism that distinguishes it from its imitators. It is the important kind of magnetism that seems to be imparted without conscious effort. It was just there, and you somehow knew that if anything new was ever introduced, it would be done by the GTO.

The product itself was already a clue to this. Never before had anyone tapped such a dynamic reservoir of meaningful desires, nor had satisfied them with such a soulful solution. Those youthful heads working on the car were far beyond the rest of us, and they just seem to stay there. About the time everyone else appears to be catching up they introduce another keen discovery and away they go again.

Their timing is uncanny. Right in the middle of the displacement mania, when engine sizes were running rampant, Pontiac offered an overhead cam powerplant and changed the standards of engine sophistication.

But the finest commentary on the fallacies of modern technology has now been presented to the American automotive world by the 1968 GTO — a car that incorporates not only the best taste in GM's "A"-body variations — and an excellent handling and performing supercar package — but also the most significant achievement in materials technology in contemporary automotive engineering all combining to substantiate it as the outstanding intermediate of the year, and the outstanding car.

It's a good lesson in the old epigram that you simply cannot create by committee. The flexible bumper concept has been around since World War II, but under the onus of bureaucratic niggling and the inertia of archaic trivia, an efficient and intelligent compatibility between materials technology development and aesthetic values has been impossible.

Pontiac saw that the only hope was to extract itself from this morass of mundane mentalities and start thinking by themselves rather than by corporate priorities. The talent was there, but it wasn't found until Pontiac had the smallest engineering department in the corporation and only five engineers in New Materials Engineering. Parkinson's Law.

For the first time in 20 years, intelligent cooperation between engineering and styling was possible. Each recognized the other's contribution, and most important, the synergism that was possible only through joint effort, finally achieved reality. Styling studios were opened to engineers, engineering labs were opened to stylists, and the entire division became materials-development conscious.

It wasn't merely a naive, vertical attempt at developing an automotive defense system that would simply rebound your adversary. Now, everything was one, and it all had to make sense aesthetically. After all, it had been proved that the human being was more than a utilitarian, corporeal mechanism. He also had cultural and aesthetic standards that any functional object had to meet. So, Pontiac put the body engineer and stylist in the same building, made sure there was intimate intellectual contact and rapport, and assigned both to the same basic projects from the start.

Before long, various experimental foams and non-rigid materials were discovered to possess possible applications values, and under the direction of DeLorean, the stage was set to feed him every new concept there was, regardless of its immediate validity.

The most logical of all new materials applications was the flexible bumper, and if used as a color and styling element, it would also allow for tasteful and different "A"-body designs, a visual body balance and a unified personality that was perfectly consistent with the neo-integrationists of modern automotive artwork in which prevailing philosophies demand elegance to be defined as the absence of ornamentation — a greater unity.

Realistic application began in 1964 when the flexible bumpers were attached to push trucks in Pontiac's yards. They not only withstood impact, but weathering and corrosion as well. The basic material, called Endura by Pontiac, had been resolved: high-density urethane-elastomer foam weighing 44 pounds per cubic foot, and with a deflection of $1/2$-inch under a 1000-psi. load, with complete recovery in 24 hours after depression by a 4000-pound load for eight hours.

The front surface of the bumper is very hard — virtually indistinguishable from steel, or, perhaps, fiberglass. This rigidity, however, decreases progressively toward the rear of the bumper so the material can compress against the metal fenders and hood where impact absorption is most critical.

Normal harmless testing on the new bumper is done at speeds of 4 mph — more than twice the speed conventional bumpers can withstand. When the new 5 mph standards are invoked, Pontiac will already be able to meet them.

At this point in development, both cost and weight are somewhat of a disadvantage, though very little. Both, however, will soon be solved.

As great an achievement as the bumper material was, Pontiac claims that the development of the paint was even more significant. Inland Manufacturing Division at Dayton had been a recognized factor in foam technology for

At 4 mph — more than twice the impact speed other bumpers can take — GTO registers no damage whatever.

years, and when named as initial fabricators for the '68 GTO bumpers, it was basically a relatively simple matter of perfecting a paint material for this specific application. It soon became apparent that the only paint suitable for the new bumper would entail an entirely new project for its development. Conventional paints simply did not possess the necessary flexibility.

The advanced quality of the paint and the technology involved is evident in the fabricating process itself. First the paint is sprayed on bare, solid nickel molds that have extremely smooth, plated surfaces. Then a .150-inch thick steel frame is placed into the mold, the cover half is dropped on, and the urethane is injected, heated, cured and removed, *all without additional finishing and polishing.* There is also no real limitation to color availability, since the present GTO range consists of 17 different hues.

Though further perfection will naturally follow, the ability of the material to conform so easily is a triumph. Indicative of even better performance is the fact that the urethane forms much easier than chrome, so possibilities of design flexibility are enhanced even more.

The rest of the division has already capitalized on the importance of the urethane-type material. Both the Firebird 400 and all "B"-bodies have an Endura emblem protecting them from initial contact.

According to Ken Valentine, staff engineer for materials, "Through the judicious use of materials, we can accomplish so many things where we would otherwise be hamstrung by regulations."

For styling, it liberated many advanced concepts that had been suppressed by conventional materials. You will have to wait a year to see them, but Pontiac claims they will definitely incorporate some of them in 1969.

Endura's contribution to styling is limited only by what the consumer is willing to accept. There is certainly no doubt that it has provided the stylist with a vastly increased scope for designs he has craved for so long. Oh, it will be misused; not every car should have it, nor every bumper. There are applications where our vanity will always demand scintillating accents, and the only way to achieve that is by contrasts to body paint and material. For instance, on limousines and luxury cars, a massive, wide, or regal countenance is normally desired, and this can best be conveyed by a chrome grille, side molding, or some other silly gimmick. But in the burgeoning hedonism of youth markets, the ease and flexibility with which a sculptured, smooth, unified, compact entity can be wrought, is invaluable.

Advantages of the new GTO bumper are already evident in styling, safety and maintenance. Equally as important is that it provides us with an innovation that is a sure way to force the hands of honesty and fairness from the windy temples of the insurance kingdom.

coupe, and noting the sweet sound from the exhausts. He stays behind all the way to the Hollywood Blvd. off-ramp, and as we leave traffic, he's still checking us out. By the time he's reached t— thought about the— less than half the— 50,000-mile warran— GTO ever checked—

That gave us the— during the next few—

The following W— County Internation— where all the loca— While we waited f— owners from a few— eve and came over— the engine is idling— lift cam is "rump-— and the guy up fro— grab a quick loo— Fat chance.

By the time we— Coxey's army of— would take all of— What's the use. W— beat them.

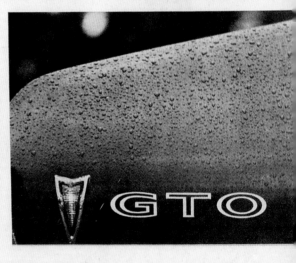

We got the feeling there was an army of woodpeckers around. Tap, tap. Tap-tap-tap-tap. "Hey man, this bumper's not rubber—is it?"

First, this sporty looking exec tools up beside us in his new Mercedes 250SL and checks out our GTO. He moves forward a bit, then drops behind. We see him in our rear-view mirror carefully considering the bright red coupe, and noting the sweet sound from the exhausts. He stays behind all the way to the Hollywood Blvd. off-ramp, and as we leave traffic, he's still checking us out. By the time he's reached the San Fernando Valley, we figure he's thought about the good looks of our machine, a price tag less than half the one he peeled off his window, 5-year/50,000-mile warranty, and the fact that no one in a '68 GTO ever checked out his SL.

That gave us the first hint of what we'd be going through during the next few weeks of driving the GeeTo.

The following Wednesday, we made it out to Orange County International Raceway for "street racers" night where all the local hot-dogs gather for grudge racing. While we waited for our turn at the line, a couple of car owners from a few lanes over gave our Ram-Air car the eye and came over. We've got the 4-speed lever in low, the engine is idling at just under a grand, the stock high-lift cam is "rump-rumping" through the exhaust system, and the guy up front is getting ready for us. "Okay, just grab a quick look fellas, and then we gotta wail." Fat chance.

By the time we can start engaging the clutch, there's a Coxey's army of hot-rodders circling the coupe, and it would take all of the 360 hp on tap to mow 'em down. What's the use. We shut it off and climbed out. Can't beat them.

We got the feeling there was an army of woodpeckers around. Tap, tap. Tap-tap-tap-tap. "Hey man, this bumper's not rubber — is it?"

"Just hit it with a hammer pal and see what bounces. You'll be pulling your arm back into its socket for a week."

Wherever we took the groovy looking super car, a 15-minute question and answer session developed. First the bit about the rubber bumper (we were always careful not to mention the line about a hammer to a carpenter). Down at the barbershop, this car can be a useful weapon when the Saturday afternoon crowds pack the joint.

All we had to do was walk in the door, quietly of course, and announce "there's the wildest looking machine parked outside you ever did see." Whoosh! All the old guys with shiny domes (why do *they* always come in on Saturday?) throw down the girly books and make it out the door so fast it takes the footwork of a ballet dancer to avoid them. What a kicker! By the time the gents file back in, our ears are lowered and we sail out the door smelling of fresh aftershave. A blast of the horn and a spin of wide-ovals, and mighty "tiger" disappears from sight.

That trick won't work for long, but it's good for now.

We became as addicted to the GTO as onlookers. It goes, rides, handles, steers, stops and looks like a car should. We halfway believe Pontiac took the best parts of all cars made, poured them into a mixing bowl, and stirred up GTO. But they didn't have to. They've been working their way toward this beautiful result for the past four years.

Niceties abound in this machine. Like the Hurst 4-speed shifter that's standard, and the hood-mounted tach that's optional. The first power shift we threw between first and second was so short and quick, we pushed the clutch pedal back in thinking we'd stopped in neutral and blown the shift. Checking the tach is easier than accepting a free drink. It reposes in a straight-forward position, and not far down from line of sight.

Finding instruments is a snap. They're all bunched in front of the driver, and the wood rimmed steering wheel seems fresh from Ferrari-land. The high positioned console

storage bin is softly padded on top, and while being too low for use as an armrest will hold gobs of essentials near-at-hand.

There's a quietness inside reminiscent of a church. Tight window sealing as well as smooth suspension pieces keep all road or traffic noise outside where it belongs.

One thing only smokers will criticize is that when the ash tray is open, it interferes with shifting into or out of first or third gear. Why no one at Pontiac found this out during testing is beyond our comprehension. We know for a fact that some of their engineers support the tobacco industry.

GTO is a beautiful road machine. Speeds of 60 to 80 mph are as steady and firm as a drive through the car wash. Any reasonable speed won't upset its balance. We've had GTOs well over 120 mph — under controlled conditions — without noting any skittishness.

Handling maneuvers will make converts of anyone who ever doubted U.S. cars could go-around-corners. In fact, most domestic supercars will do this, but that's another story and this one's for the GTO. Like the fabled tiger connected with GTO, it paws around corners flat and true, then leaps through short straights, ready to have another go at a seemingly hard turn. Only driver inability will reveal any difficulty in the car's handling spirit.

Straight-line performance is just short of stupendous. After finally breaking away from our fan club at Orange County, we dropped a best of 14.80 seconds e.t. and a speed of 96 mph in *completely* street worthy trim. This means mufflers, air-cleaner, power assist belts, and street tires intact. We pulled off the air-cleaner and bolted on a pair of Goodyear Super-Stock "slicks" on Ansen Top Eliminator wheels and immediately kicked .3-second off this time, with speed going up to 97 mph. A few more passes through the quarter-mile and we knocked off another .05-

second, finishing the evening with a 14.45-second reading and a speed of 98 mph. We still hadn't tampered with any part of the engine, and kept the exhaust running through the mufflers.

Earlier GTO's were outrunning us, but no other comparable car could finish the quarter first. It took a modified GTO to beat us, and we even had the pleasure of getting to a few of these by "reading" the Christmas Tree Chrondek starting lights a little better than their drivers.

We were asked, frequently, "What's the gas mileage?" Not to be facetious, our only reply was and can be, "If you have to ask, there's not much use in knowing." Quite frankly the car isn't built to go far on a gallon of gas. Our low reading was 7.0 mph, while the high was 14.4. This car had the 360-hp Ram-Air 400-cu.-in. V-8 with a 4.33 rear axle gear, and the 14.4 came as more of a shock than the 7.0. Mileage gets progressively better as the power descends through the range of GTO engines, hitting an all-time high with the 265-hp, 2-bbl. 400 V-8.

We had the pleasure of running-in our test GTO, as well as some with milder engines and more creature comforts such as air-conditioning and automatic transmissions. We've owned several other new cars that wore thin on our temperaments soon after their newness wore off — which usually wasn't long after noticing the first scratch. This wasn't the case here. Even when we'd clocked thousands of miles, the GTO still appealed to us as a "new" car, with the thought of its becoming "old" a nearly impossible happening.

PERFORMANCE	Automatic 400	4-speed Ram-Air
Acceleration		
0-30 mph	3.1 secs.	2.8 secs.
0-45 mph	4.9 secs.	4.5 secs.
0-60 mph	7.3 secs.	6.5 secs.
0-75 mph	10.4 secs.	9.6 secs.
Passing Speeds		
40-60 mph	2.9 secs.,	2.8 secs.,
	212 ft.	205 ft.
50-70 mph	3.6 secs.,	3.0 secs.,
	316.8 ft.	264 ft.
Standing Start ¼-mile	15.93 secs.,	14.45 secs.,
	88.32 mph	98.20 mph
Speeds in Gears		
1st...mph @ rpm	39 @ 5000	41 @ 5000
2nd...mph @ rpm	66 @ 5000	56 @ 5000
3rd...mph @ rpm	95 @ 5000	73 @ 5000
4th...mph @ rpm		92 @ 5000
Mph Per 1000 rpm	19	18.4
Stopping Distances		
From 30 mph	26 ft.	28 ft.
From 60 mph	145 ft.	150 ft.
Mileage Range	8.9 - 15.6	7.0 - 14.4

SPECIFICATIONS	Automatic 400	4-speed Ram-Air
Bore & Stroke	4.12 x 3.75 in.	4.12 x 3.75 in.
Displacement—Cu. In.	400	400
Hp @ rpm	350 @ 5000	360 @ 5400
Torque: lbs.-ft. @ rpm	445 @ 3000	445 @ 3800
Compression Ratio	10.75:1	10.75:1
Carburetion	1 4-bbl.	1 4-bbl.
Transmission	Turbo Hydra-Matic	4-speed manual
Final Drive Ratio	3.23:1	4.33:1
Steering	Recirculating Ball Bearing Gear with power assist	
Steering Gear Ratio	17.5:1	17.5:1
Turning Diameter—curb-to-curb	40.9 ft.	
Wheel Turns—lock-to-lock	4.2	
Tires	G77x14 2-ply—4-ply rated	
Brakes	4-wheel drum with power assist	Front disc/rear drum with power assist
Fuel Capacity—gals.	21.5	
Curb Weight—lbs.	3707	3650
Wheelbase—ins.	112	
Front Track—ins.	60	
Rear Track—ins.	60	
Overall Length—ins.	200.7	
Width—ins.	74.8	
Height—ins.	52.2	

OPTIONS & PRICES Manufacturer's Suggested Retail Price (hdtp. cpe), 3228.00; Engine options, 76.86-400 H.O., 342.29—Ram-Air; Automatic transmission, 236.97; 4-speed transmission, 184.31; H-D 3-speed transmission, 84.26; limited slip differential, 42.13; high performance tires, std.; special instrumentation, 84.26; hood mounted tachometer, 63.19; AM radio, 61.09; AM/FM radio, 133.76; custom wheels, 63.19; power brakes, 42.13; front disc brakes, 63.19; console, 52.66; power steering, 94.79; adjustable steering wheel, 42.13; hide-away headlights, 52.66; air conditioning, 360.20.

It didn't take too heavy a right foot to transform the rear tires to an unusual form of street art. Palladium Silver was introduced on the 1969 GTO model line.

An aggressive stance was standard on the 1969 GTO. The coupe tipped the scales in the neighborhood of 3,600 pounds, depending on options. Dual hood scoops could be made functional if the buyer just checked the proper box on the order form. The standard engine in 1969 was a 350-horsepower, 400-cubic-inch V-8.

continued from page 180
GTO history: the Ram Air IV. This soon-to-be-legendary engine was worked over from top to bottom, starting with a new aluminum intake manifold with large runners and separate cast-iron heat crossovers. The shape of the round exhaust ports was further refined to improve the flow of exhaust gasses even more than in the Ram Air III round-port engine.

Pontiac still refrained from offering a true mechanical-valve cam, a trick most other manufacturers resorted to when building high-performance engines.

Cars with solid lifters required intensive maintenance that most owners weren't capable of or willing to perform on a regular basis. Many owners thought they had the commitment needed to drive a solid-lifter car when they bought their muscle car but found that trying to use such a car for everyday transportation was more demanding than they expected.

The GTO was intended to be a daily driver, even in its hottest Ram Air IV guise, and the car retained a hydraulic cam, but in this particular case, Pontiac's engineers compromised somewhat on the design. The lifters on the

The sizable proboscis on the 1969 GTO could make parking an interesting experience. Pontiac boasted that the Endura bumper could be repaired, rather than replaced, if moderately damaged. Total GTO production in 1969 was 72,287, down a bit from the prior year's count of 87,684. Even when equipped with the standard 350-horsepower mill, the GTO was a contender on the street.

Street racers wanting a low-profile approach might be inclined to equip a 1969 GTO with the standard hubcaps and a subdued shade of paint. But there was nothing subdued about the fire-breathing Ram Air IV beneath the hood.

Ram Air IV engine were hybrids between mechanical and hydraulic designs, employing manual-lash limited-travel adjustment capabilities that increased the engine's redline by allowing higher rpm before valve float set in. Rocker ratios were changed to increase lift and the carburetor and ignition were recalibrated to take advantage of all this increased breathing and revving capacity.

The new Ram Air IV had even larger pushrods than its predecessor–$\frac{7}{16}$ inch versus $\frac{11}{32}$ inch–and an Arma Steel crankshaft, making the bottom end even stronger than in other GTOs, which was quite an accomplishment. To keep up with the new higher-revving capabilities Pontiac engineers mounted a high-capacity oil pump, a 60-psi pressure-relief spring, and new gearing in the distributor plate. Otherwise the engine was much the same as the previous Ram Air II engine, with its four-bolt

If I was looking for a little street racing action and I pulled up next to these hood scoops, I might look elsewhere. There are stories of GTO owners removing the Ram Air IV decals in an effort to lure in easy prey.

main bearings, Arma Steel connecting rods, and forged aluminum pistons. Like the Ram Air III engine, the Ram Air IV used a driver-controlled Ram Air system.

In 1969, buyers could finally select between either the 4.33:1 or 3.90:1 rear-end gear sets, regardless of whether the car was equipped with a four-speed or an automatic transmission. This made the four-speed cars more viable as daily drivers, especially for owners who logged a lot of freeway miles.

Even though the "Ram Air IV" designation makes sense as a chronological progression, the real reason the numeric portion of the alpha-numeric designation switched from "II" to "IV" was because the system

was originally intended to have four inlets for the air induction system. In addition to the two hood scoops, the new system was originally to have a pair of snorkels leading up to a pair of scoops located behind the front grilles. The additional inlets were dropped from the design before it made it to production, but the name stuck.

While the torque rating of Pontiac's hottest engine was probably realistic at 445 lb-ft at 3,400 rpm, the horsepower ratings were anything but realistic. If the 366-horsepower rating for the Ram Air III engine was conservative, the output ratings for the Ram Air IV–370 horsepower at 5,500 rpm–were practically delusional, an example of Pontiac's attempt to appease GM's corporate

Simple yet comfortable, the interior of the 1969 Ram Air IV GTO gave little indication that on the other side of the firewall was a grenade with the pin pulled. Pontiac used quality materials throughout the cockpit, including faux wood on the dashboard.

Opposite: The foam atop the air cleaner wasn't there for show, as a Ram Air IV engine needed a lot of fresh air to generate the 370-plus horsepower the factory rated the option. Only 759 were built for the 1969 model year.

Dull driving
can get
to be a habit.

Now—aren't you ready
to break away?

Wide-Track Family for '69: Grand Prix, Bonneville, Brougham, Executive, Catalina, GTO, LeMans, Custom S, Tempest and Firebird. Pontiac Motor Division

ho needs monotonous motoring? You n't. Which is why we couldn't do better an offer you a crack at either of our two orty types—GTO (better known as The reat One) and Firebird 400.

art with The Great One. When you do, u turn on a rare-sounding, 350-horse-wer V-8 (or an even more responsive am Air V-8, that's yours to order). You'll be ated in beautifully contoured buckets oking out over a hood that culminates in e same energy absorbing bumper GTO rprised you with last year. All this fabled auty sits on a Wide-Track with wide-val Redline tires ready to handle GTO's

very special way of moving. Now about that Firebird. There's a new sweep of metal at sides and rear, a tougher looking nose and you can order impressive Rally II wheels. Inside, wider bucket seats; a steering wheel with the brand-new anti-theft ignition, steering and transmission lock. And that "400" designation stands for 400 cubic inches of V-8. Specify our Ram Air setup, and those hood scoops turn functional. And, of course, everybody knows how Firebird handles. So break away from the usual. We suggest you get in touch with your local ego builder— your Wide-Track dealer.

 '69 Wide-Track Pontiac

Bias-ply tires weren't much in the traction department, but that was as good as you got in 1969. While you didn't need a Ram Air IV engine to lay waste to the rubber, it didn't hurt.

fretters and the nation's safety crusaders. In reality the Ram Air IV engine was one of the strongest non-mechanical cam cars sold in 1969, capable of running with cars with much larger engines, like Chrysler's 440. It was down on torque when compared to its larger competitors, but it was freer revving than any of those big-cube engines.

And it was lighter, making Ram Air IV–equipped GTOs less front-end heavy than its competition. With front-rear weight distribution closer to the ideal of 50-50 and its refined suspension, the Ram Air IV GTOs were some of the best-handling cars of the entire muscle car era. But the Ram Air IV option–option code 342 on the order sheet–was expensive, setting an owner back $389.62, which was more than 10 percent of the base price.

By getting the rear tires wet, then spinning them until they started smoking, it was hoped that enough heat would get into the rubber to increase the tire's traction. At least, that was the hope.

"THE JUDGE"

When Pontiac introduced the restyled GTO in 1968, it paid little attention to its rivals at Chrysler's Plymouth division. In 1967, Plymouth offered just one entrant into the muscle car market: the GTX. The GTX was an extremely capable car, but with its conservative styling and boxy lines it wasn't a car that resonated with younger buyers. Sales had been relatively insignificant when compared to GTO sales. As Pontiac prepared the new GTO for its 1968 debut, it didn't consider Plymouth's 1968 offerings a major source of competition.

Plymouth was about to change Pontiac's perception of its competitor. In one of the most audacious marketing moves of the period, Plymouth licensed the use of a popular Warner Brothers' cartoon character and named the car Road Runner. The new Plymouth, originally intended to be a stripped-down street fighter marketed to young buyers on tight budgets, featured graphics of the cartoon bird as well as a dual-toned horn designed to ape the Road Runner's distinctive "meep-meep" voice. This was not a car for a shrinking violet who wanted a restrained, inconspicuous car. If an owner wanted to abandon any semblance of restraint, he could order a 426 Hemi and, beginning in 1969, a 440 Six Barrel.

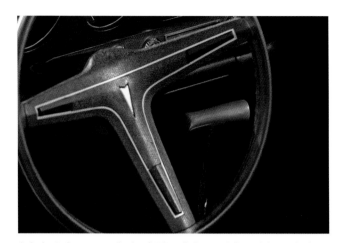

Only the Judge came with a beefy T-handled Hurst shifter. While not the best ergonomic design for a shifter handle, it was an impressive hunk of metal.

(As that name implies, "Six Barrel" referred to a trio of Holley two-barrel carburetors mounted atop a specially designed, Edelbrock-built, aluminum intake manifold feeding the high-performance 440-cubic-inch engine, which must have pissed off the folks at Pontiac; their asses were still chapped about having their beloved Tri-Power system taken away from them.)

The interior of a 1969 was somewhat monochromatic, in contrast to the vivid exterior. By 1969, image was as important as actual performance. The GTO Judge delivered plenty of both.

The Mopar crew kept their popular Road Runner lean in the 1969 model year with the fiberglass lift-off hood over the potent 440-6 engine. Traditionally a stripper with a huge engine, the modestly priced Road Runner enjoyed success both on and off the drag strip.

Opposite: Only 108 convertible Judges were built for the 1969 model year, unlike the far more common coupes; Pontiac sold 6,725 of them.

The new Plymouth, originally intended to be a stripped-down street fighter marketed to young buyers on tight budgets, featured graphics of the cartoon bird as well as a dual-toned horn designed to ape the Road Runner's distinctive "meep-meep" voice.

The standard engine in a 1969 Judge was an L74, 400-cubic-inch, Ram Air III developing 366 horsepower at 5,100 rpm, and a tire-melting 445 lb-ft of twist at 3,600 rpm. No tire of the day could survive a heavy right foot.

It's hard to believe in today's performance car environment the impact these three letters had on enthusiasts. Even drivers of non-Pontiac machinery acknowledged that the GTO started the muscle car revolution as we know it.

After Plymouth sold nearly 50,000 copies of its Road Runner cartoon cars for the 1968 model year, Pontiac realized that it had underestimated the Chrysler division.

Pontiac General Manager John DeLorean formed a committee to brainstorm ideas for the 1969 model year. DeLorean asked Wangers to sit on the committee. One of the challenges the committee faced was developing Pontiac's answer to the Road Runner, which had cut into GTO sales.

Focusing on Plymouth's initial marketing of the Road Runner as a low-priced muscle car, the committee originally devised a car called the E/T, a budget-priced GTO with a hopped-up 350-cubic-inch engine. While this car could beat a 383-equipped Road Runner through the quarter-mile (for all its hype, Chrysler's 383 B engine was, like Ford's 390-cubic-inch Mustang engine, a

By pulling this under-dash knob, a driver could manually open the flaps that controlled the Ram Air induction system. The single four-barrel Quadrajet appreciated the fresh air.

All rise for

boat anchor), DeLorean was less than happy with the committee's engine choice. In *Glory Days*, Wangers describes DeLorean's response when first seeing the car:

> *During our one-hour delivery, he sat stone-faced, not saying a word and never changing expression. At the conclusion, he looked at us all and said, very coolly, "Over my dead body. Don't you guys know this is a 400 cubic inch world? As long as I have anything to say about it, there will never be a GTO with anything less than a 400 cubic inch engine. I recognize what you are trying to do, and I support the concept, but get that !@#!*% 350 out of that car!" He had our attention, to say the least. He concluded his statement: "Bring this car up to GTO standards and then we'll figure out how to cut the price."*

This forced the committee to entirely rethink its approach. DeLorean's edict made sense. Initially the Road Runner had been marketed as a budget-priced car, and the logical way to compete with the car would be by putting a similar budget-priced car on the market. But Plymouth's plan to market the car as a stripped-down street fighter hadn't survived the transition from marketing theory to

Like the era it was born in, the 1969 GTO Judge was anything but subtle. The standard powerplant for the Judge was the potent Ram Air III.

With a midsize platform and a big engine, the 1969 Judge held firm to the classic muscle car equation. Yet the Judge option included plenty of flash to go with the fast. Sneaking up on a competitor in a Judge was pretty much hopeless.

showroom floor. Most Road Runner buyers had loaded their cars up with enough options to bring the prices up to GTO levels. The car the committee had created was competing with the original idea behind the Road Runner rather than the actual Road Runner itself.

Besides, Pontiac already had a car that was nearly identical to what the committee was proposing: the 350 H.O.-equipped Tempest. This budget-priced car, which featured a 335-horsepower version of Pontiac's excellent 350-cubic-inch engine, already had the low end of the muscle car market covered. Building a version of the GTO that would be mechanically identical to this car would only cannibalize Tempest sales and would dilute the GTO's impressive profit margin in the process.

The committee began adding standard equipment to the new package, transforming it from the least expensive GTO into the most expensive GTO. They made the 366-horsepower Ram Air III engine standard equipment, and the 370-horsepower Ram Air IV was the only optional engine. Though down 40 cubic inches and two carburetors, when equipped with the Ram Air IV engine the GTO could run with a 440-Six-Pack-equipped Road Runner when it came to quarter-mile times.

When the committee showed the revised car to DeLorean, he liked the upscale concept, still called the E/T. In *Glory Days*, Wangers describes DeLorean's reaction:

> *Clearly, he was more pleased with this new GTO concept. "All right guys, I'll buy the car." His smile broadened (as did ours). "But, let's forget about that silly name." Oh no, I thought, another DeLorean bombshell!*
>
> *"Every time I turn on the TV these days," DeLorean continued, "I hear this funny guy shouting, 'Here comes da Judge, Here comes da Judge!' So let's give them their damn Judge!" DeLorean, like many other people in late-1960s America, was a big fan of the popular NBC-TV show Rowan and Martin's Laugh-In. That "funny guy" shouting "Here comes da Judge!" was a young "Flip" Wilson. [The committee misidentified the source of the phrase "Here comes da judge." In reality comedian David "Pigmeat" Markham, an old-time Vaudevillian performer, coined the phrase.]*
>
> *From that moment on, our new car was "The Judge."*

On December 19, 1968, Pontiac issued the following press release:

Pontiac Motor Division announced today that it will introduce a new car next month that "goes one step further" [Pontiac's copy writers had a fetish for putting quotation marks around words, even when they weren't quoting anyone in particular] in the popular muscle car field, a field that Pontiac opened up five years ago with the GTO. The new supercar to be named the Judge, is specially designed to offer a unique combination of added performance, excellent handling characteristics and a very distinctive appearance.

The car described in the press release was one of the most outrageous cars of the muscle car era. The Judge option, officially coded as option WT1, set a buyer back $332.07, but for that price a buyer received a lot of standard content, such as a Hurst T-handle shifter knob and a hood-mounted tachometer. The car featured the most radical spoiler ever mounted to a production car

Above: Buyers wanting a Ram Air IV beneath the hood had to pay $558.20, as well a couple of mandatory options, such as an M40 three-speed automatic transmission or an M21 four-speed manual tranny, as well as a heavy-duty differential. With 370 horsepower, wouldn't you want heavy-duty?

Opposite: In a touch of irony, this Ram Air IV beast was equipped with the rare T87 Cornering Lamps option, to the tune of $33.70. Unlike many muscle cars of the era that could haul ass in a straight line, the 1969 GTO was capable of handling the curves better than most of its ilk.

up until that time (though Dodge and Plymouth would produce a car with a spoiler that couldn't be topped with their Daytona/Superbird couplet) along with bold tri-colored side stripes and tri-colored psychedelic "The Judge" lettering on the front fenders and rear spoiler.

The first 2,000 cars were all painted in a color borrowed from sister-division Chevrolet. Chevrolet called the color Hugger Orange, but Pontiac renamed it Carousel Red. After the first 2,000 cars had been built buyers could order the Judge in a number of colors from Pontiac's color palate, but Carousel Red became the defining color for the car; for the 1969 model year nearly 80 percent of all Judges were painted Carousel Red.

Combined with the yellow, red, and black stripes and lettering, the Carousel Red Judge practically assaulted a viewer's eyes. Magazine scribes and purists hated the Judge, judging it tacky in the extreme. One magazine writer called it "the perfect car to take on picnics. This new rear deck spoiler makes a great cutting board to slice cheese."

But the general public embraced the car because it captured the Zeitgeist of that tacky, outrageous era. Like the youth market itself, which was growing increasingly hostile as the war in Vietnam dragged on, the Judge was loud, obnoxious, and confrontational. It appeared to be spoiling for a fight, and with its potent Ram Air engines, it had the strength to win most confrontations.

MARKETING THE JUDGE

Pontiac's advertisers had a field day playing with the name "The Judge." They couldn't use the phrase "Here comes 'da judge" because Markham had copyrighted it and he wanted an exorbitant amount of money to license its use. Wangers was tasked with the job of making sure the phrase was never used, even in corporate communications.

But the name gave Wangers and his team a host of opportunities for other promotional phrases. Advertisements for the new car featured taglines like "The Judge will rule," "All rise for the Judge," and "The Judge can be bought." Pontiac pulled that last example almost immediately because of an outcry from the American Bar Association. General Motors lived in fear of just one pissed-off attorney: Ralph Nader. The thought of an entire nation of pissed-off attorneys was enough to cause GM's upper management to lose control of its collective bodily functions.

Pontiac's advertising for the Judge used self-reflective humor to counter the criticisms of magazine editors and GTO purists. One ad read, "Yeah, it looks a bit weird, but it runs like Hell!" Pontiac procured pop star Mark Lindsey backed by the pop group Paul Revere and the Raiders to create and record the music to be used in the Judge television commercials.

Pontiac took this creative approach when marketing more pedestrian GTO models, too. One memorable ad

A hood-mounted tachometer was a $63.19 option on a 1969 GTO. While its efficiency as a tach was questionable, it sure looked great. And paired with a Ram Air IV set of decals, the driver of this GTO was a big fish, a very big fish indeed.

The cable at the back of the hood feeding into the scoop assembly was attached to a knob located beneath the dashboard by the driver's knee. It was used to open and shut the Ram Air flaps as needed. A tight fit between the top of the air cleaner assembly and the bottom of the hood was ensured by the foam.

A vision in blue, this 1969 Ram Air IV GTO was an ideal way to transport five into a drive-in. The Turbo Hydra-matic 400 transmission was a rugged piece, able to handle the massive power the 400 cubic inch generated.

From its Endura prow to the dual exhaust, the 1969 GTO, especially in Ram Air IV guise, was a handsome car, capable of besting most street racing competitors. Tipping the scales at 3,760 pounds, it could rip off mid-14-second quarter-mile dashes off the showroom floor.

parodied the film *Bonnie and Clyde*, a popular film of the period that romanticized the lives of the infamous bank robbers Bonnie Parker and Clyde Barrow. Pontiac's ad depicts Bonnie and Clyde robbing a bank. (Unlike the movie, Bonnie and Clyde were not played by Faye Dunaway and Warren Beatty in the commercial. Pontiac's ad budget wasn't big enough to hire stars of that caliber.) Upon leaving the bank they are unable to start their

getaway car. They run to a nearby Pontiac dealer, and Clyde asks a salesman if he's got "something that moves." Of course he does: a Verdoro Green GTO.

BACK TO THE DRAG STRIP

Though General Motors forbade Pontiac from directly engaging in drag racing as a means of promoting the Judge, its dealer network was under no such prohibition.

Royal Pontiac took this car to Florida and ran it down the strip with an experimental Ram Air V engine, but on its second pass, the engine expired. It showed incredible potential, but General Motors saw a softening of the muscle car market, and decided to shelve the engine.

Pontiac knew that the Judge was fast enough to be competitive in the NHRA's B/Stock and C/Stock classes and knew that having the car performing well at drag strips around the country would sell a lot of cars, so the division's marketing types cooked up a promotion to get the Judge out in front of as many drag-racing enthusiasts as possible.

Pontiac enticed dealers into participating in this program by offering them a free drivetrain–engine, transmission, driveshaft, and rear axle assembly–if they

bought a Judge at regular dealer cost and agreed to race it at local drag strips. The dealers would just have to provide Pontiac with a log of the car's racing activities along with its results.

One caveat was that the car had to be Carousel Red. This ensured that the car was instantly recognizable as a Judge, and it also created the illusion that there were a lot more Judges competing at drag strips around the country than was actually the case. Almost 100 dealers participated in the program and the promotion was a huge success. The Judges didn't always win their races, and they didn't win a national championship; but they performed well and they put the car out in front of hundreds of thousands of potential customers.

TOO MUCH SUCCESS

The Judge and its high-profile marketing campaign succeeded in its intended mission of raising the GTO's profile in an increasingly crowded muscle car market. Perhaps Wangers and his crew succeeded too well in promoting the car. Pontiac had difficulty in filling all the orders it received, which caused problems with the division's dealer network. By the end of 1969, Pontiac had sold 6,833 Judges, accounting for nearly 10 percent of the 72,287 GTOs sold that year. Of that total, 108 were convertibles, and just five of those convertibles featured the Ram Air IV engine. Seven hundred hardtop Judges were equipped with the optional Ram Air IV engine.

Prices rose yet again for 1969, which may have played a role in the decreased sales. The hardtop now started at $3,156 and the base GTO convertible listed for $3,382. The popularity of air conditioning increased, with 5,970 buyers equipping their cars with air conditioners. Pontiac equipped 14,514 GTOs with the Ram Air III engine, though that number was boosted considerably by the inclusion of the Ram Air III engine as standard equipment on the popular Judge. The trend toward automatic transmissions continued, with 40,854 buyers choosing the slush box over the manual tranny and 5,970 customers ordering air conditioning, including 784 Judge buyers.

Sales of the potent Ram Air IV option nearly doubled in 1969 when compared with sales of the previous year's Ram Air II option, with 1,514 buyers selected, 165 of which were equipped with automatic transmissions. The availability of more rational 3.90:1

Royal Pontiac, always looking for a way to set their vehicles apart from other offerings, came up with a spectacular paint scheme to create visual impact. Unfortunately for Royal Pontiac, the public shied away from such eye-catching paint, preferring to blend in with the crowd as they kicked booty.

Red, white, and blue wrapped a camera-friendly 1969 GTO equipped with a legendary experimental Ram Air V developed by Pontiac Engineering and Royal Pontiac. This was a 12-second package until it spun a bearing. Brutal.

final-drive gearing on four-speed cars proved a popular change, but the main reason for the rise in sales for the GTO's top engine option was the popularity of the Judge package.

Pontiac's outrageous Judge and its potent Ram Air IV engine enjoyed strong sales in 1969, but overall GTO production fell by 15,397 units. Pontiac wasn't the only company taking a sales hit; muscle car sales declined across the board in 1969. Part of the sales decline can be attributed to the failure of General Motors management to fully engage in the horsepower wars raging in Detroit at the time. By 1969 the GTO's 400 cubic inches, the upper limit GM allowed, were starting to look a bit puny compared to the competition, and General Motors' muscle car offerings had suffered even greater sales drops than

Hurst Performance and Pontiac enjoyed a mutually beneficial relationship for years, and Hurst products, including a shifter, were used in the one-off 1969 Ram Air V GTO that underwent testing in Florida.

With Royal Pontiac performance "enhancements" beneath the hood, the 1969 GTO Judge of Jim Wangers tended to run a bit more brutally than a standard Judge. Wangers wasn't above an impromptu tussle with another muscle car. Once a drag racer . . .

Many an automotive journalist accompanied Jim Wangers to this Woodward Avenue landmark for a meal before tasting what a GTO could deliver on the street. Located a stone's throw from Wangers' office, the Fox & Hounds Inn catered to a business clientele, usually in the auto industry.

had the big-engined cars from rivals Chrysler and Ford. But another reason for the decline was occurring half a planet away, in the jungles of Vietnam.

Throughout the mid-1960s the U.S. military had been sending troops to Vietnam in increasing numbers. By the summer of 1965 more than 125,000 U.S. troops were stationed in the far-off little country in Southeast Asia. A year later that number had risen to nearly half a million. In January 1968 the North Vietnamese army began what became known as the Tet Offensive, the bloodiest battle of the entire Vietnam War. To replenish troop strength, the U.S. Army began to increase the number of young males drafted into military service. The bulk of these draftees were young blue-collar males from the prime demographic group that bought muscle

cars. As the war droned on, these potential muscle car customers were being killed in alarming numbers. More than 58,000 U.S. soldiers perished in the conflict. Shipping a half-million potential GTO customers to the other side of the world did not make Pontiac's job of selling the cars any easier.

DeLorean was promoted to general manager at Chevrolet division late in 1969 and was replaced by F. James McDonald, a native of Saginaw, Michigan, and a 1944 graduate of General Motors Institute. McDonald, who would go on to become the president of General Motors in 1981, believed in Pontiac as the performance division, but he lacked instincts for the business.

McDonald was a likeable enough fellow, but he lacked both the passion for cars and the instinctual

Trolling for a tussle, Jim Wangers' 1969 GTO Judge patiently waits on Detroit's storied Woodward Avenue for a driver with more enthusiasm than power. Wangers had the inside track at Pontiac Engineering, and combined with the able mechanics at Royal Pontiac, it was a rare day that Wangers would come in second.

understanding of the market that both Knudsen and DeLorean had. Estes also lacked a passion for automobiles, but he was a brilliant engineer as well as a fast learner. At Pontiac he learned to understand the product and the market. Plus Estes had strong convictions. When he believed in one of his employee's ideas, he fought to make those ideas a reality. It was this characteristic in Estes' personality that allowed the creation of the GTO.

General Motors—and the entire U.S. auto industry—was about to enter a dark period, and Pontiac division was about to do so without the leadership of any of the original trinity that had turned the division into the performance company: Bunkie Knudsen, Pete Estes, and John DeLorean.

At night, on Woodward Avenue, it would be easy to overlook this discreet badge on the C-pillar of Jim Wangers' 1969 GTO Judge. Such an oversight often led to a quick defeat in a drag race.

CHAPTER 5

HIGHLIGHTS AND LOW POINTS

By 1970, everyone in the automotive industry knew the muscle car era was coming to an end. Smog, which was a slang term for "smoky fog," had become a major health concern in metropolitan areas. The federal government had taken action to curb the air pollution that was choking American cities, and this action had the support of the majority of the American people.

President Richard Nixon created the Environmental Protection Agency (EPA), a federal department that sniffed out sources of smog and tried to eliminate them. As a major source of smog-creating pollutants, passenger cars became a primary focus of the EPA's attention. The federal government began requiring increasingly stringent emissions control equipment on cars, equipment that robbed the engines of power.

NO LONGER A "400-CUBIC-INCH WORLD"

The forces aligned against the muscle car movement–increasing emissions requirements, rising insurance rates, and an aging youth market–were gaining momentum by the end of the 1960s and contributed to an overall decline in muscle car sales. Every manufacturer took a hit, but General Motors muscle cars were hit hardest of all. This was in part because of the company's ban on engines larger than 400 cubic inches. In 1968, when DeLorean had told the committee that it was a 400-cubic-inch world, he was guilty of understatement. In truth, the auto industry was well on its way to becoming a 440-plus-cubic-inch world, and that world was telling General Motors its engines were too small in a way that even the flaming nitwits running the corporation could understand: by not buying GM muscle cars.

When faced with a choice between protecting customers from themselves, losing money in the process, or giving the market what it seemed to want and hopefully recapturing its share of the youth market, GM's management chose the bottom line over what it believed to be the greater good of the country. For 1970, management allowed its divisions to mount their biggest engines in their intermediate-size muscle cars.

For sheer retina-burning power, there was little that could touch a 1970 Orbit Orange, Ram Air IV automatic transmission-equipped convertible. Only 13 examples were built.

The relatively low redline on the tachometer was indicative of the huge quantities of power the Ram Air IV–equipped 400-cubic-inch engine would develop at low rpm. On the street it's torque that rules, not horsepower. In torque we trust.

400 OR 455?

When GM management finally decided to enter the mega-cubic-inch engine frenzy in 1970, Pontiac found the transition a bit more difficult than Oldsmobile, which already had a sleeved-down 455-cubic-inch V-8 engine (displacing 400 cubic inches) powering its A-body muscle cars. Pontiac lacked a sufficiently large engine; the largest engine Pontiac offered in any of its cars in 1969 displaced 428 cubic inches. Not only would Pontiac have to expend funds, which were increasingly rare as the division invested more and more money into developing emissions controls for the future, but it would also have to revise its GTO chassis to accept a larger engine.

But there was no way the performance division was going to let rival divisions Oldsmobile, Chevrolet, and Buick have larger engines in their muscle cars, so Pontiac's engineers enlarged the 428 to create a 455-cubic-inch monster motor. They accomplished this by boring the cylinders to 4.15 inches and increasing the stroke to 4.21 inches through the use of a revised crankshaft. As a result this was an under-square engine; that is, its stroke was longer than its bore was wide.

This was an unusual design for an engine meant for use in a high-performance car. An under-square engine has inherent characteristics that limit its ultimate peak power output. A longer stroke leads to higher peak piston speeds at a given rpm. A piston traveling up and down along a 4.21-inch stroke 5,200 times each minute is moving a lot faster than a piston traveling along a 4-inch stroke 5,200 times during the same amount of time.

The tape graphics served a second purpose besides being vivid graphics to an extrovert's dream car; they were reflective, so that at night, they acted as a safety measure.

Move over mountain. This is the way it's going to be.

The Humbler is here. Pontiac GTO. If the sight of it doesn't turn you on, the sound of it will.

Listen. It's a 400-cube V-8 speaking out through a new, low-restriction performance exhaust you can order. And if you'd like to be even more vocal, order the new 455-cube V-8 with automatic box. (Hill, lay low.) Or, for the big shooters, the ultimate: our 400-cube, 370-hp Ram Air IV. With a fully synched, Hurst-shifted, 3-speed cogbox. 4-speed if you so specify.

Curve, straighten out. The Humbler will take you in style. With new, firmer control shocks. New front and rear stabilizer bars. Big, wide fiberglass-belted boots.

The Humbler. This is the way it's going to be, baby.

▼ Pontiac's New GTO

(We take the fun of driving seriously.)

With "eyebrows" above the wheel arches, a functional tail spoiler, and a Ram Air induction system, a 1970 GTO Judge was hard to ignore. Fortunately, it had the goods under hood to back up the image.

Increased piston speeds lead to all kinds of engineering challenges and severely limit the ultimate rpm that an engine can attain.

Limiting revs meant limiting peak horsepower, but on the plus side, an under-square engine produces gobs and gobs of wheel-spinning torque. Pontiac's new 455 H.O. certainly did that, cranking out 500 lb-ft of the twisting force at a low 3,100 rpm.

Pontiac acknowledged that this engine would be a low-revving torque monster. Because the Ram Air fresh-

air intake system only provided benefits at higher rpm, the division didn't offer Ram Air on the new big-cube engine. Likewise the engine used D-port heads rather than the round-port heads off the Ram Air IV because the round ports only provided significant power increases at the upper end of the rev range.

Because of its reputation as the performance company, everyone expected Pontiac to produce a monster big-inch motor. Most fans were sorely disappointed with the power output of the new engine, which, with its

Pontiac ensured the GTO Judge wouldn't fall on its face in the curves with a tuned suspension, and the result was a vehicle that could be driven on a daily basis. Only 2,394 GTOs were painted Palladium Silver in 1970.

10.25:1 compression ratio, generated just 360 horsepower at 4,600 rpm. That was 10 horsepower down on Pontiac's Ram Air IV engine. Worse yet, it was 6 horsepower down on the 400-cubic-inch Ram Air III engine.

The Ram Air III remained relatively unchanged for 1970, except for a slight decrease in compression, down from 10.75:1 to 10.5:1. With its D-port heads, the Ram Air III was in many ways like a smaller (yet faster) version of the 455 H.O. The two even shared the same crankshaft. In spite of the decrease in compression, the

engine retained its power rating from the previous year. Likewise, the Ram Air IV returned relatively unchanged save for the same decrease in compression as the Ram Air III, and like the Ram Air III, the Ram Air IV retained its power ratings.

Instead of making a monster 455-cubic-inch engine to serve as its first line of defense in the muscle car wars, Pontiac left the 370-horsepower Ram Air IV engine as the top performance engine in the GTO, reasoning that with its shorter stroke and higher revving capabilities,

Firestone Wide Ovals were cutting-edge tires in 1970, and the GTO Judge came from the factory so equipped. The Judge was a popular option that year, as 3,635 hardtop coupes were fitted with the Judge option.

Unlike the tail spoiler on the 1969 Judge, the wing on the 1970 model actually developed usable downforce. The taillights were tucked gracefully into the rear bumpers, ensuring they would stay clear during a snowfall. Not that many Judges were taken out onto the white stuff.

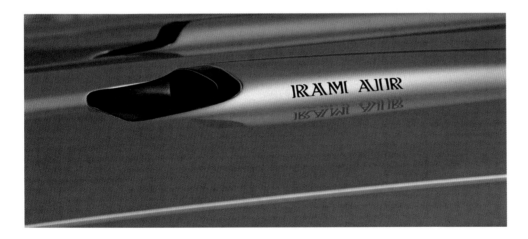

Functional hood scoops were part of the Ram Air package. The Judge option, WT1, cost $337.02, and included Rally II wheels and G78x14-inch fiberglass belted black wall tires.

the 400-cubic-inch Ram Air IV would provide livelier performance. Pontiac marketed the new 455 H.O. engine on the strength of its 500 lb-ft of torque, figuring it would appeal to more mature buyers while younger buyers would buy the high-revving Ram Air engines. The division guessed wrong and it sold just 4,146 GTOs equipped with the 455 H.O. engine.

A WILD MILD RESTYLE
Pontiac revised the exterior of the GTO more extensively than most people expected for the 1970 model year. The basic shape remained the same, but everything from the cowl forward was new. The troublesome vacuum-operated headlight doors disappeared from the option sheet, and each of the four headlamps were now recessed into the Endura bumper.

On Ram Air-equipped cars the scoops, which remained more or less in their previous position, fed air into a pair of snorkels that ran directly into foam-sealed air channels built into the new air cleaner cover. Cable-operated flaps controlled the flow of air through the scoops. A knob inside the cab allowed the

With the exception of the Judge badge on the glove box door and the T-handle atop the Hurst shifter, there wasn't anything in the interior to tell you that you had parked your butt in a 1970 GTO Judge. Using the shoulder belts required a separate belt and latch. The upper portion of the shoulder belt was stored above the door with a pair of metal clips.

Opposite: The standard engine in a 1970 GTO Judge was the 400-cubic-inch Ram Air III. Rated at 366 horsepower at 5,100 rpm, it cranked out an impressive 455 lb-ft of torque at 3,900 rpm.

Anyone desiring to make a low-key entrance would have been wise to steer clear of this vivid Judge. Orbit Orange was the least popular color in 1970, with only 618 GTOs finished in the hue.

driver to open or close flaps in the scoops, depending on weather conditions.

Muscular bulges appeared over the wheel openings, and the Endura nose became more prominent. These raised haunches gave the GTO a much more aggressive stance than the previous car. The drop in sales in 1969 indicated that maybe the GTO had gone too far with its mature, sophisticated look. With these new fenders and quarter panels the look swung back to the youthful, muscular end of the spectrum.

The rear of the car was also revised, though not quite as noticeably as the front had been. The taillights were incorporated into a long, thin bumper that ran around to the sides of the car, and the dual exhaust now exited through cutouts in the body-colored valence beneath the bumper. The passenger compartment benefited from the addition of beams to strengthen the door frames and strengthened roof pillars to better protect the occupants in case of a collision or rollover.

The interior of the car remained relatively unchanged. A turned-metal appliqué replaced the woodgrain on the bottom portion of the dash, and the top portion was now covered in simulated woodgrain. The optional eight-track tape deck remained. Cars equipped with power steering could be had with an optional Formula steering wheel that was about ten years ahead of its time. This wheel, with its thickly padded rim and three spokes with holes drilled in them, wouldn't have looked out of place on the most expensive European sports car.

The 1970 Judge convertible was typical of all vehicles of the era, as weights started to creep up due to federally required equipment. Tipping the scale at 3,850 pounds, its Ram Air IV had sufficient power to overcome the small weight gain.

With its automatic transmission and factory eight-track tape player, this Ram Air IV Judge was content in stop-and-go traffic. But under serious throttle, the real music came from under the hood.

One odd option was a taillight-monitoring device that consisted of a pair of fiber-optic lines that ran from the taillights to a small box on the rear-window parcel shelf where it would be visible in a driver's rearview mirror. When the taillights were in use light traveled through the fiber-optic lines into the cabin and lit up indicators in the box.

RETURN OF THE JUDGE

For 1970 Pontiac brought back the popular Judge option, which now cost $337.02. The Judge featured a new striping package that took advantage of the new flared fender bulges. As before, the base engine was the Ram Air III, with the Ram Air IV engine available as an option. Engine choices grew to include the 455 H.O., but this

The 400-cubic-inch Ram Air IV engine found in this 1970 GTO Judge was an example of the end of an era; an era when lifting the hood revealed the engine and little else. Notice how the ground is visible beneath the motor; in a couple of years the engine compartment would resemble a bowl of spaghetti. Unlike the D-port heads used on the standard Ram Air II engine, the Ram Air IV heads utilized a round-port design, improving the engine's breathing.

Capable of running the drag strip in the 14-second range, the 1970 Judge, with the desirable Ram Air IV option, was a sensation even in 1970. Due to the low build numbers, these cars today are worth scary money.

DeLorean's affection for the Flip Wilson character's line on the TV show *Laugh-In* gave this street brawler its name, "The Judge." Pontiac laughably rated the Ram Air IV at 370 horsepower.

proved an especially unpopular option with Judge buyers. Pontiac sold just 17 such cars.

In fact, the Judge itself seemed to be an especially unpopular car, at least in the first half of the year. Pontiac's advertising choices at least in part contributed to that lack of initial sales. Pontiac's advertising team used a bland white GTO in its advertisements for the redesigned Judge and people responded by staying away from Pontiac dealerships in droves.

Midway through the model year Pontiac attempted to resuscitate Judge sales with a new ad featuring a car in a more popular color. In 1970 the closest color to the popular Carousel Red was a color called Orbit Orange. Apparently it was close enough to the original color because it brought buyers back to Pontiac showrooms.

SALES DISASTER

After internalizing the "more-horsepower-is-better" mantra for a generation, the market didn't buy Pontiac's logic behind placing the 455 H.O. engine behind the Ram Air engines, and GTO sales fell 44.5 percent in 1970 to 40,149 units. Cost of ownership had risen again, which partly explained the decline in sales. The hardtop now cost $3,267 and the convertible cost $3,492. The Judge option cost $337.02. Pontiac sold just 3,797 GTOs equipped with the Judge package, barely enough to keep the option in the lineup for another year.

Another factor in the decreased GTO sales might have been the introduction of the dramatic new Firebird and Trans Am models. Arguably Pontiac's F-body cars from 1970 to 1973 are among the best-looking vehicles ever built. The GTO was gorgeous in its own right, but next to the smaller, sleeker Trans Am, the GTO looked a bit bloated and ungainly.

Judge buyers got the Rally II wheels, sans trim ring. It was a quick and effective way to give the premium GTO a street fighter look without Pontiac having to invest in new parts.

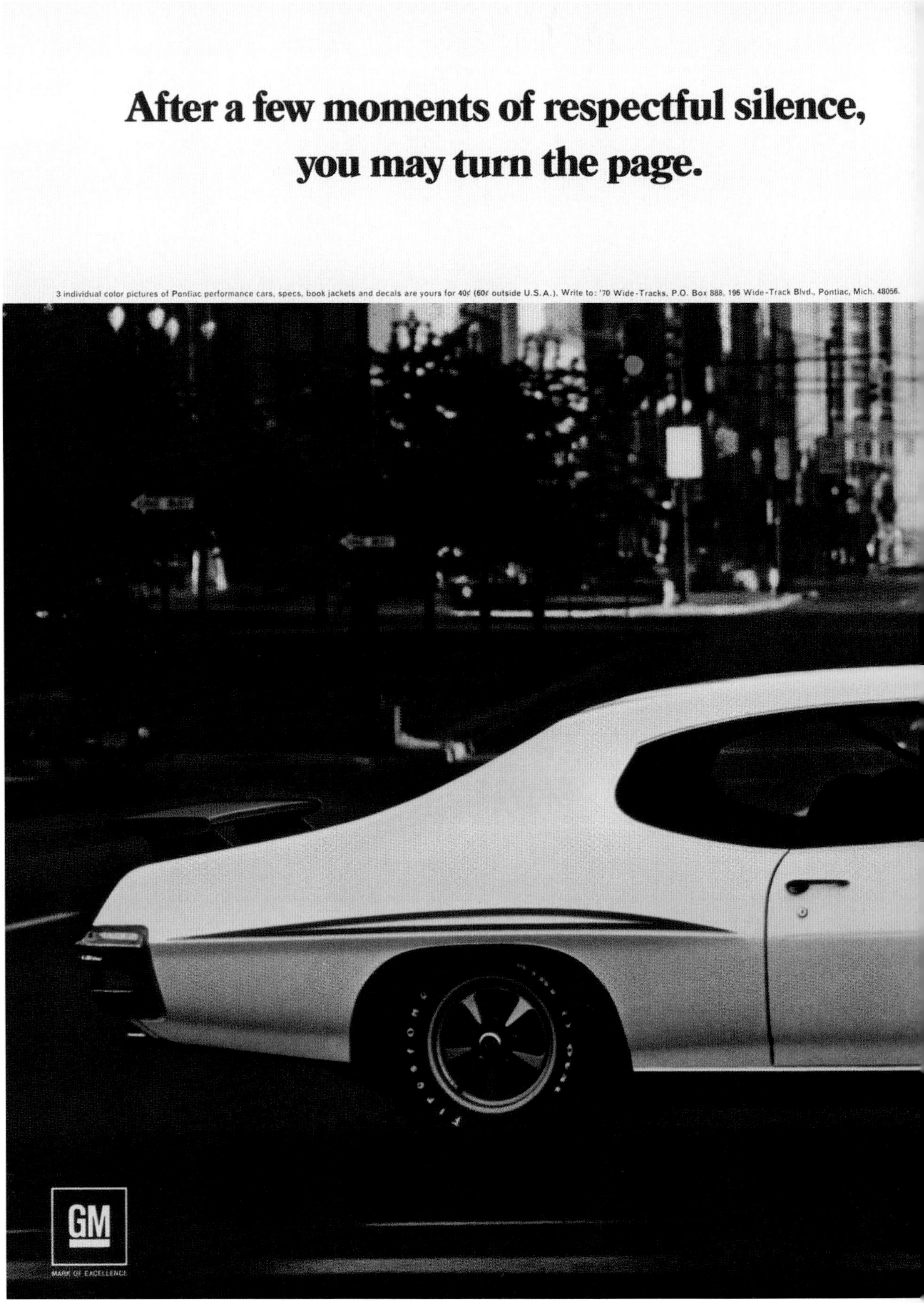

After a few moments of respectful silence, you may turn the page.
3 individual color pictures of Pontiac performance cars, specs, book jackets and decals are yours for 40¢ (60¢ outside U.S.A.). Write to: '70 Wide-Tracks, P.O. Box 888, 196 Wide-Track Blvd., Pontiac, Mich. 48056.
GM
MARK OF EXCELLENCE

EQUIPMENT
Standard: Rear-deck airfoil · Front air dam · Striping · Special mag-type wheels · Blacked-out grille · G70—14 black fiberglass-belted tires · Special "The Judge" emblems · Front stabilizer bar—1⅛" · Rear stabilizer bar —⅞" · Firm ride and handling package
Available: Variable-ratio power steering · Hood-mounted tachometer · Power front disc brakes · 7-blade thermostatic fan · Limited-slip differential (Safe-T-Track) · Heavy-duty battery · Rally gauges · Custom sport steering wheel · Formula steering wheel · Stereo tape player · Radios—AM, AM/FM, AM/FM with stereo multiplex

STANDARD RAM AIR
Displacement	400 cu. in.
Horsepower	366 @ 5100 rpm
Torque	445 lb.-ft. @ 3600 rpm
Bore & Stroke	4.12 x 3.75
Deck Clearance	.023
Compression Ratio	10.5:1
Chamber Volume	66.27 cc.
Carburetion	Quadra-jet, 4-bbl.
Exhaust	Performance duals
Valve Lifters	Hydraulic

RAM AIR TRANSMISSIONS
Standard 3-speed Heavy-duty
Make		Muncie
Ratios	1	2.42:1
	2	1.58:1
	3	1.00:1
	R	2.41:1
Shifter		Hurst

Available 4-speed Wide-ratio
Make		Muncie
Ratios	1	2.52:1
	2	1.88:1
	3	1.46:1
	4	1.00:1
	R	2.59:1
Shifter		Hurst

Available 4-speed Close-ratio
Make		Muncie
Ratios	1	2.20:1
	2	1.64:1
	3	1.28:1
	4	1.00:1
	R	2.27:1
Shifter		Hurst

Available 3-speed Turbo Hydra-matic
Ratios	L	2.48:1
	S	1.48:1
	D	1.00:1
	R	2.08:1

RAM AIR AXLE RATIOS
Standard	3.55
With Air Conditioning	3.23
Available	3.90 & 4.33

AVAILABLE RAM AIR IV
Displacement	400 cu. in.
Horsepower	370 @ 5500 rpm
Torque	445 lb.-ft. @ 3900 rpm
Bore & Stroke	4.12 x 3.75
Deck Clearance	.023
Compression Ratio	10.5:1
Chamber Volume	69.12 cc.
Carburetion	Quadra-jet, 4-bbl.
Exhaust	Performance duals
Valve Lifters	Hydraulic limited travel with manual transmission

RAM AIR IV TRANSMISSIONS
Standard 4-speed Close-ratio
Make		Muncie
Ratios	1	2.20:1
	2	1.64:1
	3	1.28:1
	4	1.00:1
	R	2.27:1
Shifter		Hurst

Available 3-speed Turbo Hydra-matic
Ratios	L	2.48:1
	S	1.48:1
	D	1.00:1
	R	2.08:1

RAM AIR IV AXLE RATIOS
Standard	3.90
Available	4.33

The Judge: a special GTO from Pontiac.

1970

(We take the fun of driving seriously. Very seriously.)

With a 10.5:1 compression ratio Ram Air IV engine under the hood, high-octane fuel was mandatory. Part of the Ram Air IV package included a standard 3.90:1 rear axle ratio; for those who felt that wasn't low enough, a stump-pulling 4.33:1 gear set was available for $21.06.

To make matters worse, the Trans Am could be ordered with the optional Ram Air III and Ram Air IV engines. When equipped with one of these potent engines, the Trans Am, which was still several hundred pounds lighter than the GTO, handily outran its bigger brother in a straight line. If that wasn't enough to place the new upstart at the top of Pontiac's performance hierarchy, the fact that the new Pontiac handled better than any American car ever built up until that time was enough to move the Trans Am right past the GTO. Thanks to a suspension designed by Pontiac's suspension guru Herb Adams, the Trans Am exhibited handling that felt more like a grand touring car from Europe than an American muscle car.

THE PERFORMANCE DIVISION?

Pontiac wasn't the only manufacturer with challenges in 1970. Everyone experienced decreased sales for the 1970 model year, but Pontiac had been especially hard hit. Sales suffered across the board and the division lost the number-three spot it had held among U.S. auto brands since 1961.

Many fans feared that the division was losing its focus on performance, as illustrated by the downfall of the GTO.

Fans had expected Pontiac to build a killer muscle car for the ages, a car that could beat all others on a spec sheet (and presumably in a street race). Instead sister division Chevrolet had built that car with its Chevelle LS-6 454SS, which cranked out 450 horsepower at 5,600 rpm and 500 lb-ft of torque at 3,600 rpm. Compared to such numbers the 370 horsepower generated by the Ram Air IV and the 360 horsepower generated by the 455 H.O. seemed positively anemic.

Sales of high-performance versions of the GTO were especially hard hit. Pontiac sold just 867 Ram Air IV-equipped hardtop GTOs and just 37 GTO convertibles equipped with the division's top performance engine. A number of those cars were Judge convertibles equipped with the Ram Air IV engine, but the records regarding the number of Judges equipped with the Ram Air IV engine in 1970 have been lost, so it's impossible to know just how many such cars Pontiac built.

Opposite: The functional hood scoops were ringed in contrasting black and could be open and shut from inside the vehicle via a driver-controlled knob. An Endura front end gave the 1970 Judge a sleek look, and the headlights in separate openings showed that the stylists paid attention to the details.

It is possible to narrow the number down by examining existing records. In 1970 Pontiac built 168 Judge convertible GTOs, 37 of which were Ram Air IV cars. At least 12 Judge convertibles left the factory with the Ram Air IV engine, because today there are 7 documented Ram Air IV automatic examples and 5 documented Ram Air IV four-speed examples remaining.

Thus the actual number has to be between 12 and 37. The exact number may never be known, but one can say with empirical certainty that it is not very damned many.

455 H.O., TAKE TWO

Pontiac may have missed an opportunity to build the ultimate spec-sheet muscle car in 1970, a car that generated the same raw numbers as Chevrolet's potent 450-horsepower LS-6 454 engine, but it compensated for that in 1971 by building one of the best real-world street engines of all time: the 455 H.O.

By 1971, both the Ram Air III and the Ram Air IV engine were gone; the top GTO engine option was a new 455-cubic-inch H.O. round-port engine, which came as standard equipment on Judge models. These were lower compression motors (8.4:1), as were all 1971 GM powerplants. The 455 H.O. featured a four-bolt main block with cast pistons, a nodular-iron crankshaft, Arma Steel connecting rods, Ram Air IV–style round-port cylinder heads, a two-piece aluminum Ram Air IV–style intake manifold, and special components such as a tuned Quadrajet and distributor.

The Ram Air induction system was an option on regular GTOs equipped with the 455 H.O. engine and only came as standard equipment on Judge models. The system was completely redesigned for 1971. In the redesigned front end, gigantic twin scoops

Pontiac built just 3,783 GTO convertibles for the 1970 model year, and total Ram Air III production, for both coupes and ragtops, was 4,644 units. These are not the kind of numbers that relegated the GTO to commonplace. Inset: The stylists at Pontiac infused the 1970 GTO with graceful lines that belied its performance history. Buyers got both beauty and the beast in one package.

resided above the Endura bumper, huge rectangular air shovels that faired into the hood as it swept back toward the windshield.

The hardware itself was refined compared to the system used on 1970 Ram Air models, with a pair of plastic funnels running down from the hood apertures and connecting to a pair of ears that were actually the air intake snorkels for the air cleaner. As in 1970 the driver manually opened or closed flaps in the scoops, depending on weather conditions. For 1971 the cable controlling the flap was shortened and rerouted because the cable location had been somewhat problematic on the 1970 car.

Not that the new engine really had much use for the additional breathing capacity offered by the Ram Air system. Rated at just 335 horsepower at 4,800 rpm and with a redline that was reduced to 5,200 rpm, the engine didn't rev high enough to take full advantage of the benefits offered by the air intake system.

From day one, the GTO was built to run the quarter-mile, and the 1970 iteration was no exception. With its standard 366-horsepower Ram Air III engine, it could jump to 60 miles per hour in 6 seconds and cover the length of the drag strip in the mid-14-second range.

The new round-port 455 H.O. looked like a slow engine on paper. In reality it was deceptively quick, thanks to a torque rating of 490 lb-ft at 3,600 rpm. This made a 1971 455 H.O.-equipped GTO an immensely satisfying car to drive in the real world. The 455 H.O. is a far more usable motor on the street than the Ram Air IV had been, and the big round-port engine had power characteristics well-suited for use in a heavy car like the GTO. In real-world use, when equipped with a 455 H.O. round-port engine, the 1971 was one of the quickest GTOs ever built. Pontiac engineers made good use of the new engine's additional cubes.

NEUTERED GOATS

With the Ram Air III and IV engines gone, along with the unwanted economy two-barrel engine, just one 400-cubic-inch engine remained in the lineup. This engine, which used D-port heads with only 8.2:1 compression, generated 300 horsepower and was the base engine on all non-Judge models. Buyers who didn't want to upgrade to the 455 H.O. engine could order an optional engine that split the difference between the two. This engine, which also displaced 455 cubic inches, was similar to the H.O. version except that it used D-port heads instead of the

H.O.'s round-port heads. With an 8.2:1 compression ratio, this engine generated 325 horsepower.

In 1971, Pontiac, like every other maker, was scrambling to develop engines that would be compatible with unleaded gasoline, which was the reason that General Motors was lowering the compression ratios of all its engines. The EPA had warned U.S. automakers that it was soon going to ban the use of tetraethyl lead as an additive in gasoline. Lead had been added to gasoline since before World War II to prevent engine detonation, allowing the use of higher compression ratios. Leaded fuel technology reached maturity during the war, allowing fighter and bomber aircraft engines to develop much more power, but lead was a nasty carcinogenic substance that caused birth defects, mental retardation, and all sorts of problems with the environment, though its role in these problems wasn't clearly understood at the time.

What was known was that the EPA planned to institute emissions requirements beginning in 1975 that would require most automakers to install catalytic converters in their exhaust systems. These converters used platinum-coated beads to reduce the toxic emissions in automotive exhaust. Lead stuck to these beads and

While the 1970 GTO could be a four-season car, the Ram Air III tended to make driving in the winter a, well, challenge. Firestone Wide Oval and snow tended not to mix. Something about massive torque . . .

Above: The callouts on the functional hood scoops were the only exterior indication that the engine below wasn't a garden variety V-8. Pontiac called this finish Starlight Black.

Left: The view out the front of the 1970 GTO was impressive, as the hood mounted tachometer and hood scoops oozed muscle car. Graceful, yes–subtle, no.

The thick wall-to-wall carpet goes well with the thick front and rear stabilizer bars.

And the floor-mounted Hurst shifter helps round out our idea of a road car—a fine balance of comfort, stability and performance.

First, a comfortable departure from tradition.

You know. The one that's always equated road-car comfort with sitting on a rock. Well, GTO's seats are Strato-buckets. Generously padded and done up in a special knit vinyl that puts air between you and the seats—avoiding the seasonal sweats and chills of regular vinyl. The carpet's a plush nylon blend. And GTO's special trim is a textured vinyl you'd swear was Spanish leather.

But it doesn't hurt to honor tradition elsewhere.

So the engine behind GTO's new Endura front bumper is a responsive 400-cubic-inch V-8 connected to a heavy-duty Muncie 3-speed transmission. If you like, order our

455-cubic-inch H.O. V-8 with Ram Air. Then the forward-mounted scoops on GTO's new fiberglass hood stop duping and start scooping.

No matter which '71 Pontiac engine you decide on, it's designed to operate efficiently on the new no-lead or low-lead gasolines. You'll get lower exhaust emissions. Plus longer life for your exhaust system, spark plugs and other engine components. If no-lead or low-lead gas is unavailable, you can use any leaded regular-grade gasoline with a research octane number of at least 91.

It corners like a kid in sneakers.

GTO has Pontiac's typical Wide-Track grip on things. And those thick

stabilizer bars fore and aft help keep it flat throughout the snakiest maneuvers. The shocks are heavy-duty, the coil springs high-rated—and both are tuned for the ideal road-car ride. Firm, but not fiercely so.

Now you know what a road car can be.

So forget all that talk about having to be miserable to enjoy one. True, some road cars are still being built that way. But you'll much prefer the one at your nearest Pontiac dealer's. It's the newest Great One. The 1971 GTO.

GM
MARK OF EXCELLENCE

'71 GTO. Pure Pontiac!

Pontiac Motor Division

In 1971, savvy buyers could still order a brutally fast Pontiac from the factory, such as the no-option T-37. This example was purchased and sponsored by Warren "Monk" King, a Denton, Texas, dealer. With its 455 H.O. engine, it could lunge down the drag strip with the best.

plugged up the exhaust systems. General Motors' decision to reduce compression levels was the first step in preparing its passenger cars for the upcoming catalytic converters and the lower-octane gasoline their use would mandate.

THE ENERGY OF DECAY

The energy keeping the GTO in Pontiac's lineup by 1971 was entropy, the energy of decay. Pontiac had gone to some lengths to restyle the car with the aggressive new hood scoops mentioned above, which, for the first time in GTO history actually provided a ram air effect because

the scoops were well-located and rose high enough above the hood to get above the dead-air zone. This one change radically altered the look of the car.

Not much changed outside the engine compartment other than the new hood scoops. As in 1970 the speedometer was calibrated to 140 miles per hour instead of 120 miles per hour, as it had been throughout the 1960s, and the vinyl seat covers could still be ordered with Comfort Weave inserts, an option that had appeared in 1970. GTO buyers could now get optional honeycomb wheels, which had been designed by Pontiac's Bill Porter using the principles

Resplendent in its Lucerne Blue and Polar White finish, the 1970 GTO Judge, *Tin Indian*, was ordered from Pontiac with every intention of being a drag car. With the heater and radio deleted on the assembly line, as well as every vestige of sound deadener, the emphasis was on light weight. Lack of weight equals speed.

R. Buckminster Fuller had developed to build his geodesic domes. For a brief time Pontiac offered seatbelts with shoulder harnesses for both the front seat and rear seat passengers. Otherwise there wasn't much new happening in the world of the GTO.

There was absolutely nothing happening on the advertising front for the GTO in 1971. Every American automaker was pouring all available resources into meeting the 1975 deadline for pollution control equipment, and General Motors was no exception. This sucked up just about every penny normally spent on advertising, promotion, racing, or anything else that wasn't an absolute necessity. In fact quite a few things that should have been considered essential were neglected during this period, like quality control, a situation that haunts American automakers to this day.

What advertising money Pontiac could scrape together went toward promoting the popular new Firebird, which had been introduced midyear in 1970. As noted above, this car offered acceleration and handling characteristics that the GTO couldn't touch. As an example of the import Pontiac placed on its sporty F-body Trans Am, that car received the 455 H.O. engine as standard equipment, while the top engine was only available as an option on the GTO.

THE LAST JUDGE AND THE LAST CONVERTIBLE

The Judge option remained on the GTO option list in 1971, but like *Rowan and Martin's Laugh-In*, it outlasted its moment of fame. The Judge received the new 455 H.O. engine and the Ram Air system as

Inside the differential is a set of 4.56:1 Shiefer gears, and with Firestone Drag 500 tires front and rear, the *Tin Indian* lived its entire life racking up mileage in quarter-mile increments.

The huge carburetor atop the prototype intake manifold is a massive 1,050-cfm Carter Thermoquad with a phenolic resin main body designed to reduce heat transfer. The heads are Ram Air IV units sitting on a Ram Air V block. This setup was going to be released to the public as the 400 Super Duty, but it didn't get beyond a handful being built by Pontiac Engineering.

Pontiac built 10,532 GTOs for 1971, and only 939 were fitted with the 335-horsepower 455 High Output (H.O.) engine. This potent powerplant cost $136.92.

standard equipment, along with the same updates as the rest of the GTO lineup.

In 1971, Pontiac sold just 3 Judge convertibles with four-speed transmissions and 14 with automatics. Sales of the hardtop versions weren't that much better at 357 units, a number that was roughly one-tenth of the previous year's sales. When sales of anything fall 90 percent in the course of one year, it's time to stop selling that thing. The Judge was no more after 1971.

The regular GTO didn't sell much better than the Judge. Pontiac sold just 10,532 GTOs for the 1971 model year. The bulk of those cars–6,421–were hardtop cars fitted with the base 400-cubic-inch motor and automatic transmissions. Counting the 374 Judges built, Pontiac built just 936 GTOs with the excellent 455 H.O. engine.

The year 1971 also marked the last time an open-top GTO would be built. The public had all but quit buying convertibles. Instead, more and more cars were being equipped with air conditioning. Pontiac sold just 678 GTO convertibles in 1971, including the 17 Judge convertibles.

Functional Ram Air hood scoops continued with the 1971 GTO. Positioning the scoops at the leading edge of the hood, rather than the midhood placement of the prior year, increased the airflow into the induction system.

Only one Pontiac assembly plant built the 1971 Judge convertibles, the Pontiac, Michigan, facility. Approximately 17 Judge ragtops were equipped with the LS5 H.O. engine.

Part of those low sales can be blamed on the steep price increases for 1971, with the hardtop starting at $3,446 and the convertible starting at $3,676. A strike by the United Auto Workers union shut down production for 10 weeks right in the prime time for building new 1971 models–from September 15 to November 20, 1970. This also contributed to low GTO sales, as well as lowered sales of all GM cars. But mostly the problem was that the GTO–and the muscle car genre–had run its course by the 1971 model year.

ABDICATING THE THRONE

It's depressing to think about what might have been had Pontiac pulled out the stops and built the ultimate GTO engine in 1970. One can't help but imagine a shorter stroke, mechanical-cam Super Duty 455-cubic-inch-plus engine with 10.75 compression ratio and featuring every tuning trick Pontiac had up its sleeve. A GTO with this imaginary engine could easily have surpassed the output of the legendary LS-6 engine mounted in the Chevelle SS 454. Figures of 500-plus horsepower should have easily been within Pontiac's reach.

It probably wouldn't have been as good a street engine as the 455 H.O., but the legacy such an engine would have left behind would mean more than its driving characteristics. Had they built such an engine for just the one year in which it would have been possible, the GTO would have been remembered not just as the first muscle car, but as the ultimate expression of the breed. It would have been the king of all muscle cars, which should have been the GTO's birthright, since it was the firstborn among muscle cars. Instead, Pontiac abdicated that throne and Chevrolet seized it.

Of course spending that much money developing an engine that would have a shelf life of just one year would have been financially ruinous for Pontiac. The division made the right choice when it put its engineering muscle into developing the 455 H.O. for 1971.

The last year of Judge production was 1971, with the last car being built in January 1971. Low demand forced Pontiac to discontinue the GTO convertible on February 2, 1971, as only 678 were sold during the entire model year.

The grille openings were fitted with a wire mesh for 1971, while the hood retainer pins cost $11.95 and the 18-inch hood lanyard went for $3.75. This year was the last that Pontiac offered a hood-mounted tachometer.

THE PERCEPTION OF POWER

Horsepower ratings fell precipitously in 1972. In some cases this was the result of detuning taking place in preparation for the coming government-mandated pollution-control equipment, but more often than not it was just because of a change in the way in which manufacturers measured horsepower output.

Prior to 1972, most American automakers rated their engines in terms of SAE (Society of Automotive Engineers) gross horsepower, which was measured using a blueprinted test engine running on a stand without accessories, mufflers, or emissions control devices. This did not provide an accurate measurement of the power output of an installed engine in a street car. Gross horsepower figures were also easily manipulated by carmakers. They could be inflated to make a car appear more muscular or deflated to appease corporate and insurance safetycrats or to qualify a car for a certain class of racing.

By 1972, U.S. carmakers were required to quote power exclusively in SAE net horsepower figures. This method rated the power of the engine with all accessories and standard intake and exhaust systems installed. This provided a more accurate measurement of a given car's potential, but the overall numbers were lower.

Left: Tri-color graphic stripes were standard on the 1971 Judge, and the colors used depended on the body color. Total Judge production during its last year was just 374 vehicles.

Below: The 455 H.O. engine was introduced in 1971 in an effort to, if not maintain engine power, minimize the loss of grunt. Rated at 335 horsepower (gross), it used its sizable displacement to generate 480 lb-ft of torque.

Even engines that had received little or no mechanical changes or additional emissions-control equipment suddenly had lower horsepower ratings in 1972. For example, a 1971 GTO equipped with a 455 H.O. was rated at 335 SAE gross horsepower. The same car was rated at 310 SAE net horsepower in 1971. In 1972, when the rating was given only in SAE net numbers, the GTO's 455 H.O. was rated at 300 horsepower. To the casual observer this looked like a 35-horsepower drop, but in reality the drop was a relatively insignificant 10 horsepower.

The situation appeared even more dramatic in non-high-performance engines. For example, the optional D-port 455 available in the GTO was rated at 325 horsepower using the SAE gross rating method. When measured using the SAE net method, that same engine produced just 260 horsepower. In 1972, when numbers were listed using the SAE net method, that number fell to 250 horsepower. In reality that was just a 10-horsepower drop, but to someone comparing the published horsepower figures from 1971 and 1972 it looked like a 75-horsepower drop. The average buyer didn't know SAE gross from SAE net; he or she only knew that the horsepower number had suddenly become smaller (in some cases a lot smaller), and bigger was better than smaller.

The psychological effect this had on what was left of the muscle car buying public was a final nail in the coffins of these cars. This was a time before online communities argued ad nauseum about the merits of different brands of valve springs. It was before the Internet, before cable television even, and genuine information was hard to come by. Most street racers operated in a fog of misinformation and old wives' tales. People believed the power ratings printed in advertising brochures because often this was the only information available regarding power output. As a result, some very quick cars built between 1972 and 1974 earned undeserved reputations as underpowered.

RETURN OF THE LEMANS GTO

After 1971's dismal sales performance, continuing to produce the GTO as a separate model was no longer a feasible proposition. The only way The Great One could survive was to go back to being an option on the LeMans. This wasn't a difficult transition, since virtually every feature except the Judge package was already offered

Does a low-compression engine mean the end of GTO?

There are those who would have you believe the GTO is dead. Doom prophets and such. Gleefully chortling over the demise of The Great One. After all, the '71 GTO has to run on those low-lead or no-lead fuels, right? And you have to lower the compression ratio to do that, right? And lowering the compression ratio lowers the general performance curve of an engine, right?

Right! But the doom people forgot to reckon with one rather important element. Pontiac engineers. Those wonderful people who brought you Wide-Track, Tri-Power, Ram Air, Rally wheels and more weren't about to let GTO become just a fond memory. Or a museum piece.

It was a real hassle. The new 400-CID and available 455-CID H.O. LS5 V-8's were worked and re-worked. Combustion chambers reshaped for a lower compression ratio. Distributors recalibrated to change ignition advance curve characteristics. In the process, the engineers found the use of no-lead, low-lead fuels can prolong the life of the spark plugs, exhaust system and other engine components. (If no-lead or low-lead gas isn't avail-

able, any leaded regular-grade gas with a research octane number of at least 91 can be used.) But the total solution centers on a thing called "tractive force."

You see, what comes out of an engine's crankshaft is only one function of a car's performance. Even on a straight, what a car will do is determined by the net result of all its drive-train components. And that's what tractive force is. The force exerted by the drive wheels.

So when all the work on the engines was completed, Pontiac started working on the other drive-train components. We altered the rear axle ratios to multiply the lowered engine torque, resulting in a tractive force as good as, or better than, last year's cars equipped with higher compression engines.

Which means you won't notice any difference in performance between

a '71 GTO with the 400-CID V-8 and last year's 400-CID V-8-powered GTO. And a '71 GTO with the exciting new 455-CID H.O. LS5 V-8 performs better than anything in Pontiac history. Both low and top ends.

Of course there's a lot more than engines that's new about the '71 GTO. There's new styling. New, more efficient Ram Air scoops. A new Endura bumper that's a real goat for punishment. We suggest you pick up a copy of Pontiac's new 1971 Performance Car Catalog for the complete story.

But for now, sleep easy. Because Pontiac hereby serves notice that the GTO is alive... and very, very well.

Prove it to yourself. With a test run at your Pontiac dealer's.

Pure Pontiac!

Pontiac Motor Division

Insurance increases and stiffer emission regulations were putting the big-block V-8-powered muscle car on the trailer. Pontiac tried to keep the visual excitement of prior years alive with the use of a huge engine, but the general public was losing interest in high-performance machines. Of course, the hardcore enthusiasts always wanted more power, but in the future it would have to be homegrown, as the factories were stepping away from muscle cars.

The final year for the GTO in this body shell, as well as functional Ram Air, the 1972 edition was the first time a convertible version wasn't offered. For the first time since 1965, the GTO package was an option, not a standalone vehicle.

Pontiac used an optional full-length Rally Stripe to inject some verve into the top-line 1972 GTO. The handsome profile could be augmented with a Cordova Top for $97. Increasingly, the option list stressed comfort and convenience items. GTO production numbers tumbled in the 1972 model year, with only 5,807 vehicles sold. Of that sum, just 645 were equipped with the 455 H.O. engine, now rated at 300 horsepower at 4,000 rpm and 415 lb-ft of twist.

on the LeMans option sheet, including the GTO bumper, hood, Safe-T-Track rear end, heavy-duty suspension components, and 455 H.O. engine.

Visually the only noticeable change in the switch from model to package was a new functional side scoop behind the front tires. This scoop ducted hot air out of the engine compartment. Otherwise the cars were virtually identical to the 1971 cars, at least at a glance. A closer inspection would reveal that the 1972 GTOs contained

less comfort and convenience equipment, unless an owner loaded up on options when ordering a car. This situation was the result of the GTO now being based on the lowly LeMans, which was a relatively Spartan car compared to previous GTOs.

Changing the GTO from a separate model to an option package for the LeMans meant that for the first time since 1967 GTO buyers could order a two-door post coupe, which had always been available on the LeMans

Gone was the rear wing and tire-melting performance. Pontiac saw the writing on the wall, and by 1972, the GTO was a performance shadow of what had been offered only a few years before. But when you compare it to other muscle cars sold that year, it acquitted itself rather well. It would sprint to 60 miles per hour in 7.1 seconds and cover the quarter-mile in 17.6 seconds.

model. Even though the convertible was dead, the buyer still had a choice of two body styles–coupe and hardtop. Not that anyone really cared–only 134 buyers elected to get the pillared coupe version of the GTO.

Another advantage to this change was that as an option package for the LeMans, the price of the GTO didn't rise much for 1972. The post coupe started at $3,434, which was actually lower than the base price of the hardtop the previous year, and the hardtop started at $3,563. The downside was that buyers had to spend a lot of money on options that had previously been standard equipment on the GTO if they wanted to bring their cars up to the luxury and convenience standard set by the earlier cars.

WW5

Pontiac offered three engine choices for the 1972 GTO, all carried over from 1971: a 250-horsepower (net) 400, a 250-horsepower (net) 455, and a 300-horsepower (net) 455 H.O. Because these engines were virtually unchanged

from the previous year, the net numbers were nearly identical to what they had been in 1971.

Buyers who didn't want to check all the individual boxes on the option sheet to get all the high-performance parts needed to make their LeMans GTOs perform like true GTOs could order option package WW4 (for cars equipped with the 400-cubic-inch engine) or WW5 (for cars equipped with the 455 H.O. engine). By ordering this one option the buyer got all the best high-performance parts offered for the GTO, like the Safe-T-Track rear end and four-speed manual transmission.

In a sign that the times were changing, the GTO got an additional entertainment option: a stereo cassette player. The eight-track tape, it seemed, was on the way out. Unfortunately, the eight-track tape would outlive the muscle car. GTO sales fell yet again, to 5,807. Only 645 buyers chose the 455 H.O. engine, and only 1,891 bought cars equipped with manual transmissions. The future of the GTO looked bleak.

Pontiac equipped the 1972 GTO with a 400-cubic-inch engine as the standard powerplant. Rated at 250 horsepower at 4,400 rpm, it churned out 325 lb-ft of torque at 3,200 rpm. That came in handy when the vehicle weighed in at 3,705 pounds.

Above: The vast majority of GTO production in 1972 centered on the standard 400-cubic-inch-equipped model. With 4,922 units built, it was indicative of the direction the performance enthusiasts were taking in their new car purchasing. More luxury, less brutal performance.

Left: It was an unusual customer that walked into a Pontiac dealer in 1972 and ordered a standard engine-equipped GTO with a manual transmission. Only 59 were built, and Hurst was still supplying the beefy shifters. As the Turbo Hydra-matic automatic was the standard transmission in 1972, a four-speed wide-ratio manual was a $190 option when paired with the standard 400-cubic-inch engine.

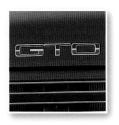  

CHAPTER 6

THE SHORT-LIVED REINCARNATION OF THE GTO AND THE DEATH OF PONTIAC

Like all of GM's A-body cars, the GTO bodywork had always been on a fixed development cycle. The same basic body shape would be used for two years, after which it would get a mild makeover. Two years after that it would get a major makeover. The car had been scheduled for a major makeover for the 1972 model year, but because of the 1970 strike, the resources being devoured by developing pollution-control equipment, and dismal sales in 1970 and 1971, GM put off releasing completely updated A-body models until the 1973 model year.

The redesigned A-body cars introduced by all GM divisions for 1973 represented the most radical makeover yet for the company's intermediate cars. The same basic frame with its 112-inch wheelbase was retained, but GM's engineers and stylist binned every single body panel. The new cars no longer came in multiple body styles. No GM division offered a convertible version of the new intermediate chassis, and the hardtop was history. Any variation of a model was created by minor (and inexpensive) sheet metal and trim manipulation.

Increasingly stringent government safety requirements meant that the pillar-less coupe body would no longer meet minimum crash protection standards set by the federal Department of Transportation. The new cars would only be offered as post coupes. Pontiac's LeMans coupe, the base car upon which the GTO would continue to be built, featured a sleek, low roofline with a fixed triangular window behind the large post between it and the driver's window. If buyers ordered the optional (and extra-cost) sport coupe, that window was replaced by a louvered metal panel.

In a step backward, the GTO lost its Endura front bumper. Instead it used the ungainly, oversized bumper from the LeMans, which outraged the GTO faithful. These massive chromed beams were designed to meet new-for-1973 5-mile-per-hour crash standards and were universally reviled. For many people, the 5-mile-per-hour bumpers, as these gargantuan units became known, signified the death of the muscle car.

The GTO sort of made up for its clumsy-looking bumper by featuring a pair of trendy NACA (National

A highly restyled A-body platform supplied the underpinnings for the 1973 GTO, an optional package built on the LeMans. The rear side windows were covered by louvers only on the sport coupe body style. The public preferred the look of the sport coupe to the tune of 4,312 sold, compared to the 494 coupes sold with the uncovered rear side window.

Advisory Committee for Aeronautics) ducts in its hood. (Pontiac's original 1973 GTO brochure mistakenly called these "NASA ducts.") These had been designed as part of a Ram Air package that had been developed for the car. This system never saw production because it made the GTO too loud to pass new drive-by noise laws being enacted at both the state and federal levels, so the ducts on the production version of the GTO were not functional.

Though the design has aged well, the look of the new A-bodies was extremely controversial at the time. More people than not hated it, but the new car was improved in a number of areas. The most notable was that the new cars put to use the lessons GM's suspension engineers had learned while developing the F-body cars—the Firebirds and Camaros. This meant that all the new A-body cars were much better handling than their predecessors had been.

Pontiac's suspension people were the best of any GM division, and throughout the decade of the 1970s the division's Trans Am was universally acknowledged as the best-handling car built in America. As a result of their expertise, Pontiac versions were the best-handling of all the A-body models.

THE GTO THAT SHOULD HAVE BEEN

Before GTO sales had tanked, Pontiac had been developing a new GTO that would have been a separate model from the LeMans. When the GTO became an option package on the LeMans, Pontiac had gone too far and spent too much money on what was to have been the redesigned GTO to kill the new car. Consequently, the division made it a completely new model; the car that was originally supposed to have been the 1972 GTO became the 1973 Grand Am.

The 1973 Grand Am was everything the 1973 GTO should have been. Instead of the economy interior from the LeMans, the Grand Am had the more luxurious Grand Prix interior, which consisted of an

Opposite: Pontiac stylists maintained the familial look on the 1973 GTO with the split grille and arrowhead logo. The dual hood scoops were for show only, as noise and emission regulations required a closed induction system.

Graceful, flowing lines on the 1973 GTO were well received by the public, as 4,806 were sold. While that number doesn't approach the sales of a few years prior, it showed that there was plenty of equity remaining in the GTO name. With a standard 400-cubic-inch engine and an optional 455, the hint of performance was present.

elegant dash layout; a Rally gauge cluster with full instrumentation (tachometer optional); a three-spoke Formula steering wheel; genuine Crossfire Mahogany trim on the dash facing, radio, and clock surrounds; and a center console between the front seats.

Those Strato bucket seats included recliners and adjustable lumbar support, features common on European sports and grand-touring cars but virtually unheard of on American cars of that time. In keeping with its high-end European theme, the Grand Am was

one of the first U.S.-built cars to come with a turn-signal-mounted headlight dimmer switch, a feature that had been common on imported cars for decades.

Because it was designed to be a GTO, the Grand Am had an Endura front bumper, as a real GTO should have. The Grand Am had Radial Tuned Suspension (RTS) that included radial-ply tires, along with Pliacell shock absorbers and larger-diameter front and rear sway bars as standard equipment. GTO buyers made do with bias-ply tires and optional Superlift air shocks rather than the more sophisticated Pliacell units.

The suspension of the Grand Am, which featured variable-ratio power steering that allowed the car to have a quicker steering ratio at slower speeds without being twitchy at higher speeds, nearly equaled the suspension on the Trans Am. As a result of its European-inspired performance and luxurious interior appointments, the Grand Am was popular among magazine editors. Meanwhile, the magazines all but ignored the GTO.

Pontiac spared no expense on the Grand Am, which came with every performance part in Pontiac's catalog either as standard equipment or as an available option, including the division's strongest engines and four-speed transmission. The new model received all the available funds when it came to marketing and advertising, too, but even with some marketing muscle

While the width of the GTO grew only 1 inch in 1973, the weight inevitably grew as well. A manual transmission–equipped sport coupe, such as the one seen here, weighed in at 3,867 pounds.

Above: Pontiac wanted to use an Endura-like nose on the 1973 GTO, but that front end ended up on the Grand Am, leaving the GTO with the chrome-plated railroad tie. It was hoped that the GTO would receive the vaunted 455 Super Duty engine, but the general manager at Pontiac, Martin Caserio, sat on the big engine for months, until it finally was released in the Trans Am. It never made it into the GTO.

Right: Slippery looking, the 1973 GTO was a one-year body style built on the LeMans Colonnade Hardtop or the LeMans Sport Coupe Colonnade Hardtop. The vast majority of GTOs built used the sport coupe as a starting point.

Overall vehicle length grew 4 inches in 1973 from the preceding year. Much of this was attributable to the federally mandated 5-mile-per-hour front bumper. While it didn't do much for the appearance of the car, it met the letter of the law.

behind it, the Grand Am proved a poor seller. Pontiac sold just 43,164 units for the 1973 model year, sold 17,083 1974 versions, and killed the car after the 1975 model year, when it sold just 10,679 Grand Ams.

In 1977, Pontiac resurrected the Grand Am concept with the Can Am, which was an option package for the LeMans that offered an optional 200-horsepower, 400-cubic-inch engine from the division's Trans Am, complete with that car's fake

shaker hood scoop. The public showed initial enthusiasm for the Can Am; Pontiac received orders for more than 5,000 units, but production problems with the fiberglass rear spoiler caused Pontiac to cease production after building just 1,377 examples.

LONG, SLOW FADE

Instead of being the car it was supposed to be—the European-inspired Grand Am—the GTO package returned for the 1973 model year as an option on Pontiac's new LeMans order sheet. Pontiac planned to return the GTO to its street-fighting roots with the new car. According to the original plan, the GTO was to receive the new Super Duty 455 engine when that became available later in the model year.

Just about the time the car hit the market, Pontiac got cold feet. It limited the application of the 310-horsepower SD 455 engine to the F-body Formula and Trans Am after production delays prevented Pontiac from building enough engines for the F-bodies, much less supplying them for the A-body GTO and Grand Am. This meant the top engine offered in the GTO would be the 250-horsepower, 455-cubic-inch, D-port engine; the round-port, 455-horsepower engine was no longer available.

The base engine would remain the 400-cubic-inch D-port engine, which had now dropped to 230 horsepower thanks to a lower compression ratio (8.1:1) and the installation of the Exhaust Gas Recirculation (EGR) system, which consisted of new pollution-control equipment that sent unburned exhaust gasses back into the intake manifold to be burned with the incoming fuel-air mixture.

Pontiac tried to pull a fast one on the EPA and designed the system with a solenoid to shut it off after running for 53 seconds. This was because the EPA only tested an engine in 50-second cycles. The EPA saw through this ploy and on March 15, 1973, ordered Pontiac to revise the system immediately. Cars built after that date featured a version of the EGR system without the solenoid.

A four-speed transmission was available but only with the 400-cubic-inch engine. This was the M20 wide-ratio transmission; the M21 transmission had gone the way of the Ram Air IV engine. Pontiac quit equipping the manual-transmission cars with Hurst shifters for the 1973 model year and reverted to the clumsy (but less expensive) Inland shifters. This move was as well received by GTO fans as were the 5-mile-per-hour chrome bumpers.

Pontiac again failed to promote the new GTO. In an eight-page press release on the 1973 lineup, much of which was devoted to the new Grand Am, the only mention of the GTO was buried in a section with the heading "Other Intermediates." The entire text read: "The GTO—offered as an option on the LeMans coupe and LeMans sports coupe."

Honeycomb wheels were a $123 option, designed by stylist John Schinella. They proved to be very popular and were soon offered on many sporty Pontiacs, including Trans Ams. The 1973 GTO used cubic inches to announce the engine displacement, as muscle car enthusiasts in America tended to gravitate to big numbers, not liters.

A full-width front bench seat meant that six could fit into the 1973 GTO, but the unlucky front center passengers needed to contort themselves out of the way of the big Hurst floor shifter. About 25 percent of GTO production that model year featured the manual transmission.

The 1973 LeMans GTO never had a chance. It was a decent car with a lot of potential, but it had too many factors working against it. People just never warmed up to the styling of the new A-bodies. It never received the bodywork, interior appointments, or proper powertrain it should have received: the Endura bumper, Grand Prix interior, and SD 455 engine. Most of all, people didn't know the 1973 GTO existed because Pontiac failed to promote the car.

All things considered, it's surprising that Pontiac managed to sell 4,806 1973 GTOs. Most buyers—4,312—chose the $3,376 sport coupe, while 494 buyers bought the $3,288 coupe. The optional engine was even less popular than the base coupe; 212 cars featured the 455 engine in 1973. It's hard to justify the extra cost of the big 455 and its increased thirst for fuel when it netted the buyers a mere 20-horsepower gain. Just 1,113 buyers equipped their cars with the four-speed manual tranny. Because of the increasing emphasis being put on fuel economy, the lowest-geared rear end available was a wimpy 3.23:1.

OIL SHOCK
Fuel economy was about to get a whole lot more important, and the fate of the GTO was about to get a whole lot worse. If an aging demographic, Draconian insurance premiums, increasing encroachment by the federal government, and what appeared to be an orchestrated effort within Pontiac to kill the GTO weren't enough to make the Goat go away, the 1973 oil crisis was.

On October 17, 1973, Arab members of the Organization of Petroleum Exporting Countries (OPEC) announced that they would no longer ship petroleum to nations that had supported Israel in its conflict with Egypt, which meant the United States and its allies in Western Europe. The effects of the embargo were immediate, and the price of oil quadrupled by 1974. The embargo ended on March 17, 1974, but the aftermath would have a chilling effect on the performance-car market well into the next decade.

HITTING BOTTOM
After suffering the worst sales year yet for the GTO, Pontiac decided to move the GTO package to the Ventura's option sheet. The Ventura was Pontiac's version of GM's X-body economy-car platform, which included the Chevrolet Nova, the Oldsmobile Omega, and the Buick Apollo.

For a non–car guy like F. James McDonald, who was still running Pontiac at the time, the decision to move the GTO option from the LeMans to the

Lacking the visual pizzazz of just a few years prior, the engine compartment of the 1973 GTO still used powerplants displacing the big numbers, in this vehicle's case, 400 cubic inches. An optional 455-cubic-inch mill was installed in just 544 GTOs.

Everyone had written off "old-school" muscle cars, then Pontiac dropped this bombshell in 1973. The 455 Super Duty engine was rated at 290 horsepower, but it takes a lot more than that to hurl a Trans Am down the quarter-mile in just 13.8 seconds at 103.6 mph. A lot more.

Ventura might have seemed like a good idea. The oil crunch had caused the buying public to purchase smaller cars with lower-displacement engines, and the lightweight X-body platform was almost 800 pounds lighter than the A-body platform. In theory this should have made the new GTO a decent performer, even with a smaller engine, and the Ventura GTO should have gotten more miles out of every gallon of gas. At least in theory. . . .

BAD IDEA, WORSE EXECUTION

The problem was that the X-bodies were truly awful cars: crude, cheap, tinny, loud, uncomfortable little beasts. When driving in a crosswind an owner could actually see the sheet metal in the hood rippling in the wind. The car was available as both a post coupe and a post hatchback. That latter body style turned the

Pontiac wouldn't put connecting rod nut torque instructions on a valve cover sticker if it didn't expect owners to delve into the greasy innards. With a handful of common performance tricks, this engine could generate more than 500 horsepower.

Federal bumper regulations forced Pontiac stylists to design a 5-mile-per-hour front bumper that met the letter of the law as well as maintaining the aggressive look that Trans Ams were known for. Packing a 455 Super Duty engine under the hood was a good way to ensure most people saw a lot of the rear of the car.

Ventura GTO into a resonance chamber that amplified the noise made by the cheap tires, substandard mechanical components, and ill-fitting body parts.

The car's handling characteristics were considered marginal in the mid-1960s, when the design had first appeared, and they hadn't aged well. Pontiac offered a Radial Tuned Suspension for the Ventura, which improved the handling quite a bit, but not enough to bring it anywhere near the standard set by the Trans Am or Grand Am, or even by any previous version of the GTO. Pontiac had made a

name for itself by selling fast cars in the 1960s. In the 1970s it had earned a reputation for building cars with stellar suspensions that were often cited for being the best-handling cars in America. The new GTO embodied neither quality. The X-body cars represented everything that was wrong with the way American cars handled. The optional Radial Tuned Suspension helped the GTO rise above its lowly X-bodied brethren, but the cars' chassis dynamics were much closer to the bottom end of the handling spectrum than they were to the top end.

THIRSTY DOG

The only engine available was a 200-horsepower 350. When hitched to the optional four-speed manual transmission the engine should have motivated the 3,400-pound car in a spritely fashion, but that was not the case. Performance was dismal; even when equipped with the four-speed transmission and Safe-T-Track rear end, the GTO was barely able to break into the 15-second quarter-mile bracket. Sixteen-second quarter-mile times were an embarrassment for the once-proud GTO. And the loss in performance didn't come with a corresponding increase in fuel mileage. The little Ventura GTO managed to coax a mere 12 miles out of each gallon.

Part of the problem was that the engine was a boat anchor, one of the worst examples of emissions-choked engines built up until that time (unfortunately, engines would get worse before they would get better). Though rated at 200 horsepower, that number was probably optimistic because of the engine's low 7.6:1 compression ratio. Another factor contributing to the car's leisurely acceleration was

Only two transmissions from the GM roster were used with the brutal 455 Super Duty engine, the M20 Muncie wide-ratio four-speed manual and the M40 Turbo Hydra-matic 400 three-speed automatic. Either box lived a high-stress life.

that even with the optional Safe-T-Track limited-slip differential, the only available gearing was a tall 3.08:1. This long-legged gearing combined with the lousy Inland shift linkage and the underachieving engine to ensure that the 1974 GTO would be a slug in the quarter mile.

RAM AIR

For all its shortcomings, the 1974 Ventura GTO did have one interesting standard feature—a functional ram-air intake system. This consisted of a through-the-hood scoop similar to that used on the Trans Am, except that this scoop was never functional on the Trans Am. Like the Trans Am, the scoop's inlet was reversed and faced backward, toward the windshield. Unlike the Trans Am, a solenoid opened a flap in the inlet under full acceleration, allowing fresh air

to enter the carburetor. This was a genuine ram-air system, though Pontiac never officially called it "Ram Air," and the car received no callouts to draw attention to the system, probably to keep it from raising the dander of insurance companies.

This scoop served decorative purposes only even on the Super Duty 455 version of the Trans Am (as well as the SD 455 version of the Formula, the only non–Trans Am F-body to receive the through-the-hood scoop design). The Ventura GTO was the only car Pontiac ever built that could pass noise emission tests with a functional version of this scoop, which earned the nickname "shaker" because it moved with the engine and appeared to be shaking in the hood when the engine was running.

Other than the scoop, the appearance of the car was rather pedestrian. When the body style first appeared in 1968 the Ventura had been considered the Tempest's homely little sister, and the intervening six years hadn't made the design look any fresher. The hatchback looked a little more sporting than the coupe because of its more flowing lines in back, though only 1,723 people chose the hatchback version of the car.

If the exterior was mundane, the interior of the Ventura GTO was positively low-rent. The round gauge pods of every other GTO ever built were gone, replaced by the sweeping speedometer that DeLorean had tried to get away from with the original GTO. A small blank face on the right could house either an optional tachometer or a clock, and a fuel gauge filled the space to the right of the speedometer. No other gauges were offered, not even a temperature gauge.

Every piece of the Ventura GTO's interior broadcast its economy-car roots. The situation in

Pontiac changed the body style of the GTO yet again in 1974 in an effort to keep interest in a heritage-rich nameplate yet deliver an automobile that was street legal while strongly suggesting performance. This was the start of serious "performance by graphics."

1955 ———————————○ **1956** ——————————————————————————————————————

- Pontiac replaces its inline flathead sixes and eights with an overhead valve V-8 dubbed the Strato-Streak V-8.

- GM President Harlow Curtice promotes Semon E. "Bunkie" Knudsen to manager of the Pontiac division.

- General Motors management gives Knudsen five years to turn Pontiac around or the division will be eliminated.

- Knudsen hires Elliot M. "Pete" Estes to be Pontiac's chief engineer.

- Knudsen and Estes hire John Zachery DeLorean from the ash heap of the failed Studebaker-Packard corporation.

1959 ———————————————————————————————————————○ **1960** ——————————

- Knudsen orders the 1959 chassis redesigned so that it will better fit the new wider bodies, resulting in the Pontiac "Wide-Track" design.

- Wangers develops plan to sell performance at Pontiac dealerships. Frank Bridges, Pontiac's sales manager, hates the idea, but Knudsen likes it and orders Wangers to develop a test dealership.

- Wangers teams up with Asa "Ace" Wilson Jr. to make Ace Wilson's Royal Pontiac in Royal Oak, Michigan, the prototype for a performance-oriented Pontiac dealership.

- Wangers campaigns the first Royal drag car, a red 1959 Catalina hard-top coupe, which features a stock 389 H.O. engine that generates 341 horsepower and 425 lbs-ft of torque.

- Complete Super Duty Package becomes available for the 1960 model year.

1962 continued ——

- Pontiac wins its second manufacturers' championship in NASCAR's Grand National series, and Bud Moore wins the drivers' championship in a Pontiac.

- Royal Pontiac offers the Royal Bobcat, a Catalina coupe equipped with performance parts from Pontiac's Super Duty Group.

- Pontiac introduces the performance-oriented Grand Prix personal luxury coupe.

- Pontiac builds 16 Super Duty Grand Prix models.

- Jim Wangers befriends George Hurst and begins using Hurst shifters in Royal Pontiac drag racers.

1965 continued ——

- Ram Air option becomes available, turning the fake hood scoop into a functional hood scoop.

- Pontiac gets more aggressive when it comes to advertising and promoting the GTO.

- Pontiac partners with Hurst to build two pace cars for the Riverside 500 NASCAR race; one car is given to race winner Dan Gurney, and the other is given away in a contest to a young Californian.

- Pontiac teams up with Hurst and Petersen Publishing to built the GeeTO Tiger, a car given away to contest winner Alex Lampone.

- *Motor Trend* magazine awards it "Car of the Year" award to the entire Pontiac lineup.

1966 continued ———————————————○ **1967** ————————————————————————

- James Roche, the chairman of General Motors, orders Pontiac to tone down its GTO advertising.

- General Motors bans multiple carburetion on most models, killing the Tri-Power option.

- Carter Thermoquad four-barrel carburetor is replaced by a more modern Rochester Quadrajet unit.

- GTO engine is enlarged to 400 cubic inches, the maximum allowed by GM corporate policy.

- Hood-mounted tachometer becomes available.

1968 continued

- Two-door post version of GTO is no longer available.

- Ram Air engine receives a new cylinder block with four-bolt main bearing caps.

- New GTO features Endura front bumper—because of production process problems, 2,108 early 1968 GTOs feature chrome front bumpers.

- Concealed headlight option becomes available.

- Last year for the side vent windows.

1969 continued / 1970

- Sales of 1969 Ram Air IV–equipped GTOs are nearly double the number of sales of 1968 Ram Air II–equipped GTOs.

- John DeLorean is promoted to general manager of the Chevrolet division.

- F. James McDonald is promoted to head of the Pontiac division.

- Pontiac gives the GTO a minor restyling with a new front end and bulges over the wheel wells.

- Hidden headlights are dropped from the option list.

1971 continued / 1972

- Last year the GTO is offered as a convertible.

- Pontiac uses all available advertising money to promote the Firebird at the expense of the GTO.

- GTO sales dip to almost nothing (10,532 units).

- GTO becomes an option package for the LeMans model.

- Automakers switch from rating power output in SAE gross numbers to rating it in SAE net numbers, leading to a huge across-the-board plummet in output ratings, even when no mechanical changes occur.

1973 continued

- Close-ratio M21 four-speed transmission is no longer available, leaving only the wide-ratio M20 unit.

- GTOs are not equipped with Hurst shifters for the first time in 1973; instead, four-speed cars use Inland shifters.

- Lowest-geared rear end is a tall 3.23:1.

- GTO option receives no promotion or publicity.

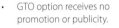

- Pontiac introduces the Grand Am, the car originally designed to be the next-generation GTO.

1980 / 1981 / 1982–91 / 1992 / 1993–2002

- Top engine in Trans Am and Formula is now a turbocharged, 301-cubic-inch engine that generates 210 horsepower.

- Power output for the turbo engine falls to 200 horsepower.

- Power output for Trans Am lags in the 175–230 range for a decade.

- Pontiac teams up with SLP to build the 350-horsepower Firebird Firehawk.

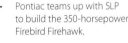

- Power output for Firebird models rises throughout the decade, culminating in the all-aluminum LS1 V-8 sourced from Chevrolet, but sales decline, and the Firebird is killed after the 2002 model year.

- Knudsen forms the Super Duty Group to develop Pontiac performance parts in-house.

- Malcolm R. "Mac" McKellar, Russ Gee, and Bill Collins are assigned to the Super Duty Group and given the unofficial assignment of developing racing parts.

- Automobile Manufacturers Association (AMA) bans factory involvement in racing.

- Knudsen openly ignores the AMA racing ban.

- United States is hit by a severe recession, and automobile sales plummet.

- Jim Wangers joins MacManus, John & Adams, Pontiac's advertising agency.

- Knudsen is promoted to manager of the Chevrolet division.

- Estes is promoted to head Pontiac.

- DeLorean is promoted to chief engineer.

- NASCAR rule changes force Pontiac to offer the Super Duty 421 engine in passenger cars.

- Pontiac builds a small number of Super Duty Catalinas and Bonnevilles with the Super Duty 421 engine, all of which come without a factory warranty and with notices saying they are for competition use only.

- Pontiac introduces optional Tri-Power carburetion for the GTO late in the year.

- *Car and Driver* publishes a road test comparing the performance of the Pontiac GTO to that of a Ferrari GTO, a test in which the Pontiac (which Jim Wangers now admits was a ringer with a high-performance 421-cubic-inch engine) beats the much-more-expensive Ferrari.

- Royal Pontiac develops a Royal Bobcat package for the GTO.

- After a slow start, GTO sales take off; Pontiac sells 32,450 units and would have sold many more had the division not been hindered by a shortage of 389-cubic-inch engines.

- Pontiac redesigns the front grille of the GTO.

- Ram Air cars are equipped with a hotter cam and heavy-duty valve springs to take advantage of the improved breathing.

- GTO is used as the basis for the *Monkeemobile*, the car built by customizer Dean Jeffries for the popular sitcom *The Monkees*.

- Wangers develops a racing promotion in which racing fans have an opportunity to drag race against the Mystery Tiger in a pair of identically prepped GTO drag cars.

- Pontiac sells 96,946 GTOs for the 1966 model year.

- Ralph Nader publishes *Unsafe at any Speed*, a book that accuses General Motors of building dangerous cars.

- Red plastic fender liners are available for one final year.

- Pontiac promotes the GTO as "The Great One."

- Pontiac introduces the Firebird, a sporty car that cuts into GTO sales.

- In part because of increased competition, GTO sales fall to 81,722.

- Pontiac introduces a completely redesigned GTO for the 1968 model year.

Knudsen tells *Automotive News*: "We're going racing, and we're going to build some really exciting cars here at Pontiac."

- Knudsen removes the "Silver Streaks," twin chrome strips that ran lengthwise down Pontiac hoods that the public called "Pontiac suspenders," which had defined Pontiac styling since 1932.

- Pontiac introduces the triple-two-barrel Tri-Power carburetion system.

- Pontiac introduces the Bonneville, a fuel-injected convertible designed to improve Pontiac's image among fans of high-performance automobiles.

- Cotton Owens wins the NASCAR race at Daytona Beach in a Bonneville, giving Pontiac its first-ever NASCAR victory.

On Monday, September 5, 1960, Wangers wins the Top Stock Eliminator run-off at the NHRA Nationals, giving Pontiac its first national drag-racing championship.

- Pontiac redesigns V-8 engines, eliminating top-end oiling problems inherent in the original 1955 design and strengthening the bottom ends.

- Pontiac offers a small number of Super Duty 421 race engines to select race teams.

- Super Duty Pontiacs dominate NASCAR's Grand National series, winning 30 races and earning Pontiac a manufacturers' championship.

- Pontiac introduces the compact Tempest, with unit-body construction.

- Pontiac rises to become the number-three nameplate in America, behind only Chevrolet and Ford.

General Motors institutes a complete ban on all corporate racing activities.

- Pontiac disbands the Super Duty Group and ceases production of Super Duty engines, after delivering 88 Super Duty cars from the 1963 model year to customers.

- DeLorean decides to build a high-performance street car to market to the bourgeoning youth market, a bare-knuckled street fighter that nearly everyone could afford. While the unsuccessful Tempest is being redesigned for

the 1964 model year as a mid-sized car with traditional body-on-frame construction, engineer Bill Collins tells DeLorean and engineer Russ Gee that it would take only 20 minutes to put a high-performance 389 in a Tempest body.

- Pontiac sneaks the rule-breaking GTO past GM's corporate management by making it an option on the LeMans, a sporty version of the Tempest, rather than making the car a separate model.

- Pontiac introduces the W62 GTO Package as an option on the LeMans for the 1964 model year.

Estes is promoted to head of the Chevrolet division.

- DeLorean takes over as division manager for Pontiac.

- GTO sales more than double, to 75,352 units.

- Pontiac completely redesigns the GTO, giving it a sleeker, more curvaceous body.

- GTO is available with optional red plastic fender liners.

- The Air Injection Reactor Control System, a smog-reducing air pump fitted to cars, is sold in California.

Pontiac offers the "economy" version of the GTO, which features a low-compression engine with a two-barrel carburetor.

- Three-speed TH-400 automatic transmission replaces antiquated two-speed unit.

- Buyers who order a consoles for a GTO equipped with automatic transmission receive a Hurst Dual-Gate shifter.

- Four-speed Ram Air cars come with a mandatory 4.33:1 gear set in the 10-bolt rear end (cars equipped with the TH-400 automatic transmission receive 3.90:1 gearing).

- Eight-track tape deck is available for the first time.

- Optional power-assisted, vented front disc brakes become available.

- Ram Air II option becomes available May 16, 1968, marking the first use of round-port cylinder heads.

- Hurst Dual-Gate shifter is used on GTOs equipped with automatic transmissions for the final time.

- *Motor Trend* magazine picks GTO as its 1968 car of the year.

- Sales rise to 87,684 units in spite of stiff competition in the muscle-car market.

- GTO receives optional Power Flow Ventilation system.

- High Output version o GTO engine is rename Ram Air III.

- General Motors lifts its ban on engines over 400 cubic inches in intermediate cars.

- Pontiac offers a 455-cubic-inch, high-output engine in the GTO. This engine uses D-port heads instead of freer-flowing round-port heads and lacks the Ram Air system.

- The 400-cubic-inch Ram Air IV remains the most powerful optional GTO engine.

- Pontiac introduces a restyled Firebird, which can be ordered with the Ram Air IV engine.

- GTO sales plummet to 40,149 units.

- General Motors lowers compression ratios on engines to prepare for coming of low-octane unleaded gasoline, low horsepower and torqu ratings in the process.

- Two-door post model is once again available (134 buyers choose this version).

- Power rating of top engine (455 H.O.) falls from 310 horsepower (SAE net) in 1971 to 300 horsepower (SAE net) in 1972.

- Pontiac offers the WW4 (400-cubic-inch) and WW5 (455-cubic-inch) performance options to bring the LeMans GTO up to previous GTO specifications.

- Cassette tape deck becomes available.

- Only 5,807 LeMans buyers choose the GTO option.

- Pontiac introduces the Super Duty 455 versio of the Firebird Formul and Trans Am.

- Grand Am receives the Endura front bumper.

- Pontiac sells just 4,806 GTOs for the 1973 model year.

- Pontiac moves GTO option to the Ventura, the Pontiac division's version of GM's corporate X-body economy car platform.

- Only engine available is a 200-horsepower 350.

- Ventura GTO features a functional version of the Trans Am's "shaker" hood scoop.

- GTO sales rise to 7,058

- Pontiac's most powerful model is the four-door, front-wheel-drive Grand Prix GTP, which features a supercharged 3.8-liter engine.

- Pontiac revives the GTO nameplate.

- New GTO is based on the Monaro, a car built by GM's Australian subsidiary, Holden.

- New GTO features a 350-horsepower LS1 engine.

- Pontiac offers the W40 package to celebrate GTO's 40th anniversary.

- In spite of rave reviews Pontiac sells just 13,56 the 15,728 GTOs impo from Australia.

Ram Air II is replaced by Ram Air IV round-port engine.

- Pontiac introduces the GTO Judge.

- Pontiac dealers are given incentives to drag race Carousel Red Judges.

- Pontiac has difficulty filling all orders for Judges.

- Sales fall to 72,287 units.

Redesigned Ram Air system results in dramatic new scoops at the front of the GTO's hood.

- Ram Air III and Ram Air IV engine options are dropped.

- Pontiac introduces a new round-port, high-output 455 as the top GTO engine.

- Optional Honeycomb wheels are introduced.

- Last year for the Judge option.

GTO remains an option package on the completely redesigned LeMans.

- GTO loses its popular Endura front bumper.

- Pontiac decides to use only the 310-horsepower (SAE net) Super Duty 455 engine in the Firebird Formula and Trans Am.

- Top GTO engine is a 455-cubic-inch D-port engine that generates 250 horsepower.

- Base GTO engine is a 400-cubic-inch engine that generates just 230 horsepower.

---------------- 1975–77 ---------------- 1978 ---------------- 1979 ----------------

Pontiac kills the GTO.

- Last year for the Super Duty 455 engines in Formula and Trans Am.

- Pontiac continues to offer high-performance versions of the Trans Am, but power output falls every year.

- The 220-horsepower TA 6.6 Trans Am is the most powerful car built in America.

- TA 6.6 engine is only available in four-speed cars; automatic-equipped cars use a low-output, 403-cubic-inch engine sourced from the Oldsmobile division.

5 ---------------- 2006 ----------------

Pontiac gives the GTO more exciting styling, with new hood scoops and spoilers.

- GTO receives a 400-horsepower LS2 engine.

- Sales fall to 11,069 units.

- GTO sales rise to 13,948 units.

- Pontiac once again kills the GTO.

Pontiac used the Ventura as the basis for the 1974 GTO. A cousin to the Chevrolet Nova, Buick Apollo, and Oldsmobile Omega, the Ventura was a sturdy, if visually underwhelming, platform. This was the last year for this body style, as the Ventura received a new look in 1975. Two body styles were offered for the 1974 GTO. The first was a two-door coupe (seen here) and a two-door hatchback coupe. The coupe sold 5,335 units, while the hatchback coupe failed to ignite buyers' interest, selling only 1,723 vehicles.

the cabin improved slightly if a buyer ordered the GTO package on the slightly more upscale Ventura Custom, but only slightly. The main upgrades offered by the Custom version were a bright rocker-panel molding that ran from wheel to wheel and the word *Custom* lettered on the C-pillar.

In almost every way the Ventura GTO was a step down not just from the previous year but from every GTO ever built, including the original model introduced over a decade earlier. It gave buyers very little reason to purchase a new GTO rather than purchase a used one.

Even though the car had evolved dramatically during its first 10 years, the GTO produced in the 11th and final year of the car's original production run was the crudest, least-sophisticated one of them all.

THE WORST OF THE BEST OR THE BEST OF THE WORST?

There are two ways to look at this car. It's either the worst GTO ever built or the best General Motors X-body car ever built. No amount of work could make an economy car designed in the mid-1960s compete

Pontiac continued to design it's vehicles with a split front grille, maintaining a visual continuity with previous years. No more Endura nose, too expensive. It was cheaper to use a chromed railroad tie for a bumper.

with a GTO from any era. On the other hand, with all the improvements, like ram-air, optional Radial Tuned Suspension, optional four-speed, and optional Safe-T-Track rear end, the Ventura GTO was a much better car than any of the X-bodies produced by GM's other divisions: the Chevrolet Nova, the Oldsmobile Omega, and the Buick Apollo.

Still, the entire experience of driving the gussied-up Ventura was very un-GTO, and the car failed to generate much excitement for Pontiac. The car sold better than it had the previous year—7,058 units—but that was because Pontiac put some promotion behind it. The price was a steep $3,214.00 for the base coupe, and the hatchback started at $3,438.61. A relatively large number of buyers (3,174) ordered the four-speed manual transmission, indicating that there was still a small market for people who liked to shift for themselves.

Because the Ventura was an economy car instead of a premium car, as previous versions of the GTO had been, the 1974 model had the most abbreviated option

Lifted off the Trans Am, the shaker hood scoop was made functional in an attempt to project serious muscle car street cred. Unfortunately, performance enthusiasts saw it for what it was, an attempt by Pontiac marketing to sell a commuter car in muscle car clothing.

The interior of this 1974 GTO was a no-nonsense environment, with front bucket seats, a four-speed shifter, and a steering wheel. High-back bucket seats were standard; no longer were headrests separate.

Unlike its Trans Am cousin that also used a rear-facing shaker hood scoop, the 1974 Ventura GTO's scoop was actually functional. Under full acceleration, a solenoid opened the scoop's rear-facing flap, allowing cool air to flow into the L76, 350-cubic-inch V-8's Rochester 4MC Quadrajet four-barrel carburetor. The engine had a compression ratio of 7.6:1 and was rated at 200 horsepower at 4,400 rpm and 325 lb-ft of torque at 3,200 revs.

list in GTO history. The Radial Tuned Suspension option, which featured many of the premium bits found on the Grand Am, would have been welcome on the 1973 car. In the case of the Ventura GTO, its capabilities were somewhat wasted on a chassis that was a refugee from the previous decade.

The popular Honeycomb wheels and Formula steering wheel weren't available on any Ventura, GTO or not, but a GTO buyer could get an optional camping tent that attached to the rear hatch on the hatchback body style. Perhaps this option, more than any other detail, illustrates just how disconnected Pontiac's new management was from the performance car market.

Thin, horizontal taillights had been used on Pontiacs for a number of years, and they helped in giving the 1974 GTO a Pontiac visual feel. However, if the GTO decals were removed, you would be hard-pressed to tell that this was a GTO.

True to the muscle car template, the 1977 Can Am was a midsized vehicle with a big engine. Tasteful striping and a shaker hood scoop set the car apart from the bland-mobiles littering the American roads.

While improved over the previous year, sales weren't strong enough to justify continuing to offer the GTO option on any platform. After 1974, the GTO became history.

PONTIAC'S FINAL EXPLETIVE

Just because it had given up on the GTO didn't mean that Pontiac had given up on performance. By 1973, it seemed to everyone that the muscle car era was dead and gone. Chrysler's Hemi had disappeared, and Pontiac's 455 was a faint shadow of its former self. But Pontiac, the brand that had kicked off the muscle car movement in the first place, wasn't about to roll over in submission just yet. In a final act of defiance, Pontiac built something that everyone else thought impossible: a true muscle car.

By this time the last performance car in Pontiac's lineup was the Firebird. The GTO was just a forgotten option on the X-body Ventura and on its way to oblivion. The sportiest Pontiacs were the Formula and Trans Am Firebirds. The Trans Am package had debuted midway through the 1969 model year, the last year of Pontiac's original Camaro-derived F-car. In 1970, Pontiac introduced a redesigned Firebird. This redesign allowed Pontiac to build the F-car it had always wanted to build, and the new Firebird quickly earned a reputation for killer handling, especially in Trans Am trim. In addition to sporty bodywork and stripes, the Trans Am package included a number of suspension improvements. The top engine in the 1970 car was a 345-horsepower, 400-cubic-inch Ram Air IV, similar to the top engine offered in that year's GTO.

Pontiac installed the excellent round-port 455-horsepower as the standard engine in the Trans Am in 1971. This was a good fit in the Trans Am, but

Tapering fender lines were a graceful solution to a long expanse of sheet metal. Functional dual exhausts released a healthy rumble, one of the advantages of having 6.6 liters of V-8 under the huge hood.

Above: Looking like a bordello on wheels, the interior of the 1977 Can Am was richly appointed and comfortable for long drives. Leather seats and genuine simulated wood appliqué on the dashboard bespoke true American luxury.

Opposite: Emission controls had pretty much taken over the engine compartment by the mid-1970s. The 1977 Can Am had a 6.6-liter V-8 engine somewhere beneath all of the hoses and wiring. Engine appearance was no longer a source of owner pride.

by 1973 the round-port engine was history, and the top engine in the Trans Am was the 250-horsepower, 455-cubic-inch D-port engine. As unbelievable as it might have seemed at the time, the year 1973 marked a resurgence of Pontiac performance, in the form of the Super Duty 455 option available on the Formula and Trans Am versions of the Firebird.

The SD 455 engine combined every high-performance piece remaining in the Pontiac parts

catalog—radical camshaft, big carburetor, four-bolt main-bearing caps, forged connecting rods, aluminum flat-top pistons—in a last-ditch effort not to let the encroaching nanny state strangle the fun out of performance cars. With a low 8.4:1 compression ratio, the engine was rated at only 290 horsepower, not, seemingly, the stuff of which muscle car legends are made.

But that horsepower rating told only part of the

Super Duty story. While the SD 455's horsepower rating seemed slight, it was rated at 390 lb-ft of torque, which is exactly the same rating as a 1971 426 Hemi when measured using the SAE net method. Any powerplant that generates as much torque as a 426 Hemi deserves a place in the pantheon of great engines. While the torque figure was probably accurate, the engines must have generated considerably more than 290 horsepower. At a time when the lighter GTO was turning 16-second quarters with its 200-horsepower engine, the SD 455 Firebirds were getting deep into the 13-second bracket. Without question these were true muscle cars.

They were the last of the true muscle cars. Pontiac got a late start building SD 455 Firebirds because of the same supplier problems that killed the engine in the GTO. The division only produced 396 examples in 1973. In 1974, Pontiac built 943 SD 455 Formulas and Trans Ams before the engine fell victim to the OPEC-induced oil shock. After that, the Super

In 1981, if you wanted a new car with performance, it had to have forced induction. The 4.9-liter Turbo Formula came with just 200 horsepower, but with its superb suspension, it was an excellent Grand Touring car.

Above: When the Firehawk hit the streets in 1992, it blew everyone away, especially Corvette drivers. Able to generate speed, cornering, and braking numbers that exceeded the Chevrolet sports car at a fraction of the price, the Firehawk was a performance steal, even at $39,995. *Lara Williams photo*

Right: Street Legal Performance (SLP) installed this "T-RAM" intake manifold, increasing the engine's output by at least 45 horsepower. The Firehawk could sprint down the drag strip in just 13.2 seconds toward a top speed of more than 160 miles per hour. *Lara Williams photo*

For 2002, the Firehawk incorporated a lower-profile Ram Air hood than did the standard Trans Am W56. With a 5.7-liter V-8 under the voluptuous hood, the Firehawk could sprint to 100 miles per hour in just 13.1 seconds. A 10.1:1 compression helped generate 345 horsepower.

Duty engine disappeared from Pontiac's option list and with it the last of the true big-engine muscle cars.

THE DARK AGES

Throughout the 1970s and early 1980s, which was the bleakest era in automotive history up until that point, Pontiac tried to maintain its reputation as GM's performance division, producing some admirable cars along the way. Pontiac engineers massaged 220 horsepower from the 400-cubic-inch engine used in the 1978 Trans Am and even resorted to turbocharging when they were forced to scale back to a small 301-cubic-inch engine for the 1980 Trans Am.

THE TURBO TRANS AM

Even though the rest of the U.S. auto industry was urinating on itself in submission, Pontiac refused to give up on its performance image. The division may

When Pontiac decided to revive its original muscle car concept, it had no rear-drive platform to which it could turn, having killed off the Firebird a couple of years earlier.

Per Pontiac tradition, a split grille was utilized on the 2004 GTO. Considering the Pontiac stylists were given a finished vehicle and told to "Pontiacize" it, they did a good job bringing it into the division.

Above: Rolling stock consisted of 17x8-inch cast-aluminum wheels, shod with B.F. Goodrich P245/45-ZR17 95W M+S g-Force T/A tires. The GTO was built at the Elizabeth, South Australia, assembly plant.

Opposite: Riding on a 109.8-inch wheelbase, the 2004 GTO stickered for $31,795, quite a performance bargain for a true 350-horsepower, 5.7-liter V-8 in a vehicle with an independent rear suspension and an available six-speed manual.

have had to give up its big-cubic-inch engines, but if it had to run a small V-8 in the Trans Am, then it would extract maximum performance from that engine by any means necessary. In 1980, that meant turbocharging the gutless little economy motor.

Pontiac's engineers mounted a Garrett TB305 turbocharger—the same unit used by Buick and Ford at the time—on the 301-cubic-inch engine and dialed boost up to 9 pounds. The turbocharger used a primitive "draw through" design; that is, the

turbocharger sucks in the fuel-air charge through the carburetor rather than forcing air through the carburetor and letting it mix its fuel charge just prior to entering the combustion chamber. This prevented the turbocharger from working to its full potential and also created intolerable turbo lag.

It was a compromised system, at best, but the possibility of a fuel leak causing a fire was too great to use a blow-through system on a carbureted car. Turbocharging would not become a practical solution

Unlike the GTOs of the 1960s, the taillight assembly comprised large, easy-to-see elements. The trunk lid comes down to the bumper cap, giving the trunk a low lift-over, easing loading and unloading.

on American cars until U.S. automakers developed advanced fuel-injection systems.

The blown engine produced 210 horsepower and 345 lb-ft of torque—impressive numbers for the period, at least on paper. In reality, the turbo lag inherent in the design meant a driver almost had enough time to chug a refreshing beverage between the moment he stepped on the accelerator and when the little engine came to a boil. In 1981, output fell to 200 horsepower and 340 lb-ft of torque. The engine was dropped after that.

STREET LEGAL PERFORMANCE

Performance wouldn't return to General Motors' performance division in earnest until the advent of the SLP Firebird Formula Firehawk of 1992. That car was the result of a joint venture between Pontiac and an outside vendor.

Pontiac updated the GTO badge from the 1960s for the 2004 version, reversing to showing engine displacement in liters. The checkerboard pattern was intended to suggest a competition heritage.

In 1986, Ed Hamburger started a company that developed automotive aftermarket parts to improve performance while still meeting emissions standards, called, appropriately, Street Legal Performance (SLP). The company's first collaboration with an automaker occurred in 1992, when SLP and Pontiac worked together to produce the SLP Firebird Firehawk, a version of the Firebird Formula that produced 350 horsepower and 390 lb-ft of torque, thanks in part to an SLP-designed Ram Air fresh air intake. This 13-second quarter-mile terror was a true muscle car, though a very expensive one at $40,000.

Unfortunately Pontiac was completely adrift by this time, lacking the visionary leadership that had made the company GM's performance division. It lacked a vision for its product and a vision for the market.

Judging from the look of the final Firebirds, the division may well have literally lost its vision; the best thing that could be said about the bodywork on the last generation of Firebirds was that the cars were peculiar looking. During a period when other automakers were emulating Pontiac's Wide-Track look by moving wheels out as far as possible on

This cockpit is all business. Old muscle cars were never this comfortable, nor were they four-season vehicles. The 2004 GTO can be driven anytime, yet the occupants will enjoy an effective climate control and an excellent sound system. Meanwhile, they are kicking butt. It's the best of all worlds.

Right: The LS1 designation is from the aluminum block's Corvette roots. Pontiac used a four-speed Hydramatic 4L60E automatic transmission as the standard gearbox. An M12 six-speed manual was the optional choice, costing $695.

Below: In a repeat of days long ago, real power lurks under the hood of the 2004 GTO. A Gen III, 5.7-liter V-8 sourced from the Corvette—rated at 350 horsepower at 5,200 rpm and 365 lb-ft of torque at 4,000 revs—propels the GTO to 60 miles per hour in only 5.3 seconds, while covering the quarter-mile in 13.62 seconds at 104.78 miles per hour. That's fast.

their vehicles, the final generation of F-body cars took the opposite route, moving the wheels in and giving the cars exaggerated overhangs, resulting in cars that once again resembled football players in ballet slippers.

In addition to an awkward stance, the last-generation Firebirds suffered from exaggerated styling cues. When the F-body cars debuted for the 1993 model year, the Pontiac version looked like some generic kid's toy rather than a real sport coupe. Sales were dismal in spite of strong performance. In an attempt to boost sales, Pontiac made the bodywork even more exaggerated. When equipped with the WS6 package, a last-generation Trans Am received not two but four Ram Air intake openings stacked up on the front of the hood, resulting in a vehicle that looked like something John Travolta might drive in *Battlefield Earth*.

Even though the various high-performance Firebirds and Trans Ams that followed the initial SLP Firehawk were some of the fastest American cars ever built, the Firebird sold poorly and was discontinued after the 2002 model year.

It doesn't take a lot of pressure from the driver's right foot to put the speedometer needle in the "go-directly-to-jail" zone. Clear, easy-to-read instruments are a departure from the stylistically interesting but unreadable gauges from the muscle car "golden" era.

The wraparound rear spoiler was standard on the 2004 GTO. While it did little in generating useable downforce, it beefed up the undistinguished appearance of the GTO. Critics panned the look of the latest GTO as lacking any real flavor, but there was little the Pontiac designers could do to the Monaro to set their version strongly apart from the donor vehicle.

As with the original ad campaign some forty years earlier, Pontiac again showed the GTO as bold, stylish, and aggressive. Unfortunately, the buying public felt the car was bland and allowed the new generation of GTOs to languish on dealer lots.

PONTIAC

2004 GTO

The return of a legend.

Introducing the all-new 2004 Pontiac GTO in Phantom Black Metallic.

2004 Pontiac GTO

Bringing back GTO® meant developing a sport coupe that could live up to the legendary name. This one does. A 5.7L Gen III all-aluminum LS1 V8 powerplant pumps out 350 horsepower, helping to make it the most powerful GTO ever built. A taut, rear wheel drive independent rear suspension was a given. And an available Tremec™ close-ratio six-speed manual transmission were a given. Yes, GTO is back. And it will once again become the benchmark by which all other sport coupes are judged.

2004 GTO

PONTIAC Fuel for the Soul™

pontiac.com/gto
OR 1-800-2-PONTIAC

MSRP¹	
GTO	Coupe
	$32,495

ENGINES	
5.7L Gen III all-aluminum LS1 V8	
350 HP @ 5200 RPM	
365 lb.-ft. of torque @ 4000 RPM	

ESTIMATED FUEL ECONOMY IN MPG²		
	Automatic	Manual
City	16	17
Highway	21	29

STANDARD CAPACITIES	
Seating	4
Cargo volume (cu. ft.)³	7.0
Fuel tank (gal. approx.)	18

STANDARD EQUIPMENT ON GTO
- Air conditioning
- Automatic rear-seat access
- Console, includes storage compartment, accessory power outlet and dual cup holders
- Cruise control
- Illuminated driver and passenger visor vanity mirrors
- Intermittent windshield wipers
- Machine-drilled accelerator, brake and clutch pedals
- Rear- and side-window defoggers
- Satin Nickel interior appointments
- Soft-Ray® tinted windows

PERFORMANCE STATISTICS
- 0–60 in 5.3 seconds with available manual transmission
- Quarter-mile in 13.8 seconds with available manual transmission
- .86 lateral g's

INTERIOR		
	Key: S = Standard A = Available	GTO
Blaupunkt 200-watt, 10-speaker audio system with six-disc in-dash CD changer		S
Programmable Driver Information Center		S
Power, programmable door locks with lockout protection		S
Sport gauge package, available in five colors		S
Keyless Entry with interior lighting package		S
Eight-way, power front driver and passenger seating with manual lumbar-support controls		S
All-leather, 2+2 bucket seating with sport-style bolsters		S
Tilt and telescopic leather-wrapped steering wheel with radio controls		S
Power windows with driver and passenger Express-Down		S

EXTERIOR	
Dual exhaust with chrome tips	S
Spoiler	S
Front foglamps	S

MECHANICAL		
5.7L Gen III all-aluminum LS1 V8 with four-speed automatic transmission		S
Tremec close-ratio six-speed manual transmission		A
Rear-wheel drive with limited slip differential and Traction Control		S
Power-assisted, variable-ratio, rack-and-pinion steering		S
MacPherson struts on front suspension with progressive/variable-rate springs		S
Independent rear suspension with semi-trailing link and progressive/variable-rate springs		S
P245/45ZR-17 rated all-season tires with 17-inch aluminum wheels		S

SAFETY	
Four-channel, four-wheel disc antilock brake system	S
Frontal driver and passenger air bags⁴	S
Emergency Mode System	S
Daytime Running Lamps	S
Programmable, automatic headlamps	S
Three-point, all-positions safety belts	S
Rear-seat child belt anchor points	S
Immobilizer theft-deterrent system for content protection	S

EXTERIOR	INTERIOR	INSTRUMENTS

Quicksilver Metallic

Phantom Black Metallic

Torrid Red

Impulse Blue Metallic

Barbados Blue Metallic

Cosmos Purple Metallic

Yellow Jacket

GM Card

ABORTED REBIRTH

Pontiac revived the GTO for the 2004 model year. Building a muscle car was easier said than done for Pontiac at that time. When Pontiac decided to revive its original muscle car concept, it had no rear-drive platform to which it could turn, having killed off the Firebird a couple of years earlier.

A GTO needed to be a rear-wheel-drive car. While there are some great front-wheel-drive performance cars on the market, such cars are sport compacts and not muscle cars. Even when you stuff a V-8 engine in them, as Pontiac did with the last iteration of its front-wheel-drive Grand Prix, they are not muscle cars. And if it was not a muscle car, it most certainly wouldn't have been a GTO.

While Pontiac lacked a proper muscle car platform, Holden, General Motors' Australian division, had the Monaro, a great potential muscle car. This car made a logical choice as a starting point for building a modern GTO. Swiss-born Robert A. "Bob" Lutz, a man who has held high-ranking positions at each of the big three U.S. automakers and is currently an advisor to GM, championed the new GTO and made it a reality through the sheer force of his will.

The 2004 GTO rode on a 109.8-inch wheelbase and harked back to the Wide-Track Pontiacs of yore. The front track measured 61.4 inches across and the rear track measured 62.1 inches wide. Like the Monaro from which it sprang, the new GTO had a world-class suspension, a thoroughly modern design with independent rear suspension, unlike classic American muscle cars (as well as the 2004 GTO's only real muscle car competitor at the time, the Ford Mustang), which transferred their power to their rear wheels through solid rear axles.

The fully independent suspension featured MacPherson struts in front and a semi-trailing arm design in the rear, with specially tuned strut valving and spring rates. Direct-acting stabilizer bars and a variable-ratio power steering system were tuned to

Pontiac built this "Dream Cruise Edition" 2004 GTO, equipped with a 389-cubic-inch V-8 rated at 575 horsepower. The carbon fiber splitter helped in directing airflow above and below the body. The two-tone upholstery was eye-catching but was never put into production. Neither was the vivid Orbit Orange hue.

provide a sporty feel and increased driver feedback. Seventeen-inch alloy wheels and performance tires, a performance-tuned suspension, and a limited-slip differential also came as standard equipment.

In addition to delivering power to the correct pair of tires through a sophisticated suspension, the new GTO had a true muscle car engine: the Chevrolet-sourced LS1 that had been used in the final generation of Firebirds.

General Motors originally mounted the 5.7-liter (346-cubic-inch) LS1 in the 1997 Corvette. It was the first GM regular production V-8 engine to feature an aluminum block. This clean-sheet design—the first complete redesign of the Chevrolet small-block engine since the first Chevy V-8 in the 1950s—was designed to be powerful, emissions-friendly, and easy on fuel. Even though it retained the classic two-valve, pushrod architecture, bucking the modern trend of

Kip Wasenko, left, GM executive director of the Advanced Design Studio, shows off the 2004 "Dream Cruise Edition" GTO to Ken Orlowski on August 17, 2004. On August 21, 2004, during the annual Dream Cruise, the two GTOs plied Woodward Avenue with a few thousand of their favorite friends.

Huge tires barely fit inside the wheel wells, while a discreet tail spoiler and side scoops are the work of GM's Advanced Design Studio. With 575 horsepower on tap, this one-off GTO was as much a neck-snapper as it was a head-turner.

Pontiac used tasteful accents to set the 2005 GTO's interior apart from the non-performance vehicles in the Pontiac roster, including GTO seat inserts and special-colored gauge faces.

four-valve, overhead-cam performance engines, the LS1 was a thoroughly modern powerplant, capable of giving any car in which it was mounted world-class performance. In GTO trim, the LS1 engine produced 350 horsepower at 5,200 rpm and 365 lb-ft of torque at 4,000 rpm.

CREATURE COMFORTS

The fit and finish of the new car were top-notch inside and out. The elegant interior of the new GTO brought to mind the best sports and grand-touring cars from Europe. The GTO came with leather seats and a leather-covered steering wheel and shifter knob, features for which even premium brands charged

extra. The front seats featured side bolsters and the "GTO" name embroidered on the headrests. Later in the model year Pontiac introduced the W40 package to celebrate the 40th anniversary of the original GTO. The W40 consisted of an exclusive paint color called Pulse Red, red GTO embroidery on the seats, and a gray gauge cluster. The last 800 2004 GTOs built featured the W40 package.

Four large analog gauges (wearing faces color-coordinated with the exterior paint) resided in a large pod behind the wheel. The dials and much of the interior were trimmed with a satin-nickel finish, and the foot pedals had holes drilled into them, as did some of Europe's most prestigious automobiles. A

With the introduction of the
dual hood scoops, the 2005 GTO
ratcheted up the muscle car look
and visually tied the vehicle to the
original 1964 GTO. The scoops on
the older car were nonfunctional
as well.

standard-equipment 200-watt, 10-speaker Blaupunkt audio system featured an in-dash six-disc CD changer.

In addition to its high-end audio system, the 2004 GTO boasted a list of standard features never before seen on a muscle car, such as air conditioning; a console with storage compartment, accessory power outlet, and two cup holders; cruise control; a rear defogger; power door locks with lockout protection; a programmable keyless entry with a laser-etched key; eight-way power-adjustable driver and front passenger seats with power-assisted rear seat access; a tilting and telescoping adjustable steering wheel; power windows with driver and passenger express-down feature;

daytime running lamps with automatic headlamp control; a theft and content deterrent system; and a computerized driver information center. The integrated driver information center, which was located below the instrument cluster, included readouts for average speed, average miles per gallon, trip odometer, trip time remaining, trip distance remaining, fuel used, and instant fuel mileage. There was even a stopwatch feature and a user-programmable overspeed alarm.

RAVE REVIEWS

The new GTO performed like no GTO (or any other muscle car) before it. When *Motor Trend* magazine

Bowing to the public's insatiable demand for more power, the 2005 GTO enjoyed a bump up in engine displacement, to 6.0 liters, as well as horsepower, now rated at 400. Transmission choices remained at a four-speed automatic or a six-speed manual.

When Formula D and D1 Grand Prix Drifting hit American shores, Pontiac was quick to enlist ace driver Rhys Millen to pilot a competitive 2004 GTO drift car. The interior was gutted with the exception of the dashboard and instrument panel, and a set of racing seats were bolted in. The tall, blue-knob-topped stalk mounted between the seats controls the rear brakes.

tested the car, the editors raved about both its acceleration and its handling:

Although it'll happily melt its rear B. F. Goodriches into rubber pudding (a standard traction-control system will step in to save your tires unless you switch it off), the GTO runs not like a shuddering, rackety muscle car, but like a sophisticated executive's express. The muscle is certainly there: Under the hood lies the same 5.7-liter LS1 V-8 that powers some Chevrolet Corvettes; in the GTO, it delivers a studly 350 horsepower at 5200

rpm and 365 lb.-ft. of torque at 4000. Coupled to the optional ($695) Tremec six-speed manual transmission (an electronically controlled four-speed automatic is standard), the Vette V-8 kicks the GTO with inspiring swiftness. Even wearing its standard M+S tires, our test car scorched from 0 to 60 mph in 5.3 seconds and tripped the quarter-mile lights in 13.62 seconds at 104.78 mph— numbers that would leave a 1960s-vintage GTO seeing yellow.

When we last tested a supercharged Ford Mustang SVT Cobra (another front-V-8, rear-drive two-plus-two priced in the mid-$30s), it bettered those numbers, reaching 60 mph in just

Like most drift cars, the 2004 Rhys Millen Racing GTO is a tire-maker's dream, going through multiple sets of rubber in an event. The steering system was modified to allow the front tires to turn more sharply than a stock vehicle.

GTOs have been visiting drag strips since the beginning, and that continued as Greg Anderson raced his Summit Racing Pro Stock GTO in the NHRA Powerade Series, and he continues to be a winning driver.

Driver Greg Anderson pops the chutes after another successful pass down the quarter-mile. Anderson has won the Pro Stock championship a number of times, and his Pontiacs are consistently among the fastest in his class.

4.8 seconds and nailing the quarter mile in 13.0 at 110.7 mph. But the track stats tell only a small fraction of the story. The aging Cobra is quick, sure, but driving it means putting up with its clunky personality and a suspension that clomps over the road as if it's wearing horseshoes. . . .

The GTO apparently has Cool Whip in its suspension. Forget that punishing big-numbers ride we've come to expect from American performance coupes—the GTO is too well-mannered to deliver constant, seat-pounding reminders of its sport-coupe intentions. Maximum handling grip—0.80 g—doesn't set any performance standards, but the GTO's real-world usability does. Several of our test drivers commented that they had driven few other coupes so poised, so well-balanced, so confidence-inspiring when you're in full-hustle mode.

NEW GOAT A NO-GO

The problem with the Monaro was that it didn't look like a real American muscle car. Lutz had an extremely limited budget when bringing the car to the U.S. market, and his team burned up most of the available funds converting the car from right-hand drive to left-hand drive. When they finished, there was little money left for restyling efforts. Pontiac added some GTO badges and a Pontiac-style front-end treatment and brought the Monaro to the U.S. market as the Pontiac GTO.

The 2004 GTO was a solid performer, but the car's appearance was nondescript at best. Pontiac's front-drive Grand Prix, by no means a stylish car, turned more heads than the plain-looking GTO. Even though the car was quick and handled better than any previous GTO, no one but Pontiac's advertising people called the new GTO "The Great One." Mostly no one even noticed it existed, and if they saw one driving on a road, they dismissed it as a Grand Prix or Grand Am.

The cars sold as slowly as the last generation of Firebirds. Pontiac imported 15,728 cars from Australia (where they were built by Holden) for the 2004 model year but sold just 13,569 of them. By the middle of the 2004 model year it had become clear that buyers weren't responding to the new GTO, and dealers were discounting the car by 30 percent of their original retail price or more.

LS2

Pontiac designers made a few token efforts at giving the GTO more presence for 2005, like punching a couple of Ram Air–style holes in the hood and bolting a Judge-like wing to the rear deck, but there was only so much they could do with a car that looked like a coupe version of the 1996 Ford Taurus.

The designers might have been hamstrung by the car's basic shape, but Pontiac's engineers had a terrific car to develop. For 2005, Pontiac borrowed the new LS2 engine from the just-released C6 version of the Corvette and stuck it in the GTO. The 2005 GTO's LS2 V-8 incorporated several significant changes compared with the LS1 used in the previous year's car. The aluminum block was an all-new casting with revised oil galleries. Cylinder bore and stroke were increased to 4.00 inches and 3.22 inches, respectively, for a total displacement of 6 liters (364 cubic inches). The engineering team developing the LS2 reduced weight and mass wherever possible, from the water pump to the exhaust headers, making the LS2 the quickest revving pushrod V-8 ever built up until that time.

The cylinder heads and camshaft were revised to deliver the airflow necessary to complement the engine's larger displacement. Camshaft lift increased to take advantage of increased cylinder head flow, and the camshaft sensor was relocated from the rear of the block to the front to provide room for new oil galleries. A new flat-top piston design with lower ring tension reduced friction, and the pistons received floating wrist pins to reduce operating noise.

More efficient ignition coils required less energy to provide a comparable spark.

A tube-frame factory race car, the 2007 GTO.R packed 410 horsepower and cost a staggering $275,000. In the field the GTO.R runs in, it's something of a bargain. And faster than snot. *Richard Prince/GM Racing*

Here's the full spectrum of GTO performance circa 2005, as the GTO.R race car poses with the GTO pace car and the potent GTO street car at the start/finish line of the famous Daytona International Speedway on June 29, 2005. *Richard Prince/GM Racing photo*

The 2005 GTO was tapped for pace car duties at the 2005 Rolex 24-hour race February 5–6 at Daytona. With 400 horsepower and a fully independent suspension, it had no trouble staying in front of the huge field of race cars.

The 2006 GTO was the last year for this storied nameplate, and the able street fighter went out with a bang rather than a whimper. With a 6.0-liter LS2 rated at 400 horsepower beneath the hood, it had the ability to back up its street-fighter look.

The compression was raised to 10.9:1, and engine redline rose to 6,500 rpm. All of this resulted in an engine that generated 400 horsepower at 6,000 rpm and 400 lb-ft of torque at 4,400 rpm, making it the most powerful GTO that Pontiac ever produced. The 2005 GTO cranked out more SAE net horsepower than the old Ram Air IV produced using SAE gross horsepower measurements.

The addition of the LS2 engine turned the 3,800-pound car into a genuine rocket. *MotorWeek* ran one through the quarter-mile in 13.5 seconds at 108 miles per hour, the quickest any as-delivered production GTO with stock tires had ever gone (notwithstanding the flawed testing done by *Car and Driver* in the original "GTO versus GTO" test in 1964).

THE SECOND DEATH OF THE GTO

The new GTO may not have had the visual flash of

Warren Johnson, "The Professor of Pro Stock," warms the tires of his 2006 GTO in preparation to streak down the quarter-mile. Johnson won the NHRA Pro Stock championship in 2006.

its illustrious GTO predecessors, but it had enough muscle to spank each and every one of them in a stoplight drag race. Besides, many people believe nondescript looks aren't necessarily a bad thing for a car capable of going 160 miles per hour. Sometimes it's better not to draw too much attention to yourself.

Unfortunately for Pontiac, the general public seemed uninterested in buying a nondescript car, and GTO sales remained dismal. An almost complete lack of advertising undoubtedly contributed to these low numbers, but it seems unlikely that even the most outrageous Wangers-esque advertising campaign could have generated much interest in the last iteration of the GTO. *Automobile* magazine summed up the situation: "Sad to say, but if Pontiac put some ridiculous 'Judge' stickers on it, made it less pleasant to drive, and added a big stupid wing, it might even sell some."

By then it was too late to make the car look like a classic Judge. Pontiac sold just 11,069 units for the 2005 model year. In 2006, that number jumped to 13,948 units, but that still wasn't enough to save the car. The last new GTO rolled off the Holden production line in Port Melbourne, Australia, on June 14, 2006. After building just 40,808 cars over a three-year period, Pontiac once again pulled the plug on the GTO.

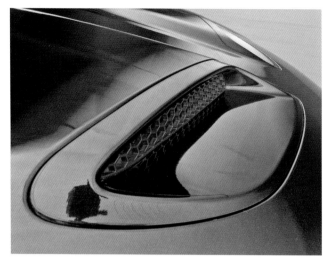

Pontiac has used a honeycomb grille material for many years, and the faux hood scoops on the 2006 GTO continued the tradition. Phantom Black was the most popular color on the 2006 model, with 3,974 units trying to slip under the radar.

A MISTAKE?

Peter M. De Lorenzo—the publisher of the influential automotive weekly Internet magazine Autoextremist. com and author of *The United States of Toyota*, an insightful portrait of the iconic American auto industry as it struggles for survival in the early

The valance panel between the functional dual exhaust tips used an embossed GTO script to notify other motorists what just blew their doors off. It's a pity the aggressive exhaust note can't be heard in a book.

The 2006 GTO was essentially a carryover from the preceding year, with a handful of new features, such as quicker power seats, darkened taillights, lit radio controls on the steering wheel, and an extra cigarette lighter/power port. The six-speed manual transmission remained a $695 option.

years of the twenty-first century—calls the revived GTO "a mistake."

"The modern day GTO was a mistake for a number of reasons," De Lorenzo says. "Not that it wasn't a good car and a terrific value by the end (when it was heavily discounted), but GM had allowed Pontiac's image to dry up in the market place and by the time the new GTO came out, there was no legacy left. [The GTO] didn't mean anything to younger enthusiasts, and for the older enthusiasts who remembered the great GTOs from the past, it didn't qualify as a real GTO. It also didn't help that the modern GTO was a lackluster, totally uninspired design that was already showing its age by the time it made its debut."

HARD TIMES AT GENERAL MOTORS

By the time Pontiac once again crucified the resurrected GTO, not just Pontiac, but General Motors itself was on the ropes. By that time GM's corporate structure consisted of a haphazard collection of paralyzing bureaucratic fiefdoms. After the departure of visionaries Knudsen, Estes, and DeLorean, the

With a curb weight of 3,725 pounds and 400 horsepower, effective brakes are important. Standard 17x8-inch alloy wheels could be replaced with optional 18 rolling stock. The 2006 GTO rode on a 109.8-inch wheelbase.

The Corvette-sourced LS2 engine featured an aluminum block and heads, displaced 364 cubic inches, and was rated at 400 horsepower at a lofty 5,200 rpm, while torque peaked at 400 lb-ft at 4,000 rpm. Its induction system was electronic sequential port fuel injection, allowing engineers to deliver good fuel economy with strong power and low emissions. However, the GTO required premium fuel.

company designed, engineered, and built vehicles in a vacuum, resulting in a lack of focus on the one thing that could save the company: the product. Lutz did a terrific job of getting the various divisions to focus back on the product. Unfortunately, he was never given the authority to dismantle GM's fiefdoms. In the sterile corporate atmosphere that permeated General Motors at the time, not only would a creative marketing genius like Jim Wangers not be given access to the top decision makers, such a person would not even have been let in the door.

Rather, for several generations GM recruited MBAs who lacked any passion for automobiles whatsoever. At the 2005 SEMA (Specialty Equipment Marketing Association) trade show in Las Vegas, the author of this book asked a Pontiac manager working to promote the then new Solstice sports car the following question: "What cars stir your passion?" The man didn't seem capable of understanding the question, much less answering it, so the author asked a more direct question: "What was your favorite car of all the cars you've ever owned?"

The man paused, thought a bit, and finally his eyes sort of lit up. "I had a Beretta in college that I really liked."

The fact that a man in his position would even admit to owning a Beretta, much less deem it the best car he ever owned, speaks volumes about why General Motors found itself in such dire circumstances.

With its low-key "6.0" badge and the GTO script beneath the bumper, the 2006 edition could be overlooked in a world of overstyled and underdelivering street cars. The GTO started life as a big engine in a midsized package, and the 2006 version followed the same formula.

GTO.R drivers Marc Bunting and Andy Lally, 2006 Grand American Rolex Sports Car Series GT class co-champions, stand with their Pratt & Miller–designed race car. This vehicle tipped the scales at only 2,700 pounds, and with 393 horsepower on tap, it was a potent combination. *GM Racing/ Richard Prince*

THE DEATH OF PONTIAC

As the first decade of the twenty-first century wound down, General Motors experienced the most difficult period in the company's long history, ultimately resulting in the unthinkable; in 2009, GM filed for bankruptcy. This time there would be no Bunkie Knudsen to step in and save Pontiac. General Motors' corporate bureaucracy makes it virtually impossible for visionary leaders like Bunkie Knudsen, Pete Estes, and John DeLorean to buck the system and build cars like the original GTO. In fact, after these mavericks had shaken up the system, General Motors instituted policies designed to weed such miscreants from corporate ranks.

The infinite onion that is GM's corporate bureaucracy ensured that even Bob Lutz, who is

The last year that the GTO.R was eligible for racing in the Rolex Sports Car Series was 2006. It capped its two-year battle on the track with a championship in 2006. Starting in 2007, its place was taken by the G6 GXP. *GM Racing/Richard Prince*

probably the closest thing to a Bunkie Knudsen in the modern auto industry, was unable to take the steps necessary to regenerate enthusiasm for Pontiac, in spite of great products like the GTO.

About the demise of Pontiac, De Lorenzo, a lifelong Pontiac fan, said, "The demise of Pontiac was the last painful chapter of the GM implosion into bankruptcy. The company's Byzantine corporate structure had become obsolete easily 25 years earlier, and its continuous downward spiral to final oblivion was played out in declining market share year after painful year. GM was still structured as if it dominated its home market, when in fact it was ill-equipped for the reality of what the U.S. market had become, which was a swirling maelstrom of chaos dominated by smarter and savvier competitors with the added complexity of a new wave of agitated consumers with little interest in American vehicles, or the inevitable excuses that went with them.

"In this environment GM simply didn't have the resources to keep its myriad brands afloat, and especially in Pontiac's case. Instead GM cherry-picked its brands, giving Cadillac, Chevrolet, Buick, and GMC the majority of the available resources, leaving Pontiac to fend for itself with only scraps of intermittent attention. The rebirth of the GTO provided brief shining moments of hope for Pontiac enthusiasts, but just when the company could have and *should* have powered-up the brand with an infusion of cash and engineering talent, it walked away. And in the end impressive vehicles like the GTO became cruel exclamation points to a legacy that GM chose to abandon.

"The only guy with the *cojones* to pull a Knudsen-like or Ed Cole–like or Bill Mitchell–type deal off was Lutz—and even he had his failings. He never did get Pontiac. I applaud Lutz for trying to jump-start the division with the modern GTO, but

There's a live one under the hood

Pontiac Tigers

rushing that car to market glossed-over the real issue for Pontiac, and that was that the division didn't stand for anything anymore. They needed to do their homework and come up with a real plan to get Pontiac going again. And they didn't do it.

"The end of Pontiac was an American tragedy for anyone with gasoline in their veins, because though it had long been sullied by an almost criminal level of neglect, gross underfunding, and a brace of clueless managers—with a few notable exceptions—within the GM monolith, it was still the last link to GM's glorious heyday, when brilliant executives led with their guts and created magnificent machines that in their unbridled audacity and flash became the mechanical conduits of America's hopes and dreams.

"For enthusiasts who loved Pontiac and it's fabulous history—and even for enthusiasts of other brands who still had great respect for the marque— the death of Pontiac was much more than the end game for yet another American nameplate. It was an end of an era in American motoring—and for America itself—that will never be seen again.

"Will there be a future for high-performance cars in this tortuously oppressive green-at-all-costs environment that the U.S. is rapidly descending into? Absolutely. It will cost more—much more in fact— but I firmly believe that the excitement of personal mobility will remain a powerfully intoxicating lure for generations to come. And that high performance in some way, shape, or form will never go out of style."

Perhaps De Lorenzo is correct, and high performance will never go out of style. Or perhaps Bob Lutz was right when he predicted that in the future the automobile would evolve into an "autonomous transportation pod," and our involvement with it will consist of getting into it when we leave and getting out of it when we arrive. Let's hope the future is more like De Lorenzo's vision than Lutz's.

Either way, no one envisions a future in which brand-spanking-new GTOs roam the streets. Bob Lutz couldn't save it, and now not even a resurrected Bunkie Knudsen, Pete Estes, or John Z. DeLorean could bring it back from the grave. Pontiac's great one, like Pontiac itself, is well and truly dead.

INDEX